CW01067086

PROCRASTINATION
and
BLOCKING

PROCRASTINATION

AND

BLOCKING

A Novel, Practical Approach

Robert Boice

PRAEGER

Westport, Connecticut
London

Library of Congress Cataloging-in-Publication Data

Boice, Robert.
    Procrastination and blocking : a novel, practical approach /
    Robert Boice.
       p. cm.
    Includes bibliographical references and index.
    ISBN 0–275–95657–1 (alk. paper)
    1. Procrastination. 2. Inhibition. 3. Writer's block.
    I. Title.
    BF637.P76B65   1996
    155.2'32—dc20   96–20684

British Library Cataloguing in Publication Data is available.

Library of Congress Catalog Card Number: 96–20684
ISBN: 0–275–95657–1

First published in 1996

Praeger Publishers, 88 Post Road West, Westport, CT 06881
An imprint of Greenwood Publishing Group, Inc.

Printed in the United States of America

The paper used in this book complies with the
Permanent Paper Standard issued by the National
Information Standards Organization (Z39.48–1984).

P

Dedicated to Virginia Branch

Contents

viii **Contents**

Preface

How did I, first an ethologist and later a psychotherapist with more respectable interests to pursue, get involved in studies of procrastinating and blocking (PBing)? I acquired some of my interest in these subjects naturally. I grew up in western Michigan among people of Dutch descent who often seemed to carry a love of efficiency (including succinct talk and thorough cleanliness) to an extreme. These were people who once actually scrubbed their streets, sidewalks, and porches. I almost hesitate to tell you that I keep my desk clean and organized, that I rarely strain to meet deadlines, that I am almost never stymied in my work. I hope you won't hold those things against me; I do them with only a modicum of self-righteousness.

The larger part of my interest in PB, however, came of necessity and caring. As a professor I have struggled to understand why so many students put off studying and writing until they must work in rushed, superficial, and miserable fashion. As an adviser, I have shared the anguish of graduate students who could not get past the immobilization of writing blocks to finish dissertations and whose careers consequently were ruined. I have labored to comprehend the reasons why most new professors work in an obviously inefficient, maladaptive manner and, so, undermine their potentials for success and happiness. Almost all of them have the time to write enough to survive with ease, but few do. Another mystery is that although the majority of new faculty procrastinate, block, and suffer, no one notices or wants to intervene—or so it seems.

My own bewitchment by the dark and diabolical subject of PB grew into something I had not planned. Why did I let myself make this risky move? I found I could no longer stand by and do what most of us do who are in a position to help: (1) They assume that people with the "right stuff" (divine predestination? strong will power genetically implanted at birth? Dutch upbringing?) deserve to survive and that those who fail are inherently weak and not worth helping. (2) They suppose because they know little about the mechanisms of PB that they could not help PBers. (3) They often assert, indignantly, that pointing out the PB of people who are failing would be an invasion of their privacy and dignity.

Instead of sticking with tradition, I decided, I would immerse myself in the little-known, scattered literature on this subject. Next I would make field studies of what PBers do and the prices they pay for their dilatoriness and avoidance. And then, in a third step, I would test my ideas on PBers who genuinely needed help. Now, after two decades of practice, research, and intervention in this fascinating endeavor, I feel ready to share what I have learned.

Why go public now with ideas that have consistently elicited indifference or strong resistance from those who could help? My first reason is that PB is on the increase (according to systematic information that I collect in areas such as preventive medicine and graduate programs), rather like the dramatic rises reported for maladies such as depression (Seligman, 1991) and failures in self-regulation (Baumeister, Heatherton, & Tice, 1994). Mental health, it seems, is on the decline, and our failures to deal honestly with PB may be part of the reason. My second reason for going public is that I still don't see books based on concepts and practices that have been proven successful in helping procrastinators and block-ers find timeliness and fluency in enduring and meaningful ways. Instead, even the most recent writing on PB treats it as a rather superficial problem that probably cannot or should not be changed (Ferrari, Johnson, & McCown, 1995). My third reason for writing this book is that my patients, colleagues, and students have en-couraged me to go public with my unusual, controversial ap-proach. They've even joked about the reasons for my dilatoriness and hesitation (usually, of course, while worrying about hurting my always delicate feelings).

Why do people who have tried this approach act so differently from those who maintain the status quo in PB? My patients and colleagues say it is because the ideas have helped transform their lives. Some have written me accounts of how they displaced usual tendencies of busyness and never-quite-catching-up with calmer, more productive ways of working ("My life was so hectic and I was so chronically behind in things that mattered that I did not believe I could become calm, organized, and generally optimistic. . . . But I have"). Some have said that these strategies helped them finish writing projects, including novels and dissertations, that had lain fallow too long ("Three years of frustration and spinning my wheels—and then less than one without my beloved procrastination, and I was finished"). Some have used their newfound freedom from deadlines and anxious inhibitions to live more happily and simply ("The more timely and patient I get, the more freedom and happiness I feel; I have more free time now than I can remember since the summer vacations of my childhood; I'm more spontaneous and daring in my work"). Just about all of these PBers, curiously, began my program seeing themselves as weak in character and unlikely to change. No one is harder on PBers than PBers themselves.

What Are Procrastination and Blocking?

Because PB is rarely discussed in open, serious ways, PBers often suppose their own dilatoriness and uneasy inhibitions are idiosyncratic and unlike anyone else's. Not until they hear clear definitions of procrastination and blocking do they begin to see the common themes that apply to most people. There is something in the naming and defining that allows the beginnings of control. So one of the first things we do in my treatment programs is to reflect on definitions. I do much the same here.

Procrastination has at least two characteristics. It means putting off a difficult, delayable, important task—an act with distant, perhaps doubtful rewards (as in writing)—in favor of something easier, quicker, and less anxiety-provoking (for example, cleaning a desk before writing). Procrastination also means delaying vital ac-

tions until the performance and the results are less than they
would have been if done in timely fashion.

Blocking is often similar. It occurs when we stumble, delay, and
panic in response to a demanding responsibility, when we avoid
the threatening task by way of nervous slowing of activity, self-
conscious narrowing of scope, even immobilization. Blocking typically occurs when we face public scrutiny (as in a writing block).
Writers who struggle with a single sentence or word for hours on
end are not just unable to come up with more. They often experience high levels of paralyzing anxiety and discouraging depression that make broad thinking difficult. Oddly, while they are
getting little if anything done, they worry aloud about having too
much to do. Just as paradoxically, they make more effort to control their momentary emotions than their essential work (Baumeister, Heatherton, & Tice, 1994). What they fail to realize is
this: finding moderate, constant ways of working more effectively
reduces the anxiety and doubt that build when mood control is
put first.

But this experience is not exclusive to blocking. The same kinds
of cognitions and feelings are often reported by procrastinators
facing public scrutiny over the jobs they are putting off. Often, as
in the case of writing blocks, procrastination and blocking are in-
extricably mixed. The writing is put off to avoid the anxiety of
anticipating failures, and the procrastination continues until deadlines near. Then tensions mount, and the panic of blocking can
set in. What began as an attempt to control an uncomfortable
mood grows into emotions that are out of control. Where procrastination stops and blocking begins is difficult to determine.

There are also instances where procrastination and blocking appear to be quite separate and different. We are, for example, more
likely to procrastinate doing housework than to block at it. That
seems obvious. But even here, if we associate the outcome of the
cleaning and arranging of furniture with public scrutiny of the
most demanding sort (a suddenly announced visit by royalty in
one hour), we could stumble and hesitate. We might anxiously
imagine we have too much to do and too little time. We could
work with impressive inefficiency. And if we keep it up, we might
block at what would otherwise be a simple, automatic task.

There is more to this topic than definitions and similarities. Procrastination and blocking are inherently interesting topics, so much so that a closer look raises some intriguing dilemmas.

The Aims of This Book

In this book I try to answer a trio of questions that usually go unasked: Why is so little help offered for such major problems as procrastination and blocking? Why do psychologists overlook obvious links between procrastination and blocking? (They are, after all, both about putting off things that create anxiety and discomfort.) And what, if we take an unusually patient look at these two related maladies, can we learn that would provide a new, more practical perspective on them?

Those queries raise others. Why is most of what has been written about procrastination and blocking conjectural and humorous? Why does so little research document the seriousness of PB (for example, people who put off treatments for diabetes and then pay dire costs including amputations; graduate students who do not finish dissertations and, so, fail in their intended careers)? Why do we know almost nothing about how to help PBers become more efficient and comfortable performers?

These questions, it turns out, suggest one more: Is PB one of the last, great, unexamined and misunderstood topics in psychology (indeed in the behavioral sciences, medicine, and our whole society)? I suspect it is.

In this book, I propose two, overriding answers for all these questions: First, PB is unique in peculiar and powerful ways that keep us from dealing with it. PB, for instance, embarrasses us more deeply than almost anything else we do or treat, especially if its failings are pointed out in terms of public disapproval. The topic of PB is curious and off-putting because it suggests an inborn weakness of character that cannot (or should not) be corrected. It implies things better left unexamined. Why? Careful scrutiny of procrastination and blocking quickly elicits a discomforting self-consciousness; we might wonder how many of these failings we will find lurking within ourselves. Worse yet, we might worry that the cures for PBing require the controlling, regimented, intrusive styles we associate with Nurse Ratchet or Felix Ungar.

Second, PB seems hard to define and study. Its practical understanding will require direct observation of PBers acting as problematically dilatory and self-conscious individuals. As a rule, psychologists avoid the time and inconvenience of lengthy field studies. Instead, they prefer to draw occasional conclusions about PBing based on quick personality tests administered to college freshmen. In that way, they can feel like scientists, testing students in laboratory conditions and linking the results, statistically, to other test outcomes such as the seeming inclination of PBers to admit perfectionism or demanding parents (Ferrari and Olivette, 1994). A problem is that researchers lose sight of PBing as a real, costly, and treatable problem.

The Core Reason for Overlooking Procrastination and Blocking

Both the causes just previewed hint at the underlying reason why psychology distances itself from PB. It may, at first glance, surprise you: Psychology, as will be shown throughout this book, abhors obviously effective interventions (Kipnis, 1994). PB, once its real-life costs and discomforts are revealed, demands the kinds of changes and manipulations that make present-day psychologists squeamish. Psychology's unspoken attitude toward close examination and intervention with PBers is more than distaste or disinterest. It is observance of a longstanding and formidable taboo whose violators incur punishment.

This little-known taboo keeps most of us only vaguely aware of what PB really is and how to cure it. You might, for example, have only an inkling of your own tendencies to shy away from the topic. Still, if you are a problematic PBer, you may have noticed an unusual reluctance to face up to your own dilatoriness and discomfort in performing difficult but important tasks ("I'd rather not dwell on it"). If you are a therapist or teacher, you may have experienced an irrational discomfort in pointing out the undue delays and anxieties of your patients and students ("They're already embarrassed; I hate to make them lose even more face"). If you are a social scientist, you might shy away from studying PB because you dislike the prospect of getting close to a problem that could demand changes in the environment that would impel PBers to behave as they should. The social sciences, including psychology, prefer description over intervention—to the point where interventionism itself is the issue that underlies the great taboo about dealing effectively with PB.

Or the taboo might incline you to suppose PB too trivial or ephemeral to study. Why? The topic of PB may, all too ironically, tempt you to delay its study while you attend to more pleasant, less unsettling things. PB might even seem like nothing more than a joke or minor inconvenience, something to be tackled by lightweight thinkers and researchers ("Procrastination and blocking? Seriously? That's what you study? I can't imagine spending my career on that, not at a major research university").

So tradition dictates a politely distant view of PB as something we quietly laugh about, self-consciously. More commonly, we overlook it. This book, *Procrastination and Blocking*, looks behind and beyond that unspoken taboo to explain psychology's neglect of procrastinators and blockers. And, having done so, it describes new, proven ways of moderating PB in favor of more timely, efficient, and enjoyable actions. *Procrastination and Blocking* offers one of the first objective, practical looks at this usually enigmatic, untouchable, crucial topic.

Who Might Read This Unusual Book?

I expect that *Procrastination and Blocking* will be read by scholars interested in the topics (for many, the linking of procrastination and blocking will be a new idea). I hope the book will be examined by people with significant problems of procrastination, such as chronic lateness, busyness, and poor habits of self-care (even though the directness of this book may discomfort those readers at first), and by blockers, including writers who falter, founder, and fail. Most of all, I would like to attract readers interested in the general dilemma of why psychology and the other social sciences have made so little progress in improving the welfare of humankind. One answer, I believe, lies in our reluctance to deal with the sorts of behavioral and environmental interventions that PB requires.

Another group of likely readers may surprise you. Based on reactions to early versions of this manuscript, I expect people who already work with efficiency and fluidity to peruse *Procrastination and Blocking*. They, more than any other group I've found, like to read about ways of augmenting their strengths. Sometimes they want the reassurance that they are not alone (or mistaken) in combating PB. As a rule, they want to engage in even less of the PB that proves painful and costly. So it is that the rich get richer.

What does this mean for you, the reader? I hope you feel ready to suspend judgment about this unconventional way of seeing PB. And I hope you will be patient about journeying through an often disarrayed but fascinating literature, even forbearing when I repeat ideas in new contexts. I can warn you about what sorts of surprises you may experience: Earlier readers of this material soon came to say they needed the redundancies that at first seemed annoying—because the notions prove unusual and thought-provoking. These readers said they were eager (despite their initial skepticism) to try some of the methods that have proven effective in moderating PB; they were even willing to consider some of my counterintuitive ideas. Understanding and change will not, as a rule, come quickly in a domain that is still taboo, but, in my experience, the result will prove rewarding.

The Scope and Demands of This Book

You may have guessed something about my perspective on procrastination and blocking in what I have already said. My approach is not only irreverent and revisionist. It is also heavily based in scholarship and research. So while this book has its practical side (including frequent quotes from participants in my programs), it also takes a long, hard look at what experts have written about procrastination and blocking. In what lies ahead, I often shift from a scholarly stance to practical matters, much as I do in my program for PBers. Moreover, I take an unusually wide view of these usually unrelated problems; here I not only liken procrastination and blocking to each other but to more general problems of impatience, impulse control, eating disorders, self-destructiveness, and medical noncompliance (all problems that require similar interventions).

Do you need to be a psychotherapist or professional scholar to grasp the material ahead? No. The literatures on procrastination and blocking are straightforward, for the most part, and easily grasped. The proven strategies for finding timeliness and fluency are surprisingly simple and effective—with a bit of patience, tolerance, and practice. How can I justify such a claim? I have tested these materials on hundreds of patients and colleagues, often in systematic projects that last up to two years. I have revised my materials and approaches to promote better understanding and outcomes among those who listen. And I have applied the ideas and techniques to a diversity of people ranging from students to struggling professionals, even already successful writers. No one else, so far as I know, can make that claim. I wish it were otherwise.

You might, then, read this book for a scholarly review of the field that brings a new perspective to procrastination and blocking, even to wider concerns such as self-control and self-defeat. Or you might read it more for the practical strategies that moderate PB. More likely, I expect, you will end up immersing yourself in both the scholarship and its application; neither has proven separable for earlier readers who came to care deeply about the topic.

Introduction

Procrastination, in my view, consists largely of opting for short-term relief through acts that are easy and immediately rewarding, while generally avoiding even the thought (and its anxiety) of doing more difficult, delayable, important things. Its effects can be seen most commonly in the everyday "busyness" of people doing what is unnecessary and supposing themselves productive but never being quite able to catch up with all the things they most need to do. Busyness, as will be discussed later, is a usual companion of procrastination. Procrastination occurs more obviously, at least in the view of casual observers, in situations such as people queuing up at post office windows just before annual IRS deadlines. It occurs less conspicuously but more seriously among those of us whose tax forms are still unfinished while we fret well past that midnight hour. And it acts most insidiously as the busyness that kept us from doing the taxes in the first place.

Blocking means getting stuck at a difficult transition point (for example, while beginning or ending a major project), usually because of paralyzing anxiety and uncertainty, often because the task will be evaluated publicly or because the taskmaster is distasteful.

In common practice, procrastination and blocking are overlapping and inseparable, even though scholars and practitioners still like to keep them separate. I'll explain as we move along (for example, both P and B are problems of excessive self-consciousness, and both are treated, when they are treated at all, with strategies that free up thinking for better problem-solving strategies such as time/decision charts, free writing, and early beginnings).

THE NATURE OF PROCRASTINATION AND BLOCKING

All of us, I suspect, have experienced procrastination and blocking at some level. We have put off crucial tasks until we rushed and regretted; we have choked when we performed self-consciously under audience pressure. We have opted for the short-term gains of keeping someone we dislike waiting (however unconsciously). We have put off medical examinations because even the thought of a visit to a doctor's or dentist's office is something we would rather not face. At the very root of PB is a fear of even experiencing the fear of suffering or embarrassment. PBers, to paraphrase Winston Churchill, have nothing so much to fear as fear itself. Fear of what? We mostly fear failures that might bring public disapproval and disgrace, but we also fear momentary discomfort.

Facing the Negative Side of PB

Even if we don't like to think about them, we know the pain and cost of procrastination and blocking. We have procrastinated over things like speaking out in groups because failure might threaten our public image; we have blocked in front of groups, as though to confirm everyone's worst suspicions. And then we have suffered the marginalization and frustration of silence. We have missed opportunities, some of them golden, because of the distractedness and busyness that go along with a lack of timeliness. We have imperiled our health for want of the self-discipline that would take us into medical settings for preventive checkups. We have broken relationships because communication about difficult matters was inelegant and was therefore put off. Some of us have ruined careers by missing deadlines or being absent. And more, much more.

Traditional Ways of Distancing PB

Yet for all the pain and waste of PB, Western society neglects and trivializes it. The current *Diagnostic and Statistical Manual of Mental Disorders* (American Psychiatric Association, 1994), the ultimate authority on behavioral problems that merit diagnosis and treatment, mentions neither procrastination nor blocking. If we recall PB at all from the scholarly literature, it is usually as jokes—"An unsuccessful treatment of writer's block," which is a title over a blank page (Upper, 1974) and Murray's Law of Delay ("That which can be delayed, will be" [Murray, 1978]).

Newspaper accounts like the following are the most common mentions of PB:

New York Times, May 7, 1983, p. 23: Creeping on at a petty pace. "I read about procrastination a month ago and intended to alert everybody."

New York Times, March 7, p. C20: Better late than never. Covers the belated observation of National Procrastination Week and the delays in getting members.

Christian Science Monitor, July 18, 1980, p. 24: On not doing things. Advocates the virtue of ignoring things and letting them take care of themselves.

Christian Science Monitor, January 7, 1982, p. 22: In defense of procrastination. "Procrastination is in the eye of the beholder. . . . The laws of procrastination read like this: 1. Everybody puts first things first—it's just that we can't believe some people's taste. 2. Everybody, finally, is a procrastinator, because who doesn't put off something? . . . workaholics put off vacations . . . the procrastinator, not the workaholic, should be our hero."

Two things occur to me in quoting these articles from an ever-growing file I keep of such things. First, these earliest examples from my collection are nearly identical to more recent instances; evidently, readers and writers do not grow tired of the same old jokes about PB. Second, the values implied in these newspaper briefs, even if presented tongue-in-cheek, are frighteningly wrong (almost as if scientists and journalists were amiably excusing tobacco companies as misunderstood, laughable endeavors). Consider, from your own experience, just some of the regrettable things that happen when correspondence and other responsibilities are put off in the hope they will go away of their own accord. And reflect on the fact, like it or not, that PBers are as likely to put off vacations as are those immoral workaholics.

Still the topic of PB will always, I suppose, attract humor as a way of relieving the pain. Some of the funniest writing around is about PB.

"And now to my book," I almost said to myself. . . . Or would have, except that it was just about time for the mail. . . . It meant neglecting My Work, but I waited and watched. . . . As it emerged, I saw it was a bright red halter, worn by what appeared to be a young Chinese woman, in short shorts carrying a clipboard . . . working her way through college by selling subscriptions. . . . So we went upstairs, and in a series of steps, she showed me what she had in mind. . . . Anyway, that's the real reason my summer in 1973 was less than productive. You don't have to believe it if you don't want to. (Gurney, 1977, pp. 110–121)

I still couldn't believe that I was here—Rex Sackett, the youngest player to ever make it through the playoffs to the Prose Bowl. . . . I looked across the Line at the old man. Leon Culp. Fifty-seven years old, twenty million words in a career spanning almost four decades. . . . the palms of my hands were slick and my head seemed empty. What if I can't think of a title? What if I can't think of an opening sentence? . . . in the next instant the two plot topics selected by the officials flashed on the board. . . . The Cranker and I broke for our typewriters. And all of a sudden, as I was sliding into my chair, I felt control and a kind of calm come into me. That was the way it always was with me. That was the way it always was with the great ones. . . . A hundred thousand voices screamed for speed and continuity. . . . I hunched forward, teeth locked. . . . I glanced at the scoreboard. . . . SACKETT 226, CULP 187. I laid in half a page of flashback, working the adjectives and the adverbs to build up my count. . . . Up on the board what I was writing appeared in foot-high electronic printout, as if the words were emblazoned on the sky itself.

SAM SLEDGE STALKED ACROSS HIS PLUSH OFFICE, LEAVING FOOTPRINTS IN THE THICK CARPET LIKE ANGRY DOUGHNUTS. . . .
    HE
    Nothing.
    Come on, Sackett! Hack, hack it!"
    HE

HE

Block. I was blocked. Panic surged through me. I hadn't had a block since my first year in the semi-pro Gothic Romance League. (Pronzoni & Malzberg, 1979, pp. 135–150)

Solemn Approaches to PB

Only a small fraction of writing about PB is serious, almost as if we usually choose not to see its realities, almost as if we prefer to keep it at arm's length. Even when occasional compilations of scholarship on PB do appear (e.g., Ferrari, Johnson, & McCown, 1995), their editors downplay its negative side. They omit mentions of patients in cardiac rehabilitation programs who pay a high price for procrastinating about their exercise regimens. They say nothing about the strong tendency of women and other minority entrants to professorial careers to procrastinate and block at writing (and, so, to fail). Instead, compilers of the literature suggest that PB is not really so bad and that people who insist on depicting it as a serious failing are themselves bad. For instance, these upholders of the taboo against looking too closely at PB assume that anyone with scientific leanings will be excessively unforgiving of PBers:

Since most people who perform behavioral science research are probably highly conscientious and punctual individuals, it is often difficult for the majority of such researchers to show interest of empathy for the plight of people who are constantly unable to meet deadlines. (Ferrari, Johnson, & McCown, 1995, p. 2)

Of course, J. R. Ferrari, J. L. Johnson, and W. McCown are only guessing. Evidence gathered about the work habits of scientists and academics suggests that they are at least as guilty of PB as other people (Boice, 1989). Those of us who have edited scientific journals and books might suppose that some of our colleagues are among the world leaders as PBers. What Ferrari, Johnson, and McCown apparently mean is that other, more behavioristic scientists than themselves are cruel and unsympathetic toward PBers. Behaviorists, after all, sometimes strive to intervene by controlling the situation and the behavior. Behaviorists are reviled for breaking the taboo this book is examining.

The favorite target of Ferrari and his colleagues is Albert Ellis, the outspoken pioneer of rational-emotive therapies that prescribe interventions for problems like PB. (Note that even though Ellis's notions about treating PBers are at least as empirically based as those of Ferrari, Johnson, and McCown, these critics demean his best-selling book as written for laypersons, when in fact, it has been widely used by therapists and other professionals)

Ellis and Knaus (1977), in a layperson's self-help book, provide one of the first quasi-empirically oriented treatments of procrastination. They liken the behavior to neurosis and they believe its illogicalness is its salient feature. Ellis and Knaus find it very curious, therefore, that a few psychologists have attempted an empirically based treatment of such an obviously dysfunctional behavior. (Ferrari, Johnson, & McCown, 1995, p. 7)

Where, in that view, do Ellis and W. J. Knaus go wrong? They mistakenly assume that PBers do not act illogically and need help (that is, intervention). What, in the opinion of Ferrari and his colleagues would be a better, more traditional stance? It would be one like their own, that portrays PB as logical and healthy:

Other researchers have challenged the universality of the irrationality of procrastination. Ferrari argued that although procrastination may *often* be self-defeating, this behavior may also be in one's own self-interest and therefore quite logical. (Ferrari, Johnson, & McCown, 1995, p. 7)

How did Ferrari come to this sure conclusion? It didn't come by way of years of clinical experience with PBers facing real-life problems, as Ellis and Knaus had done. Instead, he reached it, for the most part, by asking student procrastinators to speculate about why they procrastinate.

Then, to cinch their case against Ellis and other behaviorists, Ferrari, Johnson, and McCown conclude that those who label PB as irrational and maladaptive are merely making moral judgments (for example, they might assume that PBers are lazy). But behaviorists, including me, would argue the point differently.

What we do, first of all, is to observe and describe the behaviors central to PBing (including irrational statements such as the belief that the best work is done just before deadlines and more overt acts that prove maladaptive—for example, substituting an easy task such as cleaning the office for writing a difficult report). Then, to the dismay of our critics, we try to arrange conditions (interventions) to help reduce the incidence and costs of PB. Do we intervene because we want to alleviate a serious, easily corrected problem or because we are Machiavellian and power-hungry? It depends whom you ask.

The real issue here, it seems to me, is this: Traditional psychologists choose to keep an amiable distance from PB and even characterize it as generally harmless behavior rather than approach the prospect of intervening. Others, including behaviorists, choose to take a less reverent look at PB and are themselves accused of irrational behavior by traditionalists. At the bottom of this controversy lies the thing that is usually overlooked: those who look closely, objectively at PBers violate an old, sacred taboo—one so deep and threatening that we rarely mention it. Effective study and treatment of PB are forbidden because they require embarrassment and intervention (at least in the short run).

Effects Created by Defenders of the Taboo

Consider, once more, the position of Ferrari, Johnson, and McCown (1995)—because it resembles that of other leading producers of the literature on procrastination—and what it means in terms of helping PBers. First, these personality researchers insist that linking PB to problems such as poor self-control or self-destructive habits is tantamount to a moral judgment. Why? Traditionalists believe that PB is inborn and beyond self-control. Thus, the status quo is maintained—of characterizing PB as an inherited, fixed and unmodifiable, inconsequential personality trait.

Second, traditionalist researchers insist that all, or almost all, of PBing is somehow adaptive to the individual displaying it. So, in their view, while procrastination may be uncomfortable, its superior wisdom somehow works out better in the long run. Blocking, in a similarly traditional opinion, may distress, but it is presumably the mark and necessary price of genius in a writer (Leader, 1991). (Later it will be shown that most of these studies in defense of PB are based on questionable samples and methods.)

Third, traditionalist researchers hint that emphasizing the negative side of procrastination is an act of mean-spiritedness or ignorance, one akin, say, to equating schizophrenia with demonic possession (Ferrari, Johnson, & McCown, 1995, p. 9). Why do these defenders of the status quo insist that picturing PB negatively is cruel and medieval? They suppose that labeling either malady as undesirable is to blame the victim. Moreover, they claim that like schizophrenia, PB can never be improved until scientists take nonjudgmental, nonmoralistic positions. (This view helps bolster the notion that a forgiving, hands-off stance is better than the blaming that can come with close examination and intervention.) Examination, labeling, and intervention risk blaming the victim, perhaps necessarily so. Once we step outside the traditional boundaries of PB study, to more progressive arenas such as the study of self-control, we can find researchers far more ready to blame PBers. Consider this conclusion from some of the leading experts on self-control:

We are less inclined now than when we started this book to regard people who fail at self-regulation as innocent, helpless victims; they look more like accomplices, or at least willing targets of seduction. (Baumeister, Heatherton, & Tice, 1994, p. 249)

Are R. F. Baumeister and his colleagues the hard-hearted, overexacting scientists that Ferrari et al. warned us against? It depends whom you ask.

You might have wondered something amid all this quibbling. Are these polemics anything more than the dancing on the heads of pins for which academic writers are infamous? I think they are. This argument is substantial for reasons that can be drawn from the three traditionalist notions just reviewed: PB is cast as a fixed personality trait that some of us cannot help expressing. PB is portrayed in ways that make it seem beneficial and adaptive for most people most of the time. And, PB is excluded from any descriptions that would ask PBers to take personal responsibility for their failures. Taken together, these interconnected beliefs dis-

courage serious attempts at helping PBers change. They even im-
plicitly encourage PBers to continue PBing. They are the usual
enforcement mechanisms of the taboo against serious study of PB.

There has already been discussion of another way in which conservative psychologists discourage closer looks at what hinders
and helps PBers: such scholars publish the great bulk of articles
and books on the topic and so act most often as the judges of
submitted manuscripts. You can bet that they would not approve
Ellis's attempts to publish on PB (although he, fortunately, has
his own publishing house). And you might imagine their response
to a manuscript submitted by anyone else who takes a behavioral
approach to PB.

I believe that traditional thought about PB is overdue for re-
examination. The narrowness and exclusiveness of conservatives,
however comforting, have brought too little progress. So in what
follows, I delve even deeper into this problem while trying to
maintain some moderation and humor. I show how this reexam-
ination produces new, usual perspectives on PB that go beyond
doctrinal quarrels.

A LOOK AT WHAT LIES BEHIND THE TABOO ABOUT
STUDYING PROCRASTINATION AND BLOCKING

Procrastination and blocking, by their nature, are excuses. Of
all excuse-making patterns, they are especially awkward under
public examination; to question excuses can be a social impropriety. This disinclination to question the excuses of others in polite
society is a well-established fact amongst social psychologists (Snyder & Higgins, 1988).

Consider some other, lesser known reasons why psychologists
defer direct examination of PB. All of us rarely admit (or like to
be reminded of) our fondness for the short-term benefits of procrastination and blocking—that is, the excitement and euphoria
of working in binges under deadlines, the feeling of self-control
when we put off complying with someone else's demand, the
ready excuse for not facing public evaluation, the relief of doing
the routine and the easy while putting off the difficult. In addition,
as noted earlier, PB offers no ready ways of easy study or understanding. There are more convenient, comfortable things to study.

Traditional neglect of procrastination and blocking is carried out with the appearance of an amiable oversight. Such neglect is seemingly good-natured about overlooking these acts of dilatoriness and stumbling, and it often portrays procrastinators and blockers as lovably disorganized, forgivable people. Of course they can be; we are all procrastinators and blockers (or have been) to at least some degree. But in its amiability, the customary attitude tends to overlook or suppress the complexities, costs, and cures of these problems.

What Would We Gain in a Closer Look?

PB is so central to how well we find success and happiness (as will be shown later) that all of us, whether or not we see ourselves as procrastinators and blockers, can profit in appreciating the true costs of PBing. In fact, PB brings neither happiness nor efficiency—in the long run.

To accentuate that point throughout this book, I often focus on procrastination and blocking in a domain where we are all likely to have experienced them: writing. But what I have to say here is by no means limited to writing problems. Later I tie PB and its costs to common problems such as noncompliance with medical prescriptions.

The traditional view of procrastination and blocking as impolite topics spurs three related reexaminations here. First, this Introduction (and some of the chapters that follow) shows why most accounts, even research reports, of these supposedly amiable weaknesses are narrowly superficial and easily dismissed. Second, this overview replaces traditional excuses for PB such as distractedness or creative eccentricity with more telling interpretations—particularly a general lack of knowledge about how to work effectively. And third, this book proposes ways in which procrastination and blocking, thus simplified, interconnect with each other and with better-known phenomena such as self-defeating behaviors, bingeing, and styles of goal orientation.

By the end, I draw clearer, more observationally based definitions of procrastination and blocking, and then I arrange them in a descriptive model (something heretofore missing in the field). The PB model comprises three intertwined processes: impulsivity, mindlessness, and pessimism. It shows why the two problems of procrastination and blocking are essentially identical and helps lessen the mystery about both. The model also points to interventions for procrastination and blocking.

A Temporary Difficulty in Facing PB

The opening problem in communicating all this information (so far as I can tell from preliminary readers and reviewers) isn't that we are too close to these problems for comfort. And it isn't just the skepticism of traditionalists. It is more a matter of impatience.

Reading about PB may make you impatient. Many early readers reacted to explanations of PB, initially at least, much as they would have committed PB itself: with shortness and with demands for short-term relief. So, in an unorthodox move for an author of a scholarly book, I request special dispensations from you the reader: *Procrastination and Blocking* needs reading and reflecting without the impulsivity, unthinking rejection, and pessimism usually associated with procrastination and blocking. It wants patient waiting for implications and explanations to grow more explicit and understandable. And it rewards suspension of beliefs that procrastination and blocking are unimportant or cannot be controlled without fanatical, immoral regimentation.

Overall, benefit from this book requires the same (albeit unusual) qualities that help procrastinators and blockers themselves function better: patience, tolerance, and perhaps even the optimistic, forward-leaning stance of experts who look ahead to what can be learned, not to whether new problems and ideas fit preexisting conceptualizations (Ericsson & Charness, 1994, make a similar point). The difficulty of *Procrastinating and Blocking* is that it asks for your patience when you may be least disposed to give it.

PROCRASTINATION
and
BLOCKING

1

Why Researchers Know So Little About Procrastination and Blocking

A striking fact about procrastinating and blocking is that no other common behavioral problem has attracted so little systematic study or treatment. Not even weird, uncommon, and usually harmless fetishes have been so neglected, not even imaginary diseases and magical cures.

WHY RESEARCHERS DON'T STUDY PROCRASTINATION AND BLOCKING

Some of the causes for the tradition of neglect have already been noted. Here, a more detailed, useful examination of the reasons is considered.

Social Improprieties of Noticing, Studying, and Treating PB

The first reason in this list is not yet well known (but it is easily predicted). Only recently did researchers disclose that usual explanations of PB lean to the socially acceptable. When PBers explain their own dilatoriness and inhibitions at all, they do so in ways that put themselves in a good light. So if PBers list the causes of putting off things like studying for tests, they most often endorse fear of failure, an excuse that carries little social opprobrium

(Schouwenberg, 1992). And when they cannot write, PBers blame busyness and unfair pressures—both of which are especially acceptable excuses for professionals (Boice, 1989).

How can we know that these socially acceptable reasons are not the real cause of PB? Following are three explanations:

- PBers are often consciously *un*aware of the reasons why they delay so unreasonably and stumble so suddenly—thus, they cannot be expected to explain their PBing. (Indeed, one of the real quandaries about this area is why anyone would prefer students' self-reports of how and why they delay and block to direct observations of what behaviors make up the forms of PBing that lead to obvious and unacceptable consequences.)

- PBers' self-serving reports of experiencing problems such as fear of failure do not directly predict "trait" measures of procrastination (Lay, Knish, & Zanatta, 1992; Milgram, Batori, & Mowrer, 1993; Silverman & Lay, in press). Said another way, researchers who devise seemingly pure indications of procrastination as a personality trait ("trait procrastination") find that it does not relate reliably to the usual excuses offered by PBers.

- Writers who claim that their many responsibilities and distractions keep them from writing in fact have no more such hinderances than counterparts who do write productively (Boice, 1993c). Similarly, writers who procrastinate and block have just as much time that could have been use for writing as fluent and timely writers have. For many of the same reasons, teachers who most often block and show stage fright in the classroom are least likely to have done the normal amount of preparation (Boice, 1996b). The problem in understanding PB lies beyond usual, polite explanations such as distractions, personality traits, or the absence of Muses.

Questionable Study Samples and Tasks

Consider a second way (beyond relying on the socially acceptable explanations of students) that researchers underestimate and misunderstand PB: Most research accounts of procrastination rely on student experiences, even though schools offer few time pressures difficult enough to create immediate, substantial failure—or even the choice of not pursuing tasks (Dweck, 1986). Students (except in a few instances such as the dissertation stage) generally do not experience the truly maladaptive effects of procrastinative habits until after their school days are completed.

Still, the great bulk of research about PB is based on contrived experiments with students in introductory courses who spend an hour or two filling out questionnaires and/or role-playing imaginary or obviously artificial tasks where they can delay with no meaningful penalty.

Almost none of the traditional reports include direct observation of real-life PB; they depend, instead, on student's recollected estimates or momentary reconstructions of it. That is, they consider PB from afar, almost as if studying it were taboo.

Romanticizing PB

The third reason for misunderstanding is that researchers romanticize PB as yet another way of keeping a polite distance. Z. Leader (1991), a literary analyst, sees blocks as symptoms of giftedness and of the hesitant struggles it necessitates. He views blocks as maladies experienced in true form only by already talented and successful writers. Presumably, normal people fail to write because they have nothing to say, not because they are genuinely blocked. In this elitist view, meaningful PB is a gift of our gods or our genes and given to (or inflicted upon) only a lucky few creative folk. We would, it seems, be better off not meddling with it—and we couldn't in any useful way if we wanted to. PB strikes romantics, many of whom are themselves PBers, as a mysterious and irreplaceable burden or gift.

Romantics, as will be shown later, often imagine that creativity itself is dependent on the kinds of suffering and madness that begin with PBing. Here too they help keep PB unstudied and unknown.

The Most Costly Kinds of PB Usually Go Unmentioned

A fourth reason why researchers neglect PB is more sobering, one I have already mentioned with my usual bluntness. Traditionalists present only the most amiable side of PB. Reports of students delaying term papers and preparations for exams are all too visible in the literature. Not visible are stern accounts of people for whom PB is demonstrably costly for example, (diabetics who put off preventive treatments and suffer terrible consequences including blindness). Traditionalists fail to look at the reason why PBers risk such dangerous outcomes. The evident answer is that PBers believe they cannot tolerate a regular regimen or discipline or even the discomfort of contemplating it (Blakeslee, 1994); Western society ordinarily does little to help teach tolerance of discipline and discomfort. What kinds of proven programs are set up to help, say, diabetics past this misbelief? None I know of. How often do conservative scholars of PB attend to medical reports such as these? Rarely.

Denial

What else distances scholars from those documented kinds of costly PB? Few of us have diabetes or imagine ourselves remotely like diabetics. Even if we do, we might react with denial and distancing. In my experience, many of us assume PB is so entirely domain-specific that our styles of PBing show no generality between, say, seeking medical care and putting off income tax preparations. ("Heh! I may procrastinate, but I only do it in areas like getting a haircut or mowing my lawn. Not for important things.") Just as often my workshop participants have made the related assumption: "Lots of people probably procrastinate and block more than I do. I couldn't have gotten through all my schooling if I had real problems. You [referring to me] might do better to study and help those homeless people pushing their carts around aimlessly."

Why Scholars Know So Little About PB

So, we might not realize that PBing follows a general pattern (usually one of failing to deal with things in timely, patient, and calm fashion) and that it often keeps us from seeking timely medical examinations, from optimizing our work and relationships, even from weeding our gardens. People continue to be skeptical about this claim, for all its basis in fact, well into my programs. Even after a month or two, I find myself in conversations like this one with a stubborn PBer:

Well, yes, I do procrastinate on a few things, but not on most. I might be late for church or have to write my travel reports at the last minute, but that's not so bad, is it? I haven't done anything heinous. [*In response to my question, "What about your plans to visit the dentist or the medical imager or to the gymnasium?*]" Oh dear. Well! Don't even ask about that. I don't like to be reminded of that! Besides, I'm too busy already to be able to deal with everything right now.

Temptations of Short-Term Benefits in PBing

A sixth reason why scholars neglect and distort PBing problems owes to their short-lived but powerful rewards. I have already reviewed some of these, but they bear a quick reminder. PB offers autonomy, excitement, retribution, relief, and, of course, excuses—in the short run. Writers who chronically procrastinate report enjoying the risk of working under deadlines far more than do writers who face them only occasionally (Boice, 1994). Teachers who rush to catch up just as class periods end rate their teaching as most exciting during those moments. (Their students beg to differ with them.)

PBers often delay or withhold action as a means of controlling other people (for example, Nelson, 1988). People who keep others waiting for appointments often report a pleasant edge of exhilaration in taking control by subduing, for the moment, the anxiety they will feel when they finally show up for the event that makes them uneasy. Individuals who are chronically late (when monitored for the thoughts they express aloud during their preliminary activities) disclose a momentary pleasure in taking care of other, easier things until they find themselves at last overdue and then propelled, impulsively and with little time for regrets, into the thing they have put off.

Traditionalist researchers such as Ferrari et al. are right, to an extent, in praising the adaptiveness of PBing. Chronically busy PBers present themselves as overworked heroes who routinely sacrifice themselves for what must be IMPORTANT WORK. They also convey, however unwittingly, the message that their importance is reflected in their busyness.

PB also affords the short-term advantages of hiding abilities and avoiding evaluations, all in the interest of presenting a favorable self-image (Ferrari, 1991c).

And PB can promise special kinds of magic. PBers tend to wait passively for Muses and magic, hoping for brilliant inspirations of the sort unavailable to most people (Boice, 1994). They expect that motivation and complete ideas will come effortlessly as they sleep and dream (Epel, 1993; Ross, 1985). They like to begin projects mindlessly and aimlessly, hoping for spontaneous, unplanned successes that will prove their exceptional genius (Boice, 1994). When these things don't happen, PBers have a reasonable excuse for a result that should really please no one. They are, they will tell you, incurably perfectionistic and overscheduled.

Social Pressures for Conformity

PBers sometimes procrastinate and block in order to get along with their peers. PB enhances some kinds of social acceptance because PBers can seem more likable, less threatening, than do planful, disciplined sorts of people (Hamada, 1986). Why? An old bit of advice from Taoist writings suggests that non-PBers may often seem too self-righteous:

Stop confronting people with virtue: it is dangerous to leave a trail as you go. Hide your light, and no one will interfere with your activity. (Cleary, 1993, p. 95)

Therein lies another explanation of the taboo against studying PB: those who speak against it may seem too militant and overly virtuous to the rest of us. (This is a warning I will try to keep in mind for myself throughout this book.) Those of us who manage by going along with norms for PBing may be disinclined to see PB as a significant problem. This excerpt from the comments of a student on the evening before a final exam helps clarify the social mechanism:

What am I doing here? Playing pinball; what does it look like?
[*In response to my question about why he wasn't studying as he had planned:*] I kind of had to. I was studying but my house mates were all going out to have a beer and take a break and they came in my room and asked me to come along. What could I do? I don't want to look like a grind. [*In response to my question about how much studying he would*

get done after already being in the bar for four hours] Yeah. I thought I would only have one beer and play one game and get back to work. I didn't. Now, I guess, I have to pull an all-nighter. I hate that. Or maybe I'll just take the test cold. Maybe law school isn't right for me anyway.

So while PB has benefits in the short run, it typically exacts an even greater price in the long run. Why is that reality so often overlooked by PBers in the midst of PBing? I address that question in the next major section of this first chapter.

WHY SCHOLARS DON'T EXAMINE THE LONG-TERM COSTS AND BENEFITS OF PROCRASTINATION AND BLOCKING

Some of the confusion about PB owes to ambiguity about when and why it can be adaptive. There *are* times when waiting helps— while checking to see that the right problem is being solved, while collecting and preparing materials (Mills, 1959; Murray, 1978). So it is that Franz Kafka had a sign over his writing desk that said, simply, WAIT.

Also there are instances where blocks signal overexposure and fatigue, where they compel resting or working on alternatives or getting help (Leader, 1991). But these phenomena occur almost exclusively with people who use delays and pauses in order actively to prepare or regroup, not passively to put off a task (Boice, 1994). Again, these kinds of waiting and restarting are not problematic PB; they involve little avoidance or anxiety (indeed, active waiting induces action and calm); they result in gains, not losses, over the long run. Chronic and counterproductive PBers, in contrast, tend to wait maladaptively, while fretting and getting little else done of importance—or else they impulsively rush into something important without having prepared properly. PB, as will be shown, is more a matter of impatience and impulsivity than anything else.

How then, can scholars tell the real, excessive sorts of PB from the other? We can tell by attending to the costs and benefits, in the short run or the long run, of waiting and delaying. Problematic kinds of PB pay off mostly in the short run, typically by way of relief in doing something else easier and more immediately rewarding. What, by contrast, does a near absence of PB signify?

PB Uncharacteristic of Highly Successful People

Most of us are not aware of the fact that highly successful people are rarely PBers. The general absence of PB among people exemplary in their careers simply goes unnoticed as a rule. In fact, people who thrive in adult endeavors such as management know the costs of PB and simply don't indulge in it (Wagner & Sternberg, 1986).

Something else about these timely, organized people is usually overlooked or denied: their prowess in managing PB does not mean they go to extremes. Effective, fulfilled individuals are not fanatics. They want only to "satisfice" in many domains (for example, washing their cars just often enough to keep them pleasantly clean and neat); they find happy, successful medium points in their lives and gladly spend the moderate amounts of time necessary for expertise in one or a few areas. Few of us, I imagine, really want to practice the eighty-four hour work weeks that helped make the sociobiologist E. O. Wilson famous but unhappy (Wilson, 1994).

Lack of Appreciation for the Long-Range Context of PB

Another deceptive thing about understanding PB refers back to a point made by C. Dweck (1986): Most instances of maladaptive work patterns cause little damage until much, much later. Many junior faculty, for instance, manage sporadic publishing and academic visibility while struggling to write and to carry out other professional and personal activities. But in that hurried, mindless pattern of PBing, they fall well behind planned schedules, they do just enough work marginally to satisfy tenure committees, and they associate writing and teaching with duress. Only later, by midcareer, do the effects of inefficiency and disappointment become obvious as dispirited detachment from work (Boice, 1993b).

A related problem in understanding the wastefulness of PB is that many of us succeed, more or less, in spite of it (but without maximizing our real potentials). Why does this happen? Traditional schools, where most of us are formed, value most those individuals who can thrive with ambiguity, with incomplete directives, and with knowledge usually kept tacit (Langer, 1989; Sternberg, 1985). We expect "bright" students, professors, artists, and others pursuing academic or creative efforts to do their most impressive work in occasional spurts, between painful bouts of PB. Our proud tradition of Social Darwinism, of sink-or-swim attitudes towards managing PB, benefits too few of us.

Anti-Interventionism

Opposition to intervention also helps sustain PB as a common and neglected problem: Scholars have the most deeply seated prejudice against intervening in PB. These anti-interventionists react strongly to the attempts of scientists who want to lessen other people's PB. As a rule, traditionalist scholars judge such efforts to be oppressive, counterproductive, and immoral. They resent even the encouragement of self-control and orderliness, particularly when they are in institutions of higher education. So it is that educational analysts often insist that efficiency is no virtue (Solomon & Solomon, 1993), and writing teachers claim that good writing cannot, indeed should not, be taught (Stack, 1980). Teachers work best, according to tradition, unfettered by prescriptions. Writers with the right stuff, presumably, learn on their own or don't need teaching. And so it is that, as individuals, we may shy away from being seen as too organized or punctual. (That is, we are even discouraged from being effective interventionists with ourselves.)

Anticompulsivity

Just as scholars might too readily equate orderliness with pathological obsessive-compulsive disorders, they too hesitantly see its links to moderate forms of planfulness and organization (Bond & Feather, 1988). Consider the exaggerations directed at Taylorism, a well-meaning and generally effective attempt to increase the comfort and productivity of industrial workers about a century ago: Frederick Winslow Taylor's scientific management still evokes images of workers treated as machines, ruled by inhuman pressures for conformity, speed, productivity, and profit. And more: rigid norms and habits of order are seen as paternal strategies designed for the weak-willed and childish; workers are left feeling empty and victimized; and leisure and play scorned unless productive (Banta, 1993). In fact, Taylorism usually increased the productivity, enjoyment, and free time of the workers, artists, and writers subjected to it (Rabinbach, 1990). What, then, makes Taylorism seem so oppressive? It is interventionist. Its working conditions virtually eliminate PB, even the opportunity or wish to do it.

What effect did critics have on Taylorism? It is little known today, except in watered-down, less effective and threatening forms. Psychologists, as will be shown, prefer description to intervention, and they severely punish those, including Taylor, who attempt both.

Insufficient Information About PB

Still another reason why scholars shunt aside PB is that we often know too little about it to be helpful. We ourselves continue to procrastinate in meeting deadlines or expectations because we imagine each new experience (or domain of PB) unique; thus, we learn little from prior failures (Beuhler, Griffin, & Ross, 1994). As in other kinds of knowledge kept tacit, we have difficulty specifying and verbalizing the principles involved in PB. Instead, we imagine that the most telling correctives for PB can be learned but not taught (see Sternberg, Okagaki & Jackson, 1990) and that the right people will somehow learn. Defenders of PB are generally elitists.

As a result of this shallow understanding, researchers' advice to PBers tends to be superficial and incomplete. Popular books for procrastinators say a lot about schedules (for example, Lakein, 1974) but little about how to manage them flexibly and resiliently when unplanned emergencies come up. Blockers are counseled to put a manuscript away until inspiration strikes (Mack & Skjei, 1979) but not how to work effectively without it. Most important, the usual advice for PBers is conjectural. Neither admonition just mentioned has been shown to help PBers reliably; both bits of advice, in my own observational studies, have proved likely to elicit even more of the resentment and impatience that already underlie PB (Boice, 1994).

Insufficient Incentives for Helping PBers

The final reason why scholars neglect and misunderstand PB may be the most telling. Chronic PBers resist treatment, and once in it they make difficult patients. When PBers act in passive-aggressive, borderline, and narcissistic ways, their therapists end up feeling angry and helpless (Turkington, 1983). Resentful PBers can engender unusual hatred and sadism in those who try to rescue them (Birner, 1993). Why? PBers come to treatment exhibiting the pride of independence (and elitism) mentioned earlier; they want to solve problems on their own; and, they doubt the abilities of anyone else to help them.

Not only do PBers bring more of their neurotic symptoms along to treatment than do other patients but they are also relatively unique in maintaining a product (as distinct from process) orientation where they concentrate more on the outcomes they believe they need (for example, "I'll need to finish twenty-five pages of good prose this weekend") than on ways of learning to work more efficiently and durably ("Maybe I would get more done in the long run if I stopped planning such big goals and just settled into doing a few good pages a day" [see Dweck, 1986 for other examples of process versus product styles of problem solving]). Patients with product orientations provide few lasting incentives for therapists to continue working with them.

A *product orientation* robs patients themselves of the sustained improvement that rewards attempts to change. Lacking a process orientation, writers and other workers stray from a planful, step-by-step orientation to one of fear and anxiety where they dread loss of self-worth even more than failure itself (Langer, 1989; Lay, 1986; Tremmel, 1993). One common result has already been noted: PBers who could be working often spend their time wishing for fantasy outcomes where things including writing will be quick, easy, and brilliant (Boice, 1994). As a rule, PBers are solving the wrong problem and working in the wrong ways. Too often, they cannot help themselves or accept help from others.

Why, exactly, does a product orientation make PBers hard to help? PBers, if and when they *do* get around to, say, writing, focus more on correctness and placating internal editors than on simply putting ideas onto paper or screen and revising them later (Boice,

1993c; Bowers, 1979). That is, even when PBers do work on a priority task, they do it inefficiently, and they chance blocking because they rush impulsively and they aim more for a perfect product than for a good writing experience. A product orientation (that is, a usual precursor of PBing) also wastes time on indignant thinking about injustices and failures.

A *process orientation* in contrast, helps bring optimistic, practical thoughts of what we would really like to accomplish and more relaxed, reflective ways of working at things like writing (Ellis & Knaus, 1977). Perhaps because we are unaccustomed to teaching such strategies to ourselves and our patients, we have not offered optimal help for PBers.

Neglect of the Real Penalties for PBing

Not only do scholars easily give up on PBers for their resistance to help. Traditional scholarship, as already noted, keeps PB in the polite category of a generally inconsequential problem. To help procrastinators, we must begin by acknowledging the unacceptable prices they pay for their inefficient habits.

Some examples follow. As a result of their stubbornly autonomous and product-oriented styles, chronic PBers have the worst work habits, are most given to emotional overreactions when things go badly, and are most resistant to taking up new opportunities for job enrichment (Boice, 1994; Jahoda, 1981). PBers as new faculty members most often complain of unbearable pressures to publish or perish while remaining least likely to participate in (or speak well of) campus programs that could facilitate writing. And they display kindred failings elsewhere in their daily lives; for example, the same PBers most often report illnesses such as influenzas and least often visit the dentist or participate in screening programs to detect cancer (Boice, 1992b). In the end, these PBers are most likely to fail in their careers, by their own definition and that of peers (Boice, 1993b).

Other Problems with PBers

So what has just been described is that there is no avoiding the reality of how difficult PBers are to assist. But it may help to review some of the other forces that keep PBers from generally seeking or accepting help. For one thing, they focus on exceptions, on other PBers who succeed or who are not visibly penalized by delaying or obstructing (for example, the diabetics who postpone preventive acts like to suppose themselves members of the fortunate minority who take no precautions and suffer no amputations, kidney failures, or blindness. [Blakeslee, 1994]). For another thing, PBers often present themselves as complainers doing little to cope and so discourage others from wanting to help them (see Silver, Wortman, & Crofton, in press). They overreact to their failures in ways that make them less open to help (for example, "I have to maintain complete control; I have to do this on my own or I won't do it at all; I don't want to appear weak"). And they, more than other people, imagine that giving up old habits of PBing means sacrificing freedom and creativity, for much the same reason that manics mistakenly resist taking lithium (Boice, 1994).

Together, these reasons why we researchers distance ourselves from PB and PBers provide an important background for reviewing the literature and finding effective treatments. PB, again, may occasion unusual amounts of discomfort and defensiveness and it may be unusually difficult to depict constructively and tolerably. To ease the way, I begin with traditional interpretations and move stealthily to their more objective, less dismissable counterparts.

2

The Traditional, Amiable View of Procrastination and Blocking

Amiable excuses for procrastination and blocking go back at least to Dr. Samuel Johnson: "Every man is, or hopes to be, an idler." G. A. Kimble (1979), the authority on departmental leadership in universities, light-heartedly advises chairpeople to leave correspondence unopened until its business takes care of itself. And so on.

Exotic and dismissable reasons for PB may be just as traditional. E. Bergler (1950), the first to use the label *writing blocks*, analyzed them as a symbolic refusal of mother's milk. His views, including an equation of writing with neurosis, serve today as little more than examples of extreme positions on PB that few people take seriously. For example:

The creative writer is also masochistic, but his elaboration on the basic conflict differs from the non-creative masochist in that it results in productivity. He acts, unconsciously, *both* roles—that of the corrected *giving* mother and the *recipient* child. By giving *himself out of himself* beautiful words and ideas, he "proves" conclusively: It is not true that I wanted masochistically to be *refused* by Mother (milk, love, kindness). The opposite is true: I wanted to *get*—and lavishly, for that matter.... (p. 69)

Why is *vomiting* (directly or in different disguises, for instance, "upset stomach") so often encountered in sterile writers when they try to outsmart their writing block? Psychogenically induced vomiting is a psychosomatic dramatization of the thought: "I *refuse* to accept." Writing presupposes the *giving* attitude: the writer acts unconsciously [as] the giving mother. (p. 116)

Throughout these traditionally superficial, conjectural accountings for PB, one principle holds true. The more forgiving or dismissable the excuse, the more common. (The single most frequent excuse may be that PBers are simply too busy to catch up with or complete tasks.)

THE DARK SIDE OF AMIABILITY

But this traditional amiability is only superficial. Writers who defy tradition by writing with disciplined productivity, without a trace of PB, are often taken to task as "rate-busters." You may already know this problem in a slightly different context.

A Tradition of Suspicion Toward Efficiency

Literary researchers tend to dismiss writers who produce a lot and who work hard (for example, Charles Dickens and Honoré Balzac) as victims of their lower-middle-class origins, almost as if they knew no better than to show up their superiors (Parini, 1989). Academics often suppose, erroneously, that those of us who write a lot necessarily suffer a loss in the quality and creativity of our work, that writers who write with regimen (the opposite of PB), such as A. Trollope (1929) or A. Asimov (1979), must do superficial work. The facts say otherwise (for example, Simonton, 1994). What these critics might better conclude is that being too obviously productive and nonprocrastinative can impair social approval of the less productive in academe (Ellenberger, 1970).

Tradition holds special commendation for writers who claim they write without discipline, without really trying. R. Brown (1981), author of one of psychology's most revered texts, presents himself in just such a way.

There is, I think, no forcing the discovery of good expository structure. ... One is grateful when it happens.... It went almost directly from my pencil to the printer and was written about as fast as my pencil could move. (p. 16)

Misleading, Incomplete, and Ineffectual Information

The second problem with amiability may be greater. Even in psychology, the area ostensibly best prepared to deal with this problem, scholarly coverage of PB has followed a similarly congenial course, contenting its occasional readers with untested, often unlikely guesses about what helps. Lawrence Kubie (1965), apparently using his own experience as a guide, advocated working at writing in the evening, when tired and when the preconscious can skirt usual, conscious inhibitions. In that way, presumably, writing blocks could be averted. In fact, such a practice typically leads to unintentionally short work sessions (terminated by sleep) or to insomnia (Boice, 1994). Better ways of getting past preconscious constraints, at any time of day, are simple strategies of free writing—the practice of writing whatever comes to mind, without pausing to correct or to heed internal reviewers (it will be reencountered later).

Most other amiable methods are just as dubious: P. Goodman (1952) hoped that self-disclosure to others would unloosen and organize one's story for writing; T. T. Wiggers (1984) supposed that art therapy (for example, modeling clay sculptures of oneself working) might release feelings about being blocked; M. A. Wratcher (1988) trusted scheduling of what needs to be done for the day as a way of countering procrastination; L. Block (1984) imagined that lists of one's fears about writing would unblock one. Evidently none of these methods work in the long run. Why, then, do they persist? They are amiably undemanding of writers who may need to do much more to get past their PB. They too often lead blocked writers to suppose they have done the necessary things to unblock themselves and that, having done so, they can do nothing more.

What comes of even more scholarly, research-based literature that occasionally struggles to the surface in this "amiable" atmosphere?

FOUR TYPES OF SCHOLARLY APPROACHES TO PROCRASTINATION AND BLOCKING

The scholarly literature on PB sorts itself into four approaches that evolved in sequential fashion (Boice, 1986). In a curious way, they move from primitive, unconscious strategies to more difficult, conscious practices for unblocking. As will be shown later, the evidence suggests that the old (and now discredited) approaches work as well as the contemporary ones. I begin with the approach to blocking and procrastination that is by far the oldest and most popular.

Automaticity

Automaticity is viewed as an aid to fluency because it induces working without conscious awareness of one's actions, and it may be as ancient as trances and hopes of supernatural help. It means, in effect, working at a task such as writing or speaking while one is in a trance state, without close consciousness of what is being written or said. It means working in the moment (as in a process orientation), without concerns for the quality or social acceptability of the product. It also means taking the process one step at a time, without anxiety about having to finish the whole project at once.

The most common procedure for inducing automaticity is as follows: The coach or therapist distracts the writer or speaker from conscious attention to what is going to be written or said by having her or him listen carefully to something being read by the therapist/hypnotist. The writer sits at a table, increasingly relaxed and ready, following prior instructions, to write on a piece of paper out of sight and off to the side. The writing (often beginning with doodles and nonsense) occurs quickly because it is managed without usual conscious inhibitions and excessive self-focus. To make writing easier, the writer's arm may be suspended in a mobile sling or the wrist rested on a moving platform like a planchette (yes, just like the one from a Ouija board).

With practice, automatic writers eventually produce fast, fluent, and legible prose—often with unprecedented fluency and creativity. Some automatic writers have become facile enough to write successive lines from left and right margins. Some have written best-selling books (see Ellenberger, 1970). All automatic writers, in my experience, are pleasantly surprised at the fluency and creativity they manage in the automatic state ("This is just the opposite experience of blocking, I tell you. It is easy, painless, and incredibly imaginative. . . . All-in-all, it's an eye opener for a proud blocker like me; I had no inkling I had all this facility within me, I've been going about writing in the wrong way").

Automaticity's modern popularity began with L. Borne's best-seller, *The Art of Becoming an Original Writer in Three Days* (1858). He admonished blocked writers to shut themselves away with only pen and paper and to write whatever came to mind. Nowadays we call this prescription—for writing unhesitantly, without stopping to correct or listen to internal editors—free writing (Elbow, 1973). In its modern form, not surprisingly, this descendent of automatic writing is less obviously linked to hypnotism and less reliant on so deep a trance or a coach.

Free writing works nicely to create momentum and spontaneity, even creativity, in writers. Borne's method was a crucial inspiration for Freud as a writer and as the popularizer of free talking (that is, free association). Spiritists including William James who used mediums and automatic writing to reach the other world, saw the potential in automaticity for greatly enhanced quantity and quality of poetry and prose (Gardiner, 1908). Old-fashioned automatic writing is still used occasionally by eccentric therapists including me (Boice, 1985b). It works, so far as I can tell, much better than does free writing to uninhibit blockers, but its perils (for example, addiction to the trance sessions or transference to the therapist) are also greater. Automatic writing should be done under the guidance of a well-trained, experienced therapist; even free writing should be done in sessions of moderate length to prevent excess and depression. Too often, uncoached free writers grow unable to move beyond their daily journal entries to more formal prose. In so doing, they demonstrate a curious combination of procrastinating and blocking.

Why does automaticity work so well to get past usual PBing? It provides the kind of unhesitating, Muse-inspired ease that writers, especially PBers, fantasize about. Evidence of its effectiveness is mostly anecdotal but compelling. Sergei Rachmaninoff, for example, delayed and blocked until a Dr. Dahl implanted the automatic suggestion (while the frustrated composer was half-asleep) that he would begin to write his concerts and that the work would be easy and good. It was.

Research on automaticity has been as disconnected as it has been sporadic. William James (1885–89) and his students (Solomons & Stein [the Gertrude Stein whose later writing often showed the peculiar spontaneity of automaticity], 1896) demonstrated that automaticity dissociates actions from consciousness. This fact suggests that writing can be generated outside the self-consciousness that often accompanies and encourages blocking. Pierre Janet (1889), the undercredited predecessor of Freud, demonstrated the power of automaticity to move patients past their conscious defenses . . . and to uncover the unconscious, fixed ideas that delayed and blocked them. Over the next several decades, other psychologists reported that automaticity works, for example, more readily with visual imaging than with writing (Martin, 1917) and that it can reveal an unconscious conflict implanted earlier, via hypnosis, and then forgotten (Harriman, 1951). Milton Erickson (1937) used automaticity to help cure thinking blocks. Erik Erikson and Lawrence Kubie (1940) showed its potential for deciphering cryptic messages. The potential for automaticity appeared to be limitless. In the main, though, traditionalists resisted and discredited it.

Automaticity finally appeared as if it would take on legitimacy in psychology when Ernest Hilgard, fresh from successes as a learning theorist and behaviorist, cornered the study of hypnosis. Consider just two findings from his laboratory that could still be useful to blocked writers:

• Moderate levels of dissociation/automaticity work best (Hilgard, 1977); that is, we free write most fluently when moderately hypnotized. Too much or too little dissociation from consciousness (that is, hypnosis) is deleterious.

• Writers who show the most hypnotic susceptibility (that is, willingness to suspend disbelief and go along with the suggestions of the hypnotist) also evince the most fluency and the least reliance on consciously selected words or on background editors (Bowers, 1979). Why? These writers are already somewhat dissociated from strict reliance on self-consciousness and internal editors and, so, more suggestible and spontaneous.

Both these are fascinating and useful ideas, but Hilgard's messages about PB, perhaps because of their link to another taboo topic in psychology, hypnosis, have gone unnoticed.

The result is that practitioners seem to make little progress in using automaticity. Few PBers learn about it; its advocates are largely limited to books that prescribe light-weight, largely uncoached, involvement for undergraduate students of composition. Even this most resilient form of automaticity, free writing, has chalked up a mixed record that includes disappointment and discontinuity. The chief popularizers of free writing in the twentieth century, D. Brande (1934) and P. Elbow (1973), developed their methods with no apparent awareness of predecessors or contemporaries working on similar methods (see Boice & Myers, 1986). Nor did they see the need to prove the effectiveness of free writing.

Still, one recent account of automaticity stands out. Its application was far deeper than usual methods of free writing. M. V. Barrios and J. L. Singer (1981) were direct in testing long-standing notions that creative scientists and literary figures rely on vivid dreaming to resolve impasses. They recruited an unusually large sample of creatively blocked artists (N=48) and employed two kinds of dream induction, one for waking and one for sleeping dreamers, to implant an expectation of (1) dreaming about projects, (2) remembering the dreams, and (3) transforming dream images into bouts of fluent work. Their methods, developed from classic dream-induction procedures (themselves fascinating attempts to help PBers become more fluent and creative), led to improved conditions of work and imagination, compared to non-dreaming controls. But more important, Barrios and Singer's outcomes illuminated creative blocks by distinguishing characteristics of artists who had the most difficulty giving them up: poor attentional control and guilty, dysphoric daydreaming.

Why do the results of Barrios and Singer receive no mention in the most scholarly books on the psychology of writing (Kellogg, 1994), on writing blocks (Leader, 1991), or on procrastination (Ferrari, Johnson, & McCown, 1995)? The article was published in an unfamiliar journal (but one easily retrievable via modern search techniques), and its results were ambiguous (for example, no reliable increase in dreaming about projects was found). With replications and clarifications, Barrios and Singer's research might have had more impact; it still merits replication and extension. What else, finally, has kept psychologists from appreciating that innovative study? One reason, perhaps, is its violation of the rule against intervening in PB.

Analytic and Humanistic Approaches

In the second historical approach to writing about PB, as in the first, clear conceptualizing occurred early and was quickly forgotten. Some of Freud's most intriguing theorizing concerned procrastination (Birner, 1993). He concluded that certain symptoms might substitute for sexual gratification and that one particularly pathological form was ritualized procrastination. For Freud (1900), the capacity to learn adaptive delays in affective discharge and action (an opposite pattern from the impatience of PB) not only meant conquering procrastination. It also allowed the moderation in behavior that underlies satisfying involvements with objects including work and love.

Freud's disciples (for example, Holtzman, 1962), similarly, saw some instances of procrastination as main defenses against the dread of uncontrolled excitement of the impulses. Psychoanalysts have long sensed the connection between impulsivity and PB. Indeed, they were the first to grasp its real essence as a problem of impatience and overstimulation.

Eventually, though, psychoanalytic reports effectively turned away from these thematic ideas. Since then, mentions of PB have been dominated by specific accounts of problem solving that pay only indirect attention to the underlying mechanisms of impulsivity and fear of overstimulation. Psychoanalysts now write about how, when they themselves are blocked, the act of writing anything will prime more serious writing (Quaytman, 1969). They also write about why overcoming angry impulses toward a family member helps a writer direct energies to working (Domash, 1976) and why paradoxical intention (where the therapist motivates the patient to get to work by pretending to suppose that he or she cannot do it) ultimately solves what seemed a more complex problem (Schuman, 1981).

Those who take a humanist approach often cloak similarly practical approaches in private language. A. C. Jones (1975), though a transactionalist, reduces the problem of PB to fluctuating definitions of success and prescribes behavioral sorts of planning and goal defining as a solution. B. J. Kronsky (1979), a gestalt psychologist, advocates a process approach to "working through" artistic blocks by, among other things, helping patients learn to relax and moderate high anxiety. J. Minninger (1980), a widely admired therapist amongst humanists, champions playful, cognitively based tactics to help writers get in touch with their internal editors and their fears of fraud.

Still there is a disappointing narrowness and superficiality to the whole analytic and humanistic approach. Almost nowhere in these and similar accounts of PB are there broad recognitions of precedents or of kindred fields of study. Nowhere is there evidence that the anecdotally described interventions work reliably and enduringly.

Objectivist Approaches

The least visible of the psychologies applied to PB is, predictably, the most behavioral, "hard-hearted," and interventionist. Although behaviorism dominated much of the research by psychologists in the twentieth century, its few forays into studies of PB have not been influential. One reason, according to critics, was behaviorism's frank objectivism. From its beginnings, behaviorism excluded any role for subjective factors in PB; it gave little credence to inborn personality traits of PBing. Instead, it focused on what PBers did that was maladaptive and on what they could do differently, better.

In fact, the movement toward objectivism began well before it was called behaviorism, with pioneers such as Janet and Josiah Royce (names now esteemed only by obsessive teachers of the history of psychology like me). T. Ribot (1906), for example, always trying to draw psychology away from narrowness, pointed out the other side of the dissociation of consciousness (and its automaticity) that was a fad at the time. Association, he said, is the conscious process of planning and organizing the things we bring up with the aid of automaticity. His forgotten point was that treatments of PB needed to do more than induce automaticity and momentum; they also required conscious, mindful work at planning and organizing for efficient, timely action. J. Amar (1919), another European involved in the psychology of work, demonstrated that fluency in artistic activities, including music and writing, benefitted from efficient pacing and timely resting. PB, an opposite of fluency, was seen as the product of impulsive rushing and its problems including fatigue. PB, in this objective view, was not the price of creativity; it was the chief underminer of artistic productivity.

Fruition of those practical, objective approaches can be seen in two American classics, both now long buried.

The first is that of J. E. Downey (1918). She surveyed what helps and hinders writers (and provided the only review of writing research in a major psychology journal until that of J. R. Hayes and L. S. Flower in 1986). Her exercises for inducing fluency could still be useful today in combating PB (for example, practicing habits of observation and of building facilitative mental sets before writing).

The second overlooked landmark is the work of H. K. Nixon (1928). He rediscovered similarly practical strategies for reliable fluency (again, the opposite of PB). He was even more explicit than his predecessors in clarifying the unwelcome news that creative writing and productivity are more the result of hard work and borrowing than of inspiration or genius. His related caution merits another look: Writing, because it grows more effortless with practice and improved concentration, may seem to have magical origins. With a closer look, Nixon concluded, we can see that it is no different from other well-practiced habits.

Another objectivist remembered for his social improprieties, the best-selling novelist Anthony Trollope (Glendinning, 1993), proposed a reason why we prefer to attribute our successes to Muses or genes: we like to believe that hard work is beneath the person of genius or good family. Pride and elitism play a major but often overlooked role in PB.

This nettlesome, democratic tradition of practicalism and behaviorism persists in low profile. It continues to make the same basic points. Some of its present-day champions (for example, Perkins, 1981) observe that society pays too little notice to carefully reasoned accounts of why creative fluency is mostly good habits, not good luck. No one seems to notice. One behaviorist, because he is unavoidably visible, is criticized for attributing his productivity to objective factors such as regular bouts of writing (Skinner, 1979b).

Laboratory Research

Where modern behaviorism has made its biggest, most useful strides is in research done with laboratory animals (a domain where anti-interventionists, but not antivivisectionists, generally leave behaviorists alone). A good example can be seen in laboratory studies of impulse control in laboratory subjects.

At first glance, these studies seem remote from PB (other key researches present the same appearance, as will be shown throughout the book—perhaps because researchers fare better when publishing accounts with no obvious links to PB). A. W. Logue (1994), for instance, finds impulsivity a problem born of not having learned to wait for larger, longer-delayed rewards. In the perspective taken here, this means that PB is partly a problem of not having learned impulse control. Rachlin (1995), a kindred researcher, shows how impulsivity can be controlled with broad, rewarding patterns of behaving that make exceptional and problematic acts (what we might call PBing) too uncomfortable and expensive to entertain. Restated, that means PBers could fare better simply by rearranging their rewards so that a maladaptive act of PB would be too costly to maintain regularly. How? They can deny themselves access to something important, like television for the day, if they revert to PBing. They can make the short-term costs sizable enough to allow someone who usually procrastinates and blocks to put off PBing until long-term rewards occur. In an ironic way, then, an impressive cure for PB consists of delaying and inhibiting tendencies to PB by making them even more aversive, in the short run, than the activity that will bring the most long-term rewards. Said simply, it fights fire with fire. Finally, R. F. Baumeister, T. R. Heatherton, and D. M. Tice (1994), experts on failures in self-regulation, make a related point: PBers favor speed and immediacy over accuracy and constancy. PBers are generally more concerned about trying to manage short-term comfort than long-term effectiveness in solving important problems. So, to control their emotions, they procrastinate and block. Clearly, it seems to me, behaviorally oriented psychologists offer some uncommonly useful insights into PB.

Why Behaviorism Fell Short

Even this behavioral approach, for all its objectivism and empiricism, typifies the discontinuity and narrow superficiality traditionally associated with PB. Most quantitatively based accounts of actually helping PBers appeared during a brief period and were single-case studies (that is, of only one patient) with dubiously narrow cures and ethics. For example, H. M. Boudin (1972) induced a blocked patient to relinquish her usual reliance on amphetamines as fuel for writing by keeping her at his house and rationing food, cigarettes, liquor, sleeping location, and rest contingent on how many pages of her research report she typed, (amazingly unethical, but true) J. T. Nurnberger and J. Zimmerman (1970) used "productive avoidance" to force writing. They persuaded a blocked assistant professor who had not written in two years to agree to send prewritten checks to hated organizations on days when he did not meet writing quotas. He wrote.

Eventually, behavioral studies included larger numbers of cases but not much larger. B. L. Hall and D. E. Hursch (1982), for instance, coached four faculty members who procrastinated on priority activities to do things like post a schedule on their office doors to limit student interruptions. Two of the subjects spent verifiably more time on the task, two did not, leaving questions about why the strategy did not work more generally or how long the changes would endure. In a slightly larger study, I reported reliable gains for eight previously blocked writers who wrote each day to gain access to rewards (for example, reading the newspaper) or to avoid punishments (for example, missing a daily shower [Boice, 1982]). While all those academicians wrote reliably when contingencies were in effect but not in their absence, doubts remained about how happily they had worked or how well they would do without the program.

Why Most of the Behaviorists Who Studied PB Lost Interest

The behaviorists lost interest because they apparently concluded that they had shown just what they had hoped to: that writing is a behavior like any other, subject to usual behavioral laws, not to free will, genetic predisposition, or mysterious inspiration (Pear, 1977). In the behavioral view, neither PB nor its treatments are out of the ordinary. With that fact seemingly established, PB could be treated with already accepted behavioral therapies (or, more likely, ignored). As it turned out, behaviorists were somewhat right and somewhat wrong. Their methods work, to a point, but there is much more to overcoming PB in lasting fashion than merely inducing timely momentum, whether by way of automaticity (as in the oldest approach) or of contingency management (where writers can be forced to write by way of rewards and punishments). This point will be taken up again later.

Still, some of these early behavioral studies suggest what might have developed with sustained interest in PB. Here, for example is a study that should have been followed up (and an apparent reason why it wasn't): M. J. Dillon, H. M. Kent and R. W. Malott (1980) used a systematic supervisory plan to help twelve graduate students maintain steady, well-directed work toward their theses. Clearly, the kinds of supports these investigators created should be standard features in all graduate degree programs (for example, regularly scheduled meetings with advisers and with other thesis students and specification of necessary tasks at all stages and regular feedback about progress towards subgoals). But many professors, I think, would cringe at the strong contingency used in that study—later, obligatory mention, in students' letters of recommendation from the department, of how well they complied. And they might wonder if the induced fluency stood up; Malott and his colleagues never mention whether the subjects finished their theses. What effect did this practical research have? No other researchers have duplicated Malott's studies on PB; few have cited them. These studies, like most other behavioral efforts, were so powerfully controlling and interventionist that they may have annoyed more people than they helped.

Additional Shortcomings of Behavioral Studies

In most of the behavioral accounts of PB that continue to appear, another problem persists. Researchers otherwise notable for practicing sound design and continuity settle for less in studying and reporting interventions for PB, almost as though hurrying in and out of the topic. B. F. Skinner (1981), for example, relied on anecdotes when advising students how to find writing fluency. P. Salovey and M. D. Haar (1990) came closer to soundness in carrying out their comparisons of: cognitive (for example, stress inoculation), process (for example, free writing), and wait-list control conditions with fifty-ore writers selected for their high scores on self-report indices of writing anxiety and blocks. Part of their result is promising: The combined cognitive and process group fared better than did process-alone subjects on measures of self-reported satisfaction. But both interventions produced about the same, mediocre, improvements in laboratory-based samples of writing. So in the end, even the Salovey and Haar study leaves readers wondering what really changed for writers and what would have happened in a cognitive-alone condition (that comparison group was inexplicably missing). Their research, too, had no apparent impact on how researchers conceptualize or treat PB.

Another, less conclusive, cognitively oriented study of blocking remains far more cited and emulated. It doesn't deserve to be. M. Rose (1980) uncovered the useful notion that blockers too often follow rigid rules of composition (for example, trying to complete a manuscript in a single draft, with few revisions—what might here be called a product-oriented approach). But consider how Rose tested his ideas. After claiming that students can be trained to abandon inflexible rules (by pointing out to them the dysfunctional qualities of such rules and the value of flexible alternatives), he cites his evidence for effectiveness:

Operating this way, I was successful with Mike. Sylvia's story, however, did not end as smoothly. Though I had three 45 minute contacts with her, I was not able to appreciably alter her behavior . . . students like Sylvia may need more extended, more affectively oriented counseling sessions that blend the instructional with the psychodynamic. (p. 400)

Personality as the Basis of PB

The fourth approach to conceptualizing PB is the latest and fastest growing. It has treated PB both more amiably and more objectively than any other. Personality did not became important in accounts of PB until J. A. Daly's research on assessing writing apprehension (as a variant of the communication apprehension that had already been established in communication research). The Writing Apprehension Scale (Daly & Miller, 1975) quickly became the standard in studies that correlated writing problems with other personality variables and with measures of college-course outcome. Some correlates, such as the connection between writing apprehension and math anxiety, are disputed; some, like such apprehension's link to avoidance of higher-level writing courses, are not (Daly, 1985). For all its literature, though, notions of writing apprehension have yet to prove reliably useful in help-ing PBers or in relating broadly to other self-reported measures of PB (Peterson, 1987).

Some of the most amiable attempts at associating personality types with PB appeared first in studies of the Meyers-Briggs Type Indicator (MBTI). The MBTI is Jungian in its genesis and good-natured in its typings. G. H. Jensen and J. K. DiTiberio (1984) used MBTI profiles from thesis support groups, from workshops on writing, and from a writing clinic to draw informal conclusions about how personality types relate to blocking. They concluded, for instance, that extroverts may block because they especially dislike the isolation of writing; it seems, when stymied, they need to make normally private writing sessions extroverted enough to include more social contact and feedback. Though MBTI inter-pretations of PB make fun reading ("Which one of these profiles fits me?"), they are of doubtful reliability and validity. Jensen and DiTiberio employed a few convenient cases of clear personality types who dealt with blocking in predictably different ways to jus-tify their maps, much as phrenologists once did. In the end, they provided no evidence that interventions suggested by MBTI anal-yses help writers unblock in reliable, lasting ways.

Mainstream Research on Personality

Even when personality studies moved nearer to systematic series of investigations, the same sorts of problems persisted—the
amiable kinds that have helped keep PB a nonthreatening, dismissable phenomenon. For example, examples were given earlier
of PB explained in socially acceptable terms such as perfectionism
and fear of failure. Still, present-day investigators have been
unique in seeing the need to move beyond traditional, amiable
portrayals of PB; here is where old ways of studying PB begin to
break down. Why? Only in the last decade have PB researchers
taken the time to conduct follow-up studies where they could re-
examine their conclusions or be influenced by others pursuing similar programs. Consider how this subarea has moved toward more
objective, substantial inquiries in the investigations of five principal players.

The first is Esther Rothblum. She and her colleagues began
programmatic work in the area of personality and PB. Specifically,
she looked for reasons why PB seems more common among
women (the answer seemed to be that women have lower self-
esteem). Generally, she provided one of the first clearly empirical
pictures of procrastination and of its underappreciated causes (for
example, aversions to work). Her factor analyses, for instance,
suggested that fear of failure and aversiveness to the particular
task accounted for most of the variance in PB (Solomon & Rothblum, 1984).

Correlations between her own index of procrastinatory tendencies and other self-reported measures helped expand this interpretation: Scores on the Procrastination Assessment Scale for
Students (PASS [Solomon & Rothblum, 1988]) predicted: (1) delays in taking self-paced quizzes, (2) lower grades, (3) more anx-
iety-related symptoms and emotionality, and (4) lower self-esteem
(Rothblum, Solomon, & Murakami, 1986). The same index,
PASS, correlated significantly with procrastinating on a term paper outline, on the paper itself, and on completing a research
questionnaire, and with irrational beliefs about working in classes
(Beswick, Rothblum, & Mann, 1988).

By the time Rothblum had quit the field of PB for the arena of
gender issues (perhaps, in part, because it offers more social sup-

port and reinforcement), she published the following conclusions (1990): PBers report more fear of failure, and they fear the consequences of failure (for example, public embarrassment) more than failure itself. They go to extremes to avoid feedback about their public performances. Their fear of failure may play a bigger role in PB than does ability or study skills. While Rothblum's studies are nowadays faulted for methodological problems (Ferrari, Johnson, & McCown, 1995), her competent and literate style, her application of findings to a population that obviously deserved help, her collegial sociability, and the appearance of her writings in mainstream sources helped stimulate others to follow up on her work.

The second player is Clarry Lay (1986), who, almost at the same time as the early work of Rothblum, initiated his own program of connecting personality measures to students' reports of procrastination. Some of his explanations of PB seem obvious (like deficiency in planning), and some flatter PBers (for example, saying that procrastinators are more insistent on doing tasks for the sake of their enjoyable outcomes). But a few of his early revelations were not amiable, not the sort of thing traditional defenders of PBers would want to hear: for example, PBers report that they are more likely to engage in low-priority tasks.

In further studies, Lay revealed more unexpected complexities of PB. One was differences between procrastinators who overestimate and those who underestimate time needed to complete tasks (the former tend to be more pessimistic). Another was procrastinators who handicap themselves by spending less than adequate time on projects likely to succeed than on projects likely to fail. A third complexity was the remorse that PBers feel during exams (but fail to follow up on later). Still others are an indirect but powerful effect of negative expectations on PB; distinctions between procrastination and handicapping oneself (the latter syndrome, although it often includes dilatoriness, is supposedly different and broader in scope); and an intricate relationship between time-management skills and PB (Lay, 1988; 1989; 1990; 1992; Lay & Burns, 1991; Lay, Knish, & Zanatta, 1992; Lay & Schouwenberg, 1993).

The third participant in these sustained looks at PB and personality is Norman Milgram. Among other things, he uses self-reporting to suggest that students who plan or study efficiently report greater life satisfaction because they are less harassed and overwhelmed by things that need doing (Milgram, 1988). This article (along with publications by Bond & Feather, 1988; Britton & Tesser, 1991; Rosenbaum, 1980) was one of the first articles to cast nonPBers in so positive a light. But like Rothblum and Lay, Milgram found that PBers describe themselves in ways that protect their self-esteem and are more likely to put off and resent tasks seen as unpleasant or imposed (Milgram, Batori, & Mowrer, 1993; Milgram, Sroloff & Rosenbaum, 1988).

The fourth main participant in this subarea is Joseph Ferrari; his outpouring of articles matches the speed and impressiveness of his automotive namesake. And his correlation-based studies echo and expand the findings by colleagues just listed. Procrastinators are, by their own accounting, abnormally concerned with their public images (thus, he agrees with Rothblum in assuming that PBing does not result from a mere lack of skills such as timing). Women with low self-esteem are most likely to handicap their own performances. Compulsive PBers report higher self-consciousness and impaired self-understanding. PBers judge other PBers more harshly than do nonPBers; and procrastination can be factor-analyzed into first-level loadings of social anxiety, protective self-presentations, and self-handicapping (Ferrari, 1991a; 1991b; 1991c; 1991d; 1992a; 1992b; 1993).

Ferrari also confirms two suggestions made earlier in this chapter. First, the MBTI relates weakly to PB (Ferrari, Parker, & Ware, 1992). Second, PBers are uniquely motivated by the arousal of working against a deadline (Ferrari, 1993).

The fifth principal player in the outburst of studies about personality and PB is William McCown. He brings a somewhat more behavioral interest to this area, one that began with inquiries about the roles of anxiety and task avoidance as the events that may reinforce PB (McCown & Johnson, 1989a,b). In two weeks of daily assessments of self-reported anxiety of students facing exams, for instance, he and a colleague found that tension increases as the exam period nears. Indeed the rise in anxiety is apparently so sudden and great that students can no longer avoid it. Instead, they turn to frantic, last-minute studying. (No mention is made of blocking.)

How do findings such as these seem to support the reinforcement theory associated with behaviorism? Procrastinators generally do what is most reinforcing (at least in the short run).
Students designated as procrastinators on a questionnaire were far
more likely than nonPBers to recall the pleasure of completing
tasks with little time to spare (McCown & Ferrari, 1995). Student
procrastinators avoided studying by engaging in other, reportedly
more reinforcing tasks (McCown & Johnson, 1991).

So, does McCown, a member of the traditionalist establishment,
conclude that there is a broad value in appreciating PB from a
behavioral view? He doesn't quite. He supposes that if behaviorists were to make their case fully, they would have to prove that
the role of escape or avoidance in phobias (a link well established
in behavioral research) is the same for PB. But because traditionalists cannot or will not label PB in negative terms, they leave the
behavioral analogy safely behind them; PB, by their definition,
cannot be akin to phobias:

> We doubt that the dynamics of procrastination can be accounted for by
> the simple phobia model. Phobias and other major fears traditionally
> assumed to be "neurotic" are invariably described by the person expe-
> riencing them as generating a high degree of emotionality and an aware-
> ness of the phobic stimulus. . . . Procrastinators, on the other hand, often
> have difficulty knowing what they are avoiding. . . . Because of this high
> level of fear, phobic patients are usually quite motivated to seek treat-
> ment. (Ferrari, Johnson, & McCown, 1995, p. 31)

Consider what McCown and his colleagues are really saying here:
(1) phobias are neurotic and thus unlike PB; (2) procrastinators,
as opposed to phobics, are unaware of what they avoid; and (3)
phobics, not PBers, naturally seek treatments or interventions.

What is the factual basis for these claims? There is none that I
can find. The literature on phobias is well established and respectable, and the interventions of this field are uncommonly impressive (for example, Barlow, 1993). Even so, its advances do not
include the claim that phobics are necessarily aware of what they
avoid (even a casual acquaintance with agoraphobics, the often
house-bound people who remain reclusive rather than face the
embarrassment of fainting in the midst of crowded and large pub-

lic spaces, reveals that they commonly remain vague about the nature and causes of their malady). Nor do the leading researchers and practitioners of phobias use the label of "neurotic" to describe their patients (for example, American Psychiatric Association, 1994). Finally, experts on phobia do not suppose that phobics are particularly inclined to seek treatment (nor have they ever drawn comparisons to the tendency of PBers to seek treatment). Why then do McCown and other traditionalists make these claims? They are working imaginatively to treat PB amiably.

So in much of the other research that McCown and his collaborators (often Judith Johnson) report, the topics and conclusions are like those of the other leading experts on PB. For instance: extraverts experience more distractions in completing tasks (because, presumably, they are less socially isolated than introverts), and so they report more academic procrastination (McCown, Petzel, & Rupert, 1987). Curiously, this relationship may not hold beyond the college years. Collegiates who report procrastination are more likely to test as both venturesome (that is, extraverted) and impulsive. Adults, in contrast, seem to experience more routinization of everyday life, and so they no longer show a strong relationship between venturesomeness and procrastinating (McCown, 1995).

To his credit, McCown goes beyond the norm of traditionalism in studying procrastination among adults (usually by means of phone interviews) and in noting the limitations in generalizing findings from college students.

Methodological Conflicts Among Personality Researchers

By about 1992, as these productive traditionalists confirmed one another's general conclusions about the nature of self-reported PB, the climate began to grow slightly less amiable. Some of the change was the inevitable result of increasingly refined and diverse methodology. For example, perfectionism, a commonly reported correlate of PB, had been used too broadly; now, evidently, only its socially prescribed (that is, socially acceptable) dimension is properly seen as a direct cause of PB (Flett, Blankenstein, Hewitt, & Koledin, 1992).

Other criticisms are easier to fathom: Some of the best note the ambiguity of most traditional constructs (for example, self-esteem) favored in questionnaire-based studies of PB (McCown, Johnson, & Petzel, 1989; McCown & Johnson, 1991). The alternative suggested by the critics just cited (a position aligned with Eysenck's widely used personality measures of extroversion, neuroticism, and psychoticism in psychology) has yet to be widely adopted in other laboratories.

More important, traditionalists have begun quietly to criticize their own research on PB. Consider a typical confound in studies that purportedly show the uninvolvement of time-management problems in PBers (a traditionally favored, nonskills and nonbehavioral view among personality researchers). Usual methodologies in these studies (for example, highly structured tasks, short-term deadlines, ready cues for self-management—all in contrived situations with student subjects) may make poor management of time unlikely, even for people who would normally display it (Lay & Schouwenberg, 1993).

How Useful Is Traditional Personality Research?

At least for the present, there is a problem in trying to learn much that is valid and useful about PB from traditional personality study. Its fast pace and often conflicting conclusions, its confusing intricacies of traits and correlates that vary from one test instrument to another, its artificial conditions of inducing PB, and its growing disagreements about the best laboratory methods—all these can incline readers to dismiss it, perhaps prematurely, just as readers might disregard older, more subjective accounts of PB.

Oddly, most of these findings by present-day traditionalists who prefer personality explanations confirm what popular literature for laypersons has been saying for decades (for example, Lay's finding that PBers prefer low-priority tasks). Are there real prospects of change? Consider what the traditionalists see as a quantum leap in their approach to PB.

An Authoritative Book on PB and Personality

The zenith of the personality movement appears to be an enthusiastic, expansive book, already noted, with chapters by almost all its leading researchers: *Procrastination and Task Avoidance*

(Ferrari, Johnson, & McCown, 1995). This book, its editors and authors claim, is the first comprehensive and scientific account of procrastination (they are uncompromising in their rejection of earlier, seemingly less empirical books).

But early on, Ferrari, Johnson, & McCown add a proviso about expecting too much of applied science in the sort of approach they favor: they assume that the area is not ready for technology that would change procrastinating, at least for now. Why? True scientists like themselves (who are at last making a significant beginning in the study of PB) must stick to their laboratories and to descriptive accounts of the personality traits involved. So nowhere in their book do the authors mention behavioral studies of the sort reviewed earlier in this chapter; nowhere do they cite already published studies with direct observations of and interventions for PBers. Clearly, this is a narrow stance, one that draws no links to quantitatively tested interventions or to blocking.

Still it is an important and informative book. *Procrastination and Task Avoidance* begins with an interesting defense of PBers. For example, while the concept of procrastination existed throughout written history, it only recently acquired the unfortunate connotation we give it now. In olden times, it was conceptualized more accurately and humanely, in the view of Ferrari and his colleagues, as a matter of deferred judgments and wise constraints; negative meanings were absent until punctuality became a necessary part of the Industrial Revolution.

The central position advocated in Ferrari, Johnson, & McCown, then, is that procrastination is not an irrational behavior but rather something generally carried out in our own best interests. (Again, none of the studies from which this conclusion is drawn are based on people who procrastinated about the kinds of things mentioned before—delayed treatments for diabetes or examinations for symptoms of cancer, avoided conversations about marital problems, overdue work and failed academic careers.)

Keeping in mind other limitations of their data base (reliance on questionnaire results that allow self-serving answers and supposition that PBers can identify the causes of their dilatoriness in a meaningful fashion), what can we learn from them about the nature of procrastination? Judge for yourself from some of their more intriguing reports. In one study, patients who evidenced the

strongest symptoms of problems (for example, depression, substance abuse, phobias) had waited longest (that is, procrastinated)
before seeking treatment and had also scored highest on a personality test for procrastinatory tendencies (this unsurprising result almost, but not quite, casts PBers in a negative light). In a
second highlighted study, people who tested as narcissistic scored
highest on the same self-report index of procrastination used in
the first study. This result suggests that at least one category of
what psychiatry calls personality disorders may have links to PB.

Still, some of the personality traits can seem elusive. For instance, one of the editors finds that extroversion relates to self-
reported measurements of procrastination. On closer examination,
that factor is relabeled a lack of conscientiousness. But extroversion is well defined in personality research, conscientiousness is
not. Moreover, conscientiousness seems to invoke the very moral
judgment the editors want to avoid. The confusion in all this research is so inescapable that Ferrari and his colleagues do admit
some shortcomings. Here they address the problem of the different scales of procrastination that supposedly measure the same
thing:

Furthermore, studies should compare and contrast these scales to determine if any, or all, are necessary sufficient measures of procrastination.
... two scales assess different motives for procrastinatory behavior,
thereby suggesting they be used for different purposes. (p. 70)

Another suggestion of what could have been done better might
occur to readers accustomed to looking less amiably at PB than
do personality researchers: traditionalists may have shaped their
various self-report devices to measure attitudes and memories so
as to support their own preconceptions about what procrastination
is. (Without direct, real-life observations of their procrastinators
procrastinating, we cannot know.)

There is, though, promise of progress in *Procrastination and
Task Avoidance*. It ends with a pair of inquiries into what kinds
of interventions might prove helpful for procrastinators. While
these ideas draw only superficially on prior, proven methods in
the literature, they almost demonstrate effectiveness. In one ap-
proximation to a systematic intervention, a group of students was

subjected to a brief series of practices aimed at changing anxious cognitions and ruminations. The result was an increase in their sense of comradeship and in testimonials of improvement—but, alas, it was not accompanied by lasting proof of changes or of indications that this intervention worked any better than nonspecific treatments. The second trial intervention dealt with adult procrastinators and produced the conclusion that a great variety of therapies (behavioral, cognitive, and psychodynamic) must be employed to help them. That can hardly be called news; such deductions have been common in the literature on psychotherapy for some time.

So where, in the end, do these personality researchers leave us? We are left with only a few guesses and doubtful experiments on interventions for helping PBers and with little appreciable advance over the explanations of the popularizers they so harshly criticize (the best-known popularizers will be reviewed below). We are left with still amiable accounts of procrastination but also, in the end, with signs of disregarding the taboo against more direct study and intervention.

WHY TRADITIONAL, AMIABLE APPROACHES TO PROCRASTINATION AND BLOCKING GENERALLY FAIL

Because this research on personality types represents what is best known of psychology's inquiries about PB, it merits three brief analyses as a kind of summing up that permits the book to move on with continuity. In one analysis I ask more specifically how much its recent studies add to popular books and articles on PB. In the next, I recast the shortcomings of personality studies as generally characteristic of amiable and dismissable portraits of PB. In the third, I show further that the changes now underway in the field, however flawed, are headed in the right direction. Together these critiques set the stage for a more optimistic, broader view of developments, most of them outside conventional approaches to PB.

How Traditional Research Compares to Popular Writing on PB

I could dismiss the popular literature as conjectural, and it is. But dismissal would avoid the preliminary involvement in learning about PB that can generate intriguing ideas and make one more familiar with usually awkward topics (for example, recall my earlier point about why hypnotic susceptibility predicts fluency, not blocking). I'll try to keep redundancies mercifully concise.

There are just three books about procrastination that most people read. One is A. Lakein's (1974) perpetual best-seller, *How to Get Control of Your Time and Your Life*. He emphasizes breaking goals into doable acts, into what needs doing today, into what is most worth doing—all while finding more free time in which to do a bit of nothing. His is an ambitious program. Like experts before and after him, he cautions against a usual failing among PBers: spending too much time on routine and easy tasks because they provide the ready satisfaction of doing something well. And he, like almost everyone who has given workshops and advice about PB, advocates making a seemingly overwhelming task more manageable by first breaking it into small bits of work. Two of Lakein's points may be especially useful: First, he convincingly argues that the more planning and detailing, the better the chances for action (because planning *is* decision making, because planning is more easily controlled when it is slowed down). Second, he advocates noticing and supplanting the habitual escapes that PBers turn to when faced with aversive tasks.

Another standard book, one already noted, is Ellis and Knaus's (1977) *Overcoming Procrastination*. Ellis, who has made a career of confronting taboos in psychology, begins with typical and helpful immodesty: the prior literature on PB is mostly useless; he and his colleagues are unusually knowledgeable about this commonly slighted topic. Ellis and Knaus use notions from rational-emotive therapy (and from their extensive clinical experience) to explain why we procrastinate and block (1) self-downing (as, for instance, the result of imposing unnecessary demands on ourselves); (2) low tolerance of frustration (that is, the aversion to work later verified by Rothblum and other researchers mentioned above); (3) hostility (as a result of irrational beliefs that if others do not treat us fairly, we must retaliate by delaying and holding back).

Simply said, Ellis and Knaus see PB as just another emotional problem, one tied to perfectionism (with its excessive need for social approval), to anxiety (by overgeneralizing and taking a pessimistic view), to guilt (as a result of not facing up to shortcomings in rational fashion), and to self-fulfilling prophecies (where expectations of failure lead to just that). Ellis, like Freud, associates PB with problems of irrational impulsiveness; both Ellis and Freud can be seen as adherents of PB as a problematic tendency that pervades all of everyday living.

The third book, J. B. Burka and L. M. Yuen's *Procrastination* (1983), may provide the best model for tempering the hard realities of PB with a modicum of amiability (something that may be essential to finding an audience for such an awkward topic). They begin agreeably, by reassuring readers that the authors, too, are PBers: "We're still marveling that we finished this book only two years after the original deadline!" (p. ix). Soon after, they provide a palatable account of how PB usually proceeds (as a cycle of enthusiastic beginnings of projects, then waiting until feeling pushed, then paralysis and shame, then pleasant distractions, then hoping for magic, and so on). Their congenial attributions of causes include fear of failure (and its attendant belief that demonstrated ability equals self-worth). But Burka and Yuen intermix less socially acceptable reasons for PBing such as the need to control and the tendency to rebel. And, for the first time since the old psychologies of work, the authors offer clear attributions of skills deficits in PB, notably PBers are deficient in knowing how to tell time (for example, accurately predicting how much time a task will require) and how to use it wisely (for example, by working in small bits of time).

Standard books on blocking merit far less summarizing. The first, Bergler's *The Writer and Psychoanalysis* (1950), was noted earlier for its exaggerations (for example: "The writer is the most antisocial human being conceivable," p. 239). The second book, K. Mack and E. Skjei's *Overcoming Writing Blocks* (1979), gives advice that seems generally sound (for example, breaking tasks into manageable bits), but its arrangement into a plethora of every idea that might help is disorienting. In fact, *Overcoming Writing Blocks* tends to overwhelm and distance writers I have tracked through blocks (Boice, 1994). The third book is Leader's literary analysis, *Writer's Block* (1991). He describes his effort as solely a theoretical and historical enquiry. It, more than any of the works discussed here, keeps PB at an intellectual, amiable level. For instance, Leader defines writing blocks as somewhat like Mark Twain's metaphor of "the tank running dry," as different from

John Keats's "delicious diligent indolence," as more than a matter
of W. P. Thackeray's sitting unable to write or do anything else;
they are as much a matter of misery as of silence and are closer
to an accumulated fatigue from having fought resistance for so
long. While Leader displays an impressive grasp of literary people
and their presumed blocking experiences, he offers little of a practical bent for most readers. His view of blocking is anything but
egalitarian.

What do these six examples of popular literature offer us besides guessing and prejudice? They presage almost all of the issues
considered in recent research on PB. Perhaps because popular
accounts have an extensive basis in observations of PBers, they
disclose key things still neglected by personality researchers (for
example, customary patterns of escape from pressures that initiate
bouts of PBing as noted by Lakein, 1977). Even so, popular accounts of PB have done little to help make it a legitimate, widespread topic of study and treatment. Nor have their authors
checked to see why some interventions work better than others.

G. Ainslie (1975), a behavioral researcher on self-control, dem-
onstrates the kinds of verification that could add credibility to
both popular and laboratory accounts of PBers. He used laboratory research to figure out why breaking tasks into small, manageable units helps: If the entire sequence of steps to completion
consists of doable tasks, then there is reason to proceed. But if
the last step, however far off, seems undoable, we tend to avoid
the tasks that precede it. (His insights about the steps in finding
impulse control have gone largely unnoticed in the field of PB,
popular or laboratory.)

Other General Shortcomings of Research on PB and Personality

The single biggest failing of traditional research studies on PB
results, as usual, from observing a propriety: politely not watching
what PBers actually do. Reconsider one of the limitations of basing almost everything we know about PB on self-reports (as opposed to direct observation): Self-estimates are often self-serving
and misleading. When, for instance, faculty members are asked,
retrospectively, to estimate how they spent their work weeks, they

portray themselves as constantly busy and overworked. When the same academics face occasional, unannounced observations (and regular self-recordings) of what they do, it turns out that they typically spend far less time working on priority projects like scholarly writing and far more on unnecessary things like rereading memos or worrying than they had claimed earlier (Boice, 1987). What at first they describe as a problem of too little time they eventually appreciate as a failing of efficiency.

So when we expect PBers themselves immediately to see and openly report the most basic aspects of their dilatoriness and opposition, we may demand far too much of them. Most PB occurs so surreptitiously, and with so little social feedback, that PBers can take the easy way out in offering seemingly obvious and socially acceptable explanations for it (Boice, 1985a). This fact may be part of the reason why traditional researchers have not suspected that PB has general, simple roots. What could direct observation add to the picture? It might lead to the realization that PB may in fact be little more than a problem of not knowing how to work efficiently (not as easy an admission as fearing failure or loving perfectionism). D. Meichenbaum (1985), a pioneer in cognitive therapies, comes to a similar conclusion in the area of teaching thinking: progress begins with elemental performance skills that counter tendencies to expect failure and to work amid negative affect. So do K. A. Ericsson and N. Charness (1994), who observe that expert performance (another antithesis of PB) comes only with deliberate, sustained practice of skills, not as a result of ingrained factors such as talent or personality.

Consider how this skills-based notion of PB, one not readily appreciated until PBers are seen repeatedly in action, relates to one inference reviewed earlier. Rothblum concluded that her subjects' endorsement of fear of failure and task aversion showed that PB was not primarily a matter of skill or deficient ability. She implied, congenially, that if anxieties and distastes were somehow removed, PBers might perform without a hitch. She may not have considered the alternatives.

A Pause for a Preliminary Proposal

Why not assume that all of PB's self-reported manifestations can be explained as deficient skills? Or assume that anxieties and distastes are symptoms of deeper causes? Perhaps fears and delays are understandable outcomes of not knowing how to do some things efficiently and happily, of not knowing how to cope with inevitable disappointments, of not knowing how to proceed amid difficulty and unpleasantness?

In a preparatory way it can be shown how these questions suggest simple, practical notions to fit the usual cycle of PB as it can be observed in real life: We put off things that make us uncomfortable and uncertain (because we do not know efficient ways of starting without already being motivated), the more so when we have histories of failing and suffering at them. We raise the stakes of perfectionism by supposing that the longer the delay, the better the result must be (without knowing how to ignore such pressures by working in a process, not product-oriented, mode). Add to that another complexity: Most of us accept traditional notions of talent, particularly the expectation that it can be demonstrated, in the right people, almost spontaneously. Then as we put off what should be done, we grow more and more embarrassed about seeking useful help (because we know too little about how to get involved in the social, cooperative aspects of work to begin with). We even grow more likely to blame the people who have assigned the task.

So it is that we wait until we can no longer dally and make ourselves susceptible to excessive self-consciousness and blocking (because we do not know how to use waiting times for the preliminary acts that make transitions to formal work painless). When we make a habit of doing the difficult, delayable things under deadlines and in hurried fashion, we do not learn to judge how long they take, how to do them with the benefit of reflection and revision, or how to enlist others to do some of the work. We also learn little about the value of regular practice. And because our work patterns do not permit us consistently to display our best work, we unnecessarily risk criticism, even rejection. Finally, the more we experience this inefficient and painful sequence, the more likely we are to experience fear of failure, task avoidance, test anxiety, time pressures, socially prescribed perfectionism, low self-esteem and negativity. (And the less likely we are to break the vicious cycle of experiencing and excusing PB.) What has looked complicated from a polite distance may be a mere matter of deficiencies in skill and practice seen up close.

Of course, the lack of skills need not rule out influences of genetics or early experience. Predispositions to the erratic behaviors that might include PB run in families (Simonton, 1994). Authoritarian (but not authoritative) fathers may incline daughters to PBing (Ferrari & Olivette, 1994). And so on. Instead, a skills approach explains why some people with such predispositions and situations succumb to PBing while others do not. And it gives hope to the "predisposed" among us of moderating their PBing. In my view, behavior is the result of *both* heredity and environment. Baumeister, Heatherton, & Tice (1994) draw a similar conclusion for broader failures in self-management:

But these biological, genetic, or background differences that predispose people to anger, thrill seeking, alcoholism, obesity, and so forth do not lead directly to ruin. Rather they suggest areas in which self-control is especially important. (p. 250)

Recent Trends in Personality Research That Portend Change

Returning from the preliminary proposal, notice that surprising as this simple, skills-based view of PB may seem from traditional interpretations, it can fit in with recent changes in the field. Personality researchers seem to sense the need for direct observations and more fundamental explanations of PB. (So, as will be shown, do people working outside PB's usual boundaries but on related subjects.) S. Silverman and C. Lay (in press) make the boldest move. While accounting for their findings that "trait" PB relates weakly, indirectly to most of the usually listed causes for PB (such as fear of failure, perfectionism, self-handicapping), they assume that PB relates more to matters of habit, of conscientiousness, of escape from self-awareness, of factors not yet discovered (at least in personality studies). They almost, but not quite, talk about skills of working—in addition to the seemingly immutable but forgivable personality traits they usually emphasize. McCown et al. (1989; 1991), again, link PB to well-established and psychometrically sound dimensions of Eysenck's personality theory and find, among other things, that PBers make excessive time commitments and poor time estimates. Said another way, McCown and his colleagues have helped move the field closer to a definition of PB in terms of skills.

Broadening of personality notions also may be seen in M. J. Bond and N. T. Feather's (1988) development of a Time Structure Questionnaire (TSQ). Perhaps because these investigators make little direct mention of PB (and talk instead about deficits in plans and in routines), their work has found wide currency in social psychology. No doubt, the clarity and compelling usefulness of their instrument and findings have played an even bigger role. For instance, they use self-reporting to identify five main factors in the TSQ, all of them more like skills than traditional personality traits types: (1) sense of purpose, (2) structured routine, (3) present orientation (compared to ruminating about missed opportunities in the past), (4) effective organization, and (5) persistence. The TSQ correlates significantly and positively with self-esteem, healthy optimism, and efficient study habits. The TSQ, as a measure of planfulness and of organization, correlates negatively with depression, distress, anxiety, and physical symptoms of illness. Said another way, the TSQ, with its factors like skills, seems to interrelate with usual measures of dilatoriness and distress better than do trait measures of procrastination.

There may be an evolutionary trend in all this. As we look more at the deficiency in skills underlying PB, those of us who study and treat the phenomenon will inevitably examine what PBers actually do, what prices they (and those around them) really pay. Chapter 3 describes the promising results of taking a more direct, impolite look at PB.

3

The Objective, Less Amiable View of Procrastination and Blocking

Objective accounts of procrastination and blocking are not new, just uncommon and unknown. All along, a few observers of PB dared to point out its documentably avoidant, anxious, hostile, manipulative, and irresponsible components; some onlookers have even noted that chronic PBers sometimes find success without doing their best work (Bird, 1983). In the last ten years, influential researchers have begun to suggest links between their findings about maladaptive behaviors and PB (for example, Baumeister and Scher's 1988 review of self-defeating behaviors). So where, in the midst of these rumblings, will objectivity first make a meaningful foothold in the study of PB? Conceivably it will reveal the usually hidden costs of PB.

EXAMINING THE REAL, LONG-TERM ECONOMICS OF PROCRASTINATION AND BLOCKING

Hints of costs first came to light with attempts to expose myths about PB such as these: that it is laughable, that it signals genius, that it is the only avenue to freedom and free time (for example, Nixon, 1928). In one of the best confrontations with these misbeliefs, M. Jahoda (1981) exposed one of the most amiable. She found that the unemployed do *not* enjoy their free time. Without regular work and time structure (and the shared social experiences that go with them), we lose our sense of time and of meaning (see also, George, 1991). We evidently need the rules and feedback of enforced activity for personal status and identity; our worst moods occur when we are alone and nothing needs doing (Csikszentmihalyi, 1990). We rely on clear goals (plus regular success at meeting them) to achieve meaning and happiness (Baumeister, 1991).

E. J. Langer (1989) has made a similar point prominent in psychology. Mindfulness (that is, a purposeful, planned, process-oriented consciousness that is inimical to PB) helps us foresee errors and their costs by way of self-disciplines such as reflective rules and mnemonics. R. Tremmel (1993) concludes that not until we assume a stance of reflective practice (where we take conscious responsibility for our moment-by-moment decisions) can we avoid impulsive, wasteful, defensive tendencies. In emerging views like these, then, PB is anything but excusable or adaptive. Instead, it is more clearly expensive and wasteful—but correctable.

Is PB an Embarrassing Weakness?

Something else has begun to surface in this rethinking of the subject. PB is being seen less as a personal weakness and embarrassment, less as the result of an unfortunate heritage—and more as a problem of unlearned skills and poor working conditions. Even behavioral scientists are capable of compassion.

Still, this is a preliminary trend at best. It has yet to label the opposite of PBing (what I am, so far, calling nonPBing) or to deal with its moderate, adaptive levels. It hasn't yet confronted the indelicacies of talking about PB openly and prominently. Only the barest of beginning mentions of actual (as opposed to hypothesized) difficulties of trying to help PBers have yet appeared in print.

K. D. McCaul, R. E. Glasgow, and H. K. O'Neil (1992), health psychologists, broke ground in this difficult field. In their programs of dental hygiene that could save patients' teeth, they found that none of their preventive treatments (not even recent, semi-interventive favorites in psychology such as feedback, social reinforcement, and self-efficacy strategies) persisted beyond formal contacts with patients. They concluded that what suffices to initiate may not be maintained over the long run. PB is so difficult to change under ordinary circumstances (even under the threat of losing one's teeth) that it can seem implanted from birth. S. Blakeslee's (1994) report, cited earlier, is similarly unique in documenting the suspicion that people who most need help may be least likely to accept it or benefit from it. A large, well-funded federal program failed to lure many patients to a daily regimen that reduces dire complications of diabetes. Why? Potential participants reported believing that tight controls would be too difficult ("I can only do it so long. I get angry." . . . "who wants to be perfect?" p. B8).

Why, amid the traditional and dominant claims that PB could be generally adaptive (Ferrari, Johnson, & McCown, 1995), should we care about the semi-efficiency of semi-interventive approaches? We may need constant reminders of the things we already know, or should know. There are real costs to people who put off preventive and care-seeking behaviors. And, there are often reversible problems behind that PBing. For example, women who delay contact with the health-care system after their symptoms are detected are more likely to show advanced stages of breast cancer at diagnosis. Do they procrastinate and block because they are morally weak or have unfortunate personality types or because they are unskilled at taking preventive steps? The research shows that these PBers are most clearly unsophisticated and uncertain about how to proceed. Without the direction of a regular practitioner who admonishes patients about what to do next, and without regular habits of seeking preventive care, anxiety seems to block potential patients from timely action (Lauver & Ho, 1993). Said another way, PB appears to be a matter of not acting efficiently, efficaciously, that is, with knowledge, confidence, and experience of coping with disagreeable things.

Another Look at Why the Costs of PB Are Socially Acceptable

Why do so many of us pay (or indirectly condone) these costs? How can we overlook PBing that keeps people from confronting cancers only after they have advanced too far? Here too, we know the gist of the answers. First, we are customarily socialized to tolerate excuses for inaction and irresponsibility, our own or others'

(Snyder & Higgins, 1988). PB is cast as the most natural and forgivable of human weaknesses. Second, techniques of finding self-control hold little interest for people not yet experiencing high levels of stress and strain; we tend to react rather than act (Koeske, Kirk, & Koeske, 1993). Third, we often dislike being part of forced or induced compliance (even of its appearance). And fourth, few of us are yet brave enough to collect and publish information about the tacit knowledge necessary to break cycles of PB.

Elsewhere I document some of the professional costs of publicly examining and reporting attempts to intervene in PB (for example, Boice, 1996e). Here I make the point briefly: Reviewers and editors of research journals say things out of character ("Is there no room for the art in this? Must you reduce everything to numbers and facts?"). Reviewers of book manuscripts are unusually reactionary in their rejections ("Hasn't everything worth saying already been published about this topic?"). Editorial decisions seem based more on political than on methodological considerations.

Near-Exceptions to the Usual Taboo

There are times when most psychologists *do* provide useful counsel those who might become PBers and fail in crucial situations. How do we get around our usual reticence about discussing efficacies when assisting novices in psychology? Traditionally, we rely on advice from a long-successful member of our profession or culture who cites mostly his or her own personal experiences and who says little about counterparts who were not so fortunate or skilled (for example, Rheingold, 1994). That is, exemplars offer nonthreatening advice while overlooking the research literature on topics such as writing productivity, teaching skills, mentoring, career development, student development. The hero describes the art, not the practical science, of success (for example, "I was lucky to fall in with congenial colleagues and I was receptive to the stimulation of the place").

So this particular tradition of amiability, like the others noted here, eschews facts and scholarship. It prefers anecdotes of vague, nonthreatening paths to success. It says little about the unpleasant things that must be overcome. It puts no responsibility for failure on the reader who might not be able to follow suit. Consistent with the taboo it honors, tradition criticizes faculty who move beyond personal anecdotes to systematic data about how our careers develop. For instance, S. J. Kraus (1993), though depicting himself as a hard scientist who accepts only the results of laboratory research, prefers anecdotes to facts about what fosters the beginnings of careers. Why? I conclude that facts about how PB undermines efficacy are discomfiting and impolite.

Reconsider, just briefly, a reason why these amiable leanings are problematic. They discourage examination of PB's costs, they discredit attempts at interventions, and they rely on anecdotal reports. To obtain useful information about costs and interventions, we must move beyond the purely descriptive accounts of personality researchers like Ferrari et al. or bench scientists like Kraus. That step leaves us with only a slim but promising start toward breaking the taboo about PB.

Empirical Evidence About Costs of PBing

Too much of the direct evidence about costs of PB is mine; I will be succinct in this overview: Novice faculty members, for example, often procrastinate and block by putting off writing until they find ideally large, undisrupted blocks of time for it ("You can't get any really good scholarly writing done unless you have a whole, big block of time when there no disruptions. . . . I usually need a whole week, maybe during semester break, to do my best work"). But these "ideal" openings for writing are unlikely during a professor's first two or three years on campus, a period in which most newcomers devote excessive time to preparing for their classrooms ("I don't know where the time I expected to have for writing went. It just never appeared. I was always busy, too busy getting caught up on teaching. Maybe later, once I'm settled down as a teacher, I'll have time to write"). Curiously, PBers in these and in related studies (defined in terms of dilatoriness in writing beyond planned dates of completion and well short of the schedule they would have to follow to survive the retention and tenure process) have been observed to work harder overall, with more visible strain and audible complaining, and with less accomplishment than counterparts who did little PBing (Boice 1982, 1983b; 1989; 1992a; 1993c; 1995a; 1996a).

DIRECT-OBSERVATIONAL STUDIES OF PROCRASTINATION AND BLOCKING EFFICACY

Direct-observational, field-based studies scrutinize what PB actually is, what PBers do that is distinctive and maladaptive compared to nonPBers. This telling step, thus far, is uncommon among researchers and practitioners of PB. It is even, much as noted earlier, discouraged by traditional reviewers and editors unwilling to publish the results.

But direct observation is essential to practical progress in understanding and treating PB. Without it, researchers must continue to rely on speculations, anecdotes, and self-reports. With it, as will be shown, a new, more useful understanding of PB emerges.

Approximations to Direct Observation

There are beginnings toward discerning what makes PBers unique, even in some of the traditional literature: PBers, compared to nonPBers, report more remorse for PBing (Lay, 1989); part of the pattern of PBing is a regret, once the price is being paid, of having delayed and suffered. Such regrets and promises never again to procrastinate and block, unfortunately do little to fuel real change. PBers display more defensiveness about exploring relevant issues such as self-esteem (Ferrari, 1991b); express more regrets about not having enough time for reading and reflection, for loved ones, for exercise (Boles, 1985); and predict more trouble when faced with open-ended projects than with work that includes clear deadlines (Lay, 1990). But these are indirect and preliminary observations at best.

Turning Points in Objectifying PB

Better, more direct, information about what distinguishes PBers is found, so far, in work *not* obviously identified with the field of

PB. Consider four examples of what PB, given legitimacy, could rightfully claim as its own territory:

In the first example, B. J. Zimmerman (1986) studied high-achieving students to specify what he calls self-regulated learning strategies (what might be labeled as the process-oriented, mindful styles that characterize nonPBers). Exemplary students exhibit better strategies of (1) self-evaluation, (2) organization and transformation (for example, use of outlines), (3) goal setting and planning and seeking information, (4) keeping records and monitoring progress, (5) restructuring environments to facilitate work, (6) rehearsing and summarizing, (7) seeking social assistance, and (8) reviewing records and notes. Ninety-one percent of Zimmerman's sample of undergraduates could be correctly identified as high achievers on the basis of their scores on self-regulation. Moreover, these highest achievers were the least likely to use only one of the strategies listed above. PB may have no one preventive.

In the second example, M. F. Fox (1985) combined personality measures and her own, evidently informal observations to specify what makes some academics especially productive writers: autonomy and self-direction, stamina, curiosity, playfulness with ideas (while staving off closure), and collegial communication. Said another way, they know how to work.

The third example of a kindred, somewhat observational approach is R. J. Sternberg's research. He provides useful but usually tacit knowledge to students who otherwise do not fare well in school. Specifically, he tries to foster intelligence(s) and to counter beliefs that ability is immutable and inevitable. Consider, in a preliminary way, his findings on what makes students intelligent (these are discoveries that help illuminate what nonPBers do that PBers do not) (Sternberg, 1985). Excellent students, for example,

- display good reading skills because they master time allocation (that is, they waste little time with inappropriate responses; they are more flexible in using time because they are better at time-sharing between subtasks)
- redefine the problem to make it soluble, by planning a sequence of acts and steps
- automatize some of the operations essential to problem solving

Restated, skilled and successful students know how to work, how to be efficacious.

Elsewhere, Sternberg looks at fluency in creativity as a kind of excellence in knowing how to work. Said simply, creativity is intelligent, efficacious fluency. The more easily, consistently, and smartly we work, the better the chances for creativity. In this view, creativity is the opposite of PBing *and* it is learnable. Sternberg and T. I. Lubart (1991) liken creative fluency to T. M. Amabile's (1983) classic notions of creativity-relevant *skills* (for example, ability to alter a preconception readily, to work with persistence and energy).

Moreover, Sternberg hints that deficiency in specific kinds of intelligence may underlie PBing. Consider, for instance, graduate students who, before their third year, had excelled because of two kinds of strongly developed and highly valued skills: remembering facts and principles, and criticizing information. Suddenly, they may fall short when faced with new demands for intelligence of a creative sort, one that requires coming up with their own ideas for figuring out studies of their own and ways of implementing them (Sternberg, 1990). Graduate students in this predicament procrastinate and block when they face dissertations, not only because they fear failure but more fundamentally because they do not know how to manage themselves, the tasks, and the acquisition of social supports in this complex, easily delayed activity.

Sternberg and his colleagues applied discoveries such as these in one of the first large-scale programs that suggest ways of making broad principles of PB relevant to an educational system. Sternberg, L. Okagaki, and A. S. Jackson (1990) began by identifying the reasons why many students lack practical intelligence for success in school (because of lack of the same kind of skills that seem to cause PB): (1) teachers rarely verbalize their expectations of students (for example, how to allocate time in doing homework, how to talk and not talk in class); (2) poor students come to school without knowing how to manage their work (they do not understand how to break bad habits, to organize, to finish tasks on time); and (3) unsophisticated students do not know how to cooperate with others (for example, they do not understand social networks, how to put themselves in another's place). The breakthrough in explicating these three factors is the identification of usually tacit, untaught skills of succeeding in school . . . and of what happens to students who fail to learn them.

The fourth example where investigators include direct observations of what PBers do comes from outside psychology proper, in composition research done with a psychological bent by S. Perl and others. This richly descriptive approach begins most obviously with Perl's (1978) account of five unskilled college writers who were impaired by habits such as rushing into composing without planning beforehand and of delaying while "editizing" such as checking too soon for spelling. Simply put, the problem writers showed deficient skills, especially in their restricted, narrow manners of approaching and beginning the task.

Even more useful research on how students work at writing comes from L. S. Flower and J. R. Hayes (1980), a composition teacher and a psychologist who produce the most influential publications in this growing field. These two have set the precedents for cognitive methods used to uncover what writers say they think as they write, of why and where they struggle or succeed (see Kellogg, 1994). This is a procedure with unusual promise for understanding why PBers do what they do as they do it. One summary account of interest here distinguishes expert and poor writers (Hayes & Flower, 1986). Experts (who, once given Hayes and Flower's descriptions, might be labeled as efficacious non-PBers) more often

- work planfully. They construct better initial task representations (for example, story lines) and goals that will guide writing.
- use subgoals set up in hierarchical but flexible fashion.
- proceed as efficient problem solvers by generating elaborate networks of ideas with compelling, interconnected goals.
- revise by working on their manuscripts "less locally"—while attending to the whole scope of their writing, not just to isolated sentences and paragraphs. (Similarly, experts plan and compose in bigger units.)

Hayes and Flower also identify the place where blocking most often occurs, at the juncture between preparing and writing (unless planful prewriting activities help ease this usually painful transition between planning and prose). What could cause that abrupt transition? As a rule, the culprit is procrastination in doing the necessary prewriting. It is a dilatoriness that results in last-minute, hurried attempts to begin with formal prose.

How Notions of Efficacy in Terms of Skills Relate to the Literature on PB

We can, with only a modest stretch, connect these breakthrough findings to the traditional PB literature. For example, the roots of fluency in uninhibited, wide-ranging styles of planning and working (see the fourth point in the list from Hayes and Flower, above) are reminiscent of the effects of hypnotic susceptibility that were noted much earlier with Hilgard (in the discussion of automaticity). This "letting go" turns out to be particularly associated with writing styles where writers focus more on large patterns and images, less on local details of sentences or immediate correctness (Bowers, 1979). And it goes along with the learnable skill of putting off the ever present, internal editors until later, once the ideas are on screen or paper and ready for revision.

The findings that (1) PB most often occurs at the transition between planning and prose (by Flower & Hayes) and (2) PBers act in predictably inhibited, blocked ways at that time (by Hilgard) are of enormous potential importance in understanding and treating dilatoriness and uneasy inhibition. The discussion will return to them.

EXPLICITLY DIRECT STUDIES OF PB

None of the investigators above, even the most praiseworthy, examined the nature of PB itself; explicitly direct studies of PB have been so uncommon that we might think they were forbidden.

Where, then, might such inquiries begin? I, for one, found it easiest to begin by identifying what PB was and wasn't, by comparing what exemplary, efficacious performers did compared to their counterparts.

MORE THOROUGH, DIRECT STUDIES

In a decade of tracking cohorts of new faculty members through the daily activities of their academic workweeks, usually for their first few years on campuses (Boice, 1992b), one result surprised me most. Fully two-thirds of these newcomers to professorial careers experienced difficult beginnings that belied the excellent credentials they brought with them from leading universities and prominent mentors. How, I wondered, could such obviously competent people behave so maladaptively? (I even found myself entertaining notions of inborn personality traits as explanations.)

During their first three years, these slow starters accomplished little (often none) of the writing they knew they would need for retention and tenure—and, more important, for the national visibility and self-respect they felt they would need for a successful career. Instead of making the smooth, productive, and confirming beginnings they had planned, they struggled amid busyness, spending far too much time preparing for immediate demands such as teaching (for example, often twenty to thirty hours a week preparing for six hours in classrooms—and then having too much to say in class and saying it too quickly for students to understand). The things they had designated, on arrival, as most important were subject to PB: socializing with colleagues, exercising for fitness, and scholarly writing. This PBing persisted even during the long weekends and vacations that PBers had then planned to use to catch up.

What did PBers do instead of tending to their original priorities? They spent surprising amounts of time "catching up on sleep" ("I've never been so busy and stressed out in my life and never so tired. I sleep late whenever I can, sometimes for whole weekends, it seems"). They binged at teaching preparations, often working in tense, hurried sessions of lecture writing followed by rapidly presented, poorly rated classroom presentations. They, far more than efficacious peers, spent times scheduled for writing doing other, more immediately rewarding things such as composing memos and making calls. Said simply, they spent less time on the task of writing but they worked even harder than efficacious peers.

The costs of inefficiencies for struggling novices seemed clear. The work lives (and, almost invariably, the personal lives) of these PBers were hectic and unproductive compared to those of efficacious peers; PBers chronically put off work at writing, by their own admission:

You want to know how I'm doing? Not so well as I hoped. I'm overwhelmed and miserable and I'm forced to work in overwhelming conditions and pressures. I don't have time to write and I'm hopelessly behind
schedule. . . . This place expects you to be good at both teaching and writing and there isn't time for both.

Compared to quick starters, PBers spent far more time complaining and worrying; they, far more than their counterparts,
spent mornings and afternoons on campus doing other, easier
things:

I suppose so, I could be getting more done than reading these journals
in a kind of distracted way. You know why I'm doing this right now? As
soon as I finish, I'm going to work some more on my letter to the chair
[person]. I can't feel right here until some broken promises are set right.
It's a matter of principle; I'm going to make them give me all the lab
equipment they promised.

There are, I came to see, other more subtle problems at work
for slow starters. Senior colleagues more often saw these struggling newcomers as aloof and disinterested in teamwork; the slow-
starting new faculty, in turn, saw colleagues as unhelpful. PBers
were more likely to experience documentable bouts of illness and
measurable struggles with depression and anxiety. They fell far
below departmental or campus expectations for scholarly output
(the norm for retention or tenure was usually one manuscript finished and submitted to a prestigious outlet per year).

In one study, I coached a group of the slowest-starting new
faculty and a matching complement of quick starters (who typically comprise 10 to 15 percent of my overall study samples) to
examine their thoughts and feelings as they worked at writing.
Specifically, I trained them in a retrospective-thinking-aloud procedure that had proven useful in identifying personal accompa-
niments of adaptive versus maladaptive work styles (Boice, 1993b;
Perkins, 1981). The two groups of ten newcomers to academic
careers displayed strikingly different accounts of their cognitive
and emotional experiences as writers. Slow starters, once practiced
enough in the technique to get past superficial reporting, most

commonly reported thoughts about easier things they could do and about reasons why writing would be difficult and risky:

Well, this is what I thought: "I could go get some coffee first in the lounge and then I might feel more like writing." I did. But I didn't get back to writing that day. I ended leafing through the student newspaper and looking out the window. I thought: "I can write tomorrow; for now I'll enjoy the moment; it's a beautiful sunny day and too nice to write."

While quick starters often reported initial thoughts of a similar sort ("I really don't feel like writing, it can be such a pain"), as a rule they did so only briefly. Once they put negative thoughts aside ("This is getting me nowhere"), they were most likely to think more optimistically about writing ("I said to myself, 'Quit wasting time and just get on with it; this complaining is getting tiresome. Once I get it going, I'll feel better about it'"). And, then, unlike the slow starters, they turned to the writing task itself ("Let's see. What was I saying last time? Oh yeah, I know....").

Quick starters less often reported anything more than mild emotions associated with attempts to write. Slow starters, by contrast, often reported emotional experiences that seemed to delay and inhibit writing (notice too how much of the old tendency to resort to "reporting" emerges in this typical recollection):

You know I wasn't always really thinking, really. I felt too consumed with anger and sheer restlessness to do much clear thinking. . . . The feelings were about the unfairness of being pressured here to write so much. I came here to teach. So I was feeling really annoyed, hateful toward [names her departmental chairperson], you know? I would try to put it out of my mind and look at my keyboard. I said [to myself]: "Just forget about that and just stop thinking about the unfairness of it all." But I couldn't. I just didn't feel like writing in such an unfair situation and I didn't.

Slow starters, perhaps because they strained as writers, more commonly asserted their fondness for teaching. But, possibly due to the ways they overprepared and rushed, they fared far worse at teaching on a variety of measures—despite their enormous investment in time spent preparing lecture materials, compared to quick starters. The discussion will return to more details of studies like these later.

For now, this is the summary point I hope to make: The nature of the PBing involved was readily apparent as specific acts and tendencies. Direct observations of new faculty by trained observers revealed high levels of agreement about which faculty were judged as PBers. They reliably displayed more of the following patterns during everyday work activities. (I rank them from most to least common amongst those we saw and heard during times when individual slow starters had agreed to schedule writing sessions.)

- busyness and impulsive rushing (often to the point of quick signs of fatigue such as keyboard errors)

- a product orientation (talking about how many pages needed to be completed for the day, about likely reactions of journal reviewers to what might be written), while avoiding essential, delayable activities (usually actual writing)

- anxiety (seen as fidgeting, tense facial expressions, and ease of distraction) when facing work that would be public

- unrealistic beliefs stated spontaneously about how priority work will get done (for example, "Sometimes I can write a whole paper in a flash, almost without trying") and hostile attitudes towards pressures for orderliness and timeliness ("You know the kinds of people here who set up these tenure standards don't understand that someone like me has a child at home. Those are people who put work before family life. They need to understand that someone like me will be in a better position to be productive later. . . . Nothing annoys me more than people who think that writing is something that you can do on a schedule set by someone else.")

These same four characteristic ways of thinking and working were not only interesting for their salience in distinguishing PBers from their peers. They also provided me with an organized sense of the mechanisms of PBing for the first time. When my co-observers and I took a closer look at those distinctively PBing styles, a reasonably limited set of specific measures sufficed to characterize them. Those observable, easily assessed components also help show the skills needed to overcome PB:

[PBers were here designated independently in terms of missed deadlines for administrative forms, of late appearances for classes and departmental meetings, of low and inadequate outputs as scholarly writers, of missed deadlines for submitting grant applications and returning scholarly reviews, and of observed periods where planned, important work such as lecture preparation or writing was not performed even though the faculty member was in a position to do the work.]

Please note that this relisting emphasizes self-reports, most of them spontaneous, by PBers. You might wonder: is this a contradiction of my earlier disapproval of personality researchers who rely heavily on self-reports? Perhaps it is to an extent. But bear in mind that here I was not asking PBers to specify when and why they acted in ways that I counted as PBing. Instead, I noted their comments of ongoing cognitive and emotional processes—along with other recordable things they did. These, then, are the specific measures my co-observers and I agreed to use:

1. *Busyness and impulsive rushing*: (*a*) number of recorded spontaneous comments by the person under observation about being or feeling busy and about needing to catch up; (*b*) number of observed instances where high-priority work (what Covey (1989) labels nonurgent or delayable but important activity) was needlessly avoided and then started with no preliminaries such as planning on paper or discussing ideas with colleagues; (*c*) number of recorded instances where the subject engaged in priority work such as teaching preparation or writing with no breaks and for at least 90 minutes (that is, binged).

2. *Product orientation while avoiding essential activities*: (*a*) recorded instances of the subject worrying audibly while working (or preparing to work) about desired outcomes (comparing ways of working to reach the outcomes); (*b*) observed occasions where subject worked at quick, urgent activities in place of planned priorities (that is, important but not immediately urgent activities [Covey, 1989]) in the midst of self-congratulatory comments about how much was getting done.

3. *Anxiety about facing actions that are or will be public*: (*a*) recorded instances of subjects saying that they could not carry out a planned, urgent, but delayable activity because the prospect made them too anxious; (*b*) noted occurrences of subjects expressing anxiety about engaging in an anxiety-provoking activity such as public speaking or writing for review and publication—while putting off action about the

aversive, priority act in favor of the quick and the easy (for example, office cleaning; e-mailing).

4. *Unrealistic beliefs about how priority work will get done, and hostility toward pressures for orderliness and timeliness.* (*a*) subject's audible and seemingly irrational comments about how a priority task will come to completion (for example, "Maybe it will all come to me when I'm up there at the [conference] podium . . . and I'll pleasantly surprise myself; it can be done, you know; I like to do things my way, not by the dictates of uptight people who think every thing has to be done so compulsively . . . I like surprises."); (*b*) recorded instances where the subject rejected conventional deadlines and expectations (for example, "What the administrators here don't appreciate is some people, like me and some others I know, cannot work at an arbitrary pace, like machines. I may need five years, maybe more, to get a good paper written—whatever it takes is what it will take; no one is going to tell me how to do my best work").

I won't get into all the data and statistics from these observational studies here; instead I'll review the general results from a variety of studies using the kinds of measures just listed. Then, I'll present one of my more tolerably brief journal articles (Boice, 1996a), one with slightly modified and simplified measures, to show more specifically how PB relates to slow starts and to costs and benefits for new faculty members.

Three General Findings with Slow Starters

First, all of these measures of PBing proved to be reliably higher for new faculty independently judged to be in danger of failing in their careers. That is, the indices seem to be useful ways of measuring real-life PBing with real consequences. Second, these specific measures were the only kinds that reliably distinguished problem PBers from peers (in comparison to other, more traditionally favored indices favored by personality researchers such as expressions of socially prescribed perfectionism and fear of public failure). Third, those reliable indices of PBings proved easy to observe and reliably consistent across observers given a modicum of pretraining . . . even, in later studies, for PBers rating themselves on specific acts and thoughts. (Few PBers had, incidentally, noticed most of these tendencies in themselves prior to observing and recording their occurrences in systematic fashion for at least three months).

The nature of these general findings about PBers starting professorial careers becomes clearer in the study that follows. Here I want to share some of the specific procedures and outcomes of the experiment with you.

An Investigation with Direct Observations of the Costs of PBing

Because we have few useful precedents for defining PB in terms of actual *behaviors* of dilatoriness and uneasy inaction, I used a study setting well-known to some of you, one that tolerates PBing but exacts high prices for its excessive practice: the first six years of professorial careers at large universities (Boice, 1996a). Many novices describe this period as the hardest years of their lives.

Therein, we may have a reasonably unambiguous indication of substantial PBing at hand, in the final evaluations by retention, tenure, and promotion (R/T/P) committees about whether novice faculty members published enough to meet campus or departmental expectations. (At the two campuses I depict here, that expectation was about one manuscript accepted in a mainstream, refereed outlet per year since arriving on campus.) For the sake of finding a place to begin more direct studies of PB, then, I proposed defining it in terms of that simple outcome. The question that remains was this: What kinds of behavior patterns related to usual definitions of PBing actually and distinctively precede failures in the R/T/P process?

Participants

Overall, I followed 104 new faculty through a pattern of systematic observation for those first six years at two large state campuses (Boice, 1992b). All were newcomers to professorial careers; all of them fell under the scope of my observations every other week while they worked in their offices, laboratories, and classrooms. I relied most on what I had seen them doing or on checking what they had done recently (for example, writing new pages of prose).

The thirty-two new faculty I depict here consist of two groups: (1) one sample of sixteen individuals who displayed regular, moderate habits of writing in year 1 on campus (that is, wrote during most weeks on three separate days), and (2) another of sixteen peers whose first years on campus were marked by a clear preference for writing only occasionally but in binges (that is, more than ninety minutes of intense, uninterrupted work (see Boice, 1996a, for more details).

The sample size was limited by (1) the need to match the numbers and demographics of the two groups, (2) the number of subjects whose work was largely on campus (and so, directly observable) and had been recorded without large lapses, (3) the willingness or ability of R/T/P committees to communicate clear reasons to me about their decisions, (4) the exclusions of individuals from the second group whose R/T/P decisions seemed to have been confounded by problems of personality or support (for example, a promised laboratory was not provided), and (5) limiting the final groups of regular and of binge writers, respectively, to individuals who passed the retention or tenure process with ease or else failed it. The last restriction is not as circular as it sounds: none of the regular writers failed to gain tenure or promotion with ease; only two binge writers were excluded because they (with the help of litigation) gained tenure. Why make this final adjustment? It helps make the link between PBing and a costly outcome.

Methods

I describe these qualitative, observational strategies, including checks for reliability in coding, elsewhere (Boice, 1982; 1983c; 1992b; 1994). Briefly, I began visiting the offices of newly hired faculty within a week or two of their arrival on campus; all but a few of these newcomers volunteered to be monitored by me on a regular but usually unannounced basis. I timed visits to observe them actually writing manuscripts (or else procrastinating and blocking on them). I focused on work habits, time allocation, plans made and kept, and behavioral indications of being rushed and behind schedule. The specific nature of the things I watched and noted becomes clearer later, when I indicate acts and patterns that distinguished the two main outcomes in the R/T/P process (that is, unambiguous success or not).

Results and Discussion

My first concern was with differentiating the sixteen new faculty designated as regular writers from those in the binge group over the longer run. (If the numbers relating to scholarly output were not clearly related to levels of productivity and to the decisions of R/T/P committees, my assumption that bingeing risks PBing would be questionable.) In fact, the two groups were so dissimilar that there was little overlap in the range of the scholarly outputs of regular writers ($\overline{X}$ = .81 manuscripts accepted or published, SD = .62) versus successes ($\overline{X}$ = 5.31, SD = 2.02; $t[30]$ = 8.33, p <.001) during the six-year study period for each study participant.

Put simply, binge writers averaged less than one refereed publication during their entire six-year probationary period while successful writers managed about five publications. With the criterion problem reasonably settled, I looked for behavior patterns of the PB kind that related to this general outcome in reliable fashion. Virtually everything about work and coping styles that I had chosen to record in regular fashion distinguished the two outcome groups. I outline the most powerful and telling of those differences as follows:

1. *Measurements of work habits and time spent on writing.* All thirty-two subjects kept verified records of time spent at scholarly writing or its preliminaries (for example, library research, outlining, free writing) and of daily outputs in typed-page equivalents. While some of the reports began in apparently exaggerated fashion, my insistence on seeing new pages of prose or notes and on checking whether they were working at writing during prescheduled times brought the participants to what I deemed reasonably accurate accounts (see Boice, 1987, regarding problems of monitoring faculty workweeks). Figure 3.1 portrays these work habits and outputs in a general way for the first three years on campus— as overall means of time spent writing per week, as means of weekly outputs of manuscript pages or their equivalents, and as manuscripts finished and submitted to refereed outlets.

Regular writers evidenced significantly less time spent at work on writing during their first three years, overall, than did binge writers (about two and a half hours versus almost seven hours a week). Bingers' excuses for delaying writing were uniformly sim-

Figure 3.1
Productivity Measures (years 1–3 vs. years 1–6)

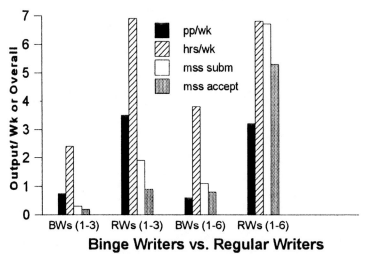

Binge Writers vs. Regular Writers

Productivity measures for new faculty who usually binged as writers (BWs) compared
to peers who wrote regularly (RWs). Two measures, pages of scholarly prose and
hours of work at writing, were taken weekly; two measures, manuscripts submitted
and manuscripts accepted, represent the first three years on campus (left two clusters
of bars) or the first six years on campus (right two clusters).

ilar (for example, "I do my best work under deadlines"; "I'll write
when I'm not so busy").

Bingers produced fewer verified pages of manuscript prose during the first three years compared to regular writers (about three-
quarters of a page a week versus three and a half, respectively).
Bingers finished and submitted fewer manuscripts to refereed outlets compared to regular writers (about a third of a manuscript,
on average, over three years versus two manuscripts, respectively).

Figure 3.1 also depicts the same indices complied through year
6 on campus (right-most clusters). Even though all but four bingers increased their work time and outputs during parts of years
5 and 6, they still fell far short (a third as many pages per week,
half as many hours invested in writing over the six years, a fourth
as many manuscripts submitted) of their more efficacious counterparts in the longer run.

Figure 3.1, finally, displays outcomes in terms of manuscripts accepted or already published in refereed outlets through the sixth year on campus. Binge writers fared worse at the three-year mark (an eighteenth as many) and in terms of the six-year total (a sixth as many).

Overall, these measures of productivity and work habits, through year 3 and then through year 6, indicate that differences between PBers and regular writers were strong in the beginning and remained so in the long haul: For years 1–3, $F(4,27) = 18.87$, $p = <.001$; for years 1–6, $F(4,27) = 38.67$, $p = <.001$.

So, spontaneous predictions by new faculty who proved to be PBers—that they would catch up later and do even more and better work by the end—were *not* verified. Regular, nonPBing writers completed and submitted far more manuscripts to approved outlets (Figure 3.1); they also had proportionately more of what they finished accepted for publication (about 70 percent as compared to 50 percent). Here, then, is a direct indication of the greater price paid by workers who more often put off and blocked at an important task, perhaps the first such report to appear in the PB literature.

In what I have just said, I implied a greater incidence of dilatoriness (that is, not working on the task at preset times for writing and/or not meeting planned outputs) and of blocking (obvious displays of anxious inaction in response to important writing tasks) among failures than for clearly successful new faculty. Next I present behavioral data to support that implication.

2. *Behavioral measures of PBing that distinguish successes in the R/T/P system.* Post-hoc analysis of instances (checked for interobserver reliability as mentioned earlier) qualifying as either P or B suggest that they predicted the outcome in distinctive ways. Figure 3.2 shows the results for the first few years (left-most clusters) and then for six years overall (with an equal number of twenty-two observations, made every other week—except for vacation times—in each year): (*a*) Instances where writers were putting off scheduled writing in favor of seemingly urgent, no more important activities (see Covey, 1989) were about three times more common among new faculty who failed or struggled in the R/T/P process than for those who passed with ease (see "not W" in Figure 3.2). (*b*) New faculty who would fail also evi-

Figure 3.2
Observational Measures of PBing (years 1–3 vs. years 1–6)

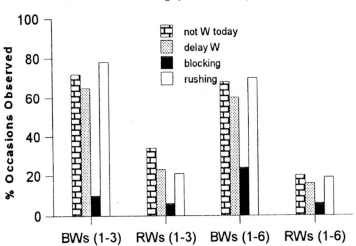

Direct-observational measures of procrastinating and blocking (PBing) for writers who binged (BWs) and regular writers (RWs) by the end of the first three years (left two clusters of bars) and then over the first six years (right two clusters).

denced about three times as many weeks without any writing output. (c) PBers three times more often displayed signs of blocking during my observations (despite a low incidence during the first three years when they were rarely attempting to write). That is, when PBers finally decided to write and tried not to do anything else in its stead, they more commonly did nothing or very little (for example, recasting a first sentence or paragraph for an hour; staring at a blank screen). (d) PBers were three times more likely to be rushing at their work (writing or its alternatives) during scheduled writing periods.

Once more, differences in patterns of apparently maladaptive behaviors were clear over time: For years 1 to 3: $F(4,27) = 38.67$, $p = <.001$. For years 1 to 6: $F(4,27) = 71.95$, $p = <.001$).

Behaviorally, then, PBing (as contrasted to writing with constancy and moderation) can be seen to include consistent acts of (a) not writing in favor of working at more immediately demanding, immediately rewarding tasks (most commonly for these new faculty, preparing lectures); (*b*) delaying writing so that planned outputs are chronically overdue; (*c*) blocking at writing when nothing else can be done; and (*d*) rushing impatiently at whatever work is underway (for example, accompanied by above-average rates of movement, by signs of fatigue, and by errors such as keyboarding mistakes).

Still another striking difference between PBers and efficient writers is one not suggested by the traditional literature. PBers were also far more likely to display a broad work pattern related to the acts just listed. When they wrote at all, they commonly wrote in binges (distinctive and temporally patterned ways of working) writing in extended sessions until they reached a state of hypomania (a lesser kind of mania that induces rushing, euphoria, and decisiveness—in the short run) (Boice, 1995as). H. Rachlin (1995) uses a similar concept, an abstract behavioral pattern dominating a particular outcome, to characterize the most crucial basis of self-control problems.

3. *Bingeing.* Specifically, PBers were far more likely than regular, timely writers to display binges of three or more uninterrupted hours of writing during which they resisted my attempts to interrupt them. I mapped the occurrence of bingeing by checking with my writers by phone or surprise visits during times I knew they might be working (in addition to observations made in person during the usual, scheduled writing times). And I relied, to an extent, on the charts of work time they kept on a daily basis (these I helped verify by way of my more random checks of faculty activities). When these new faculty reported binges to me (typically with pride over their sudden productivity), they corroborated them with actual pages produced.

Figure 3.3 shows that efficient writers binged at a fifth the rate of their less productive peers in years 1 to 3 ($F[1,30] = 4.34$, $p = <.05$). By the end of year 6, PBers were still bingeing at a rate four times greater than for regular writers ($F[1,30] = 53.55$, $p = <.001$). So bingeing was reliably indicative of the outcome of PBing (and obviously linked to more molecular acts of PBing including rushing, exaggerated priorities, and impatience). The opposite of bingeing, a common pattern of working in brief, daily sessions, was used almost entirely by the most productive writers

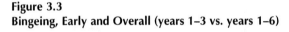

Figure 3.3
Bingeing, Early and Overall (years 1–3 vs. years 1–6)

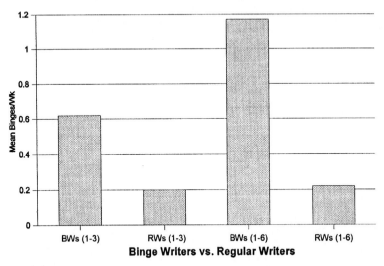

Average rates of bingeing (working at writing in rushed, uninterrupted sessions of more than three hours) for writers designated as bingers (BWs) after year 1 on campus and for peers labeled as regular writers (RWs) at the same time during the first three years (left two clusters) and for the six years overall (right two clusters).

in these first three years (Boice, 1994). Bingeing proved more distinctive of PBers than any other measure taken here.

Overall, bingeing at writing was associated with far less output, despite the veneration in which PBers claimed they held it (for example, "You can't get enough good writing done in little pieces; you need big, undisturbed blocks of time"). Rachlin concludes that such patterns, once acquired, take on a powerful attractiveness due to the short-term rewards they offer; moreover, these habits have a life of their own because they are temporally complex and hard to interrupt. In this case, Rachlin would say, the PBers may not have deliberately chosen the bingeing pattern; instead, they were probably forced into it by not knowing how to work in a steady, regular pattern. Baumeister, Heatherton, and Tice make a similar point: Binges, once started, bring immediate sensory pleasure that keeps us working in intense, uninterrupted ways. The farther we get into a binge, the less we monitor our actions, the more readily we accept irrational beliefs about the best ways of working ("I can only do great writing in binges"; once I start bingeing I cannot stop until I collapse"), and the harder it is to stop bingeing. Binges, then, take on large and powerful patterns.

Where, in the end, do these behavioral analyses of procrastination and blocking leave us? We are left with a clearer sense of PBers' acts that prove unacceptably costly and with less reliance on PBers' own interpretations of what they do (for example, supposing their problems consist of inborn, somewhat admirable tendencies to perfectionism). We also have new indications that at least part of PBing consists of broad behavioral patterns (for example, complex habits of bingeing on delayable work such as writing in great marathons and under major deadlines). And we have a suggestion that a general pattern of working regularly and in moderation may be the most useful alternative to PBing. This view of PB (and its possible curative) in broad patterns promises practicality in moderating the PBing that undermines the careers of too many novice professors. It could provide the beginning of solutions for more general forms of PBing such as self-defeating behaviors (Baumeister & Scher, 1988). Perhaps, then, PBing is not just something to be characterized as a fixed trait, to be overlooked because mentioning it might embarrass the person in the short run.

Still, this rather direct look at what PBers do that distinguishes and handicaps them is only part of what we need to know. A more complete picture awaits equally thorough study of what the most efficacious amongst us do (and how we can all learn to be that way).

Observational Studies of Quick Starters

Only after years of studying the most problematic of PBers did I appreciate the value of concentrating some of my observations on their efficient opposites. In fact, quick starters are as easy to distinguish as are problem PBers, at least among new faculty. Once quick starters come under observation, their kin in other spheres become obvious. The parallel literatures indicate that newcomers to careers in management or to college education include quick starters, nonPBers, whose habits and attitudes might be worth teaching to slow starters (Boyle, 1995).

This talented tenth of professorial newcomers more or less, clearly excels in at least three areas by the second or third semester on campus. They are rated (by themselves, their peers, their senior colleagues, their students, and their editors—depending on the activity) as performing well above average in:

• *task management* (Quick starters fare unusually well on standardized student ratings of teaching, and on related indices; they write and publish more; they spend less time at teaching preparation, and more on research and social life.)

• *self-management* (Quick starters less often complain of stress or busyness, they exhibit fewer mood swings, or miss fewer work days due to illness, than do PBers.)

• *social management* (Quick starters solicit a mentor and other social supports in timely, active fashion, some of it before their formal arrival on campus; soon after, they serve as mentors to their peers as they themselves receive guidance.)

That is, quick starters arrive already adept at (or predisposed to learn quickly) the same three categories of skills that Sternberg and his colleagues see as vital for student success. What Sternberg calls tacit knowledge (that is, unstated, unaware intelligence of how to work in school) may be the skills that promote nonPBing. We could call the assemblage of such skills *efficacy* (that is, the management skills for efficient, successful work plus the knowledge of where to find the confidence and support to proceed [Bandura, 1986; 1990]).

Task Management

Quick starters, not surprisingly, generally see frequent PBing as a wasteful luxury that they cannot afford (and they are much more consciously aware of PB and of time use than are chronic, problematic PBers). Exemplary new faculty tend to allocate their time far more wisely and more economically than do normal new faculty. The quick starters usually work at lecture preparation and at writing in brief daily sessions, despite their often feeling too busy because of other, more immediately pressing activities. They balance time spent on teaching preparation with that spent on scholarly writing, and they spend only a modicum of time (that is, an hour or two) on both most days. They generally spend as much time talking about writing as doing it.

Self-Management

Quick starters, again, fare better at moderating their emotions. They rarely display prolonged depression (as measured via the Beck Depression Inventory and by direct-observational records of mood and pessimism). Quick starters only occasionally depend on hypomania to find motivation. Why? Hypomania proves inefficient to long-term productivity and creativity, something that quick starters themselves have figured out (more about this later). They sometimes even recognize that hypomania is also a common precursor of depression and of more PB (Boice, 1994).

Indeed, quick starters shine in terms of moderation and stability: they generally work at tasks like scholarly writing or teaching preparation without rushing or anxiety. What replaces those progenitors of PB? Instead they experience mild happiness (for example, occasional smiling while writing and teaching), enjoyment (for example, more spontaneous comments of a positive sort, fewer that are pessimistic), constancy, and moderation.

Social Management

Finally, quick starters exhibit better skills at socializing (they are more likely to seek collaboration that leads to professional connections and success) and at persuading others to do some of the work (for example, they far more often enlist undergraduates as research and teaching assistants).

Self-Efficacy

But what is most memorable in day-to-day observations of quick starters is the thing they themselves value most, which encapsulates all three categories just summarized: that is, quick starters display few signs of busyness or the fatigue it brings. Accordingly, they show more patience and readiness to talk with students about academic and research topics (the very faculty involvement that engenders the most student progress [Pascarella

& Terenzini, 1991]). And they evidence more free time, more time spent socializing with colleagues and more time spent exercising and at hobbies. Moreover, many quick starters are quietly but keenly aware of realities about PB and concede that some PBing is inevitable. Instead of worrying about it obsessively, they simply try to limit it to infrequent, low-cost acts.

When quick starters procrastinate and block, their delays and reluctances characteristically occur (1) in response to *varied* problems (in contrast to the same old thing), (2) sporadically, and (3) for *specific* reasons seemingly *external* to them (and not representative of their usual problem-solving styles). This configuration of making attributions about failures resembles C. R. Snyder and R. L. Higgins's (1988) prototypical, healthy excuse-making pattern: external, variable, specific (EVS). The EVS pattern is important because it apparently minimizes depression (and, we might think, the sort of PB that comes with the passivity of depression). So an exciting discovery about quick starters is that they model what might be called adaptive PB. They typically do it with little embarrassment, few excuses, and limited expense.

Chronic PBers, in contrast, remain unskilled at seeing that their PBing is not, in fact, sporadic and unique (that is, it does not really fit the EVS pattern); instead, their PBing tends to chronicity and generality. Why don't they see the reality? They don't see it because they, more than other people, treat each new deadline as novel, each new challenge as unlike the others which they have faced with PB. Quick starters, in contrast, show more accuracy in noticing PB and its general patterns; they (unlike PBers) generally explain acts of PB as domain-general, not as domain-specific ("This [referring to the delayed preparation of a paper] is really no different from putting off appointments with the dentist; I sometimes struggle with such things, but not for long because the struggle doesn't feel good").

Information about what distinguished quick starters as efficacious in my studies (in contrast to problem PBers) can be translated into balanced, accomplished, healthy living and working. That next major step, of putting more of what has been learned about the skills of efficacy in action, is the topic of the next chapter.

4

Interventions for Procrastinators and Blockers

One thing led to another. Once I was involved in documenting the costs and benefits of efficacy and PBing, I moved almost unthinkingly to a focus on interventions. Why? The costs of PBing are so enormous for the groups I study and love that I could no longer bear to limit my studies to descriptions and theorizing. Even so, I made the move gradually. In particular I wanted to see if I could find ways of setting up effective interventions that were not too obviously distant from traditional considerations of PB. Progress is of little use if no one listens.

Even though traditional scholarship does not emphasize interventions for PBers, it does make occasional exceptions (always, it seems, keeping PB at an amiable level). It offers several such strategies, the best-known and most widely used in academe called release time. Let me explain.

As a rule, the "release" is from a course or two in the teaching load of a new faculty member; the putative purpose is to provide more time for writing to those PBing it (new faculty do, after all, commonly complain that they are too busy to meet campus expectations for scholarly productivity). The strategy sounds good to faculty who want to alleviate their PB or at least its costs. (Release time is by far the favorite response of professors asked what kinds of support for scholarship they would prefer.) Moreover, release time fits nicely with tradition. While it provides incentives (relief from teaching, free time for writing) for writers, it does so with a minimum of force or intrusiveness; writers are given the opportunity to spend more time writing, and they themselves decide how to take advantage of it. One thing, though, bothered me about this strategy: it had never been tested for its effectiveness.

TESTING INTERVENTIONS IN PROCRASTINATION AND BLOCKING

A Test of Release Time

To get a good look at what happened to new faculty awarded release time (and, for the sake of comparison, at peers who were not), I steeled myself to track them through a variety of everyday work situations. I suspected that some of what I would witness would be potentially discomfiting to my subjects; and it was, although all my subjects soon grew used to my presence, even to the point of acting inefficiently in my company.

Consider just one of these studies, carried out in a setting where new faculty received grants of release time in order to facilitate the scholarly writing for publication that would be necessary for survival in the retention or tenure process (Boice, 1987). The study campus was a large, public, and comprehensive university that hired some forty to seventy new faculty a year in tenure-track appointments. Because the university had a four-course teaching load (per semester) and because its new faculty struggled and often failed to manage the requisite outputs as writers (about 1.0 to 1.5 publications in refereed outlets per year), administrators believed new faculty's claim that teaching loads left them no time to write. That assumption helped frame the question I put to test: Would, in fact, released time (amounting to a one-course, or more, reduction in teaching load for a year) make a difference in writing output? I joined the awardees in hoping that it would.

Results

These are the reliable outcomes put simply: Individual faculty on release time closely maintained the same amounts of time spent writing, accumulated the same outputs of pages of scholarly prose, and submitted the same numbers of manuscripts for publication as they did in years before and after their grants. The best predictor of scholarly output during and after the release time was work habits and productivity in the year preceding it. Release time by itself, then, induced no substantial changes in scholarly productivity.

The direct observations suggested the reasons why. When I tracked a sample of eighteen faculty through their workdays before, during, and after these release-time grants (and coached and rewarded them to compile valid records of their time use in my absence—augmented by surprise visits by an observer), all of us could see what happened to the extra time that had been granted. It was spent on low-priority activities that seemingly demanded immediate action (for example, overdue home repairs or repeated rewritings of lecture notes to avoid possibilities of making factual mistakes in class). It was also used for delinquent things like rest and recreation.

Discussion

Why didn't the intervention of release time yield more time spent on scholarly writing? The reason is that what these frustrated writers needed was not more time but *better skills* for using the time already available to them. If these faculty members didn't know how to use their potentially available time to manage priority tasks like writing beforehand, why would the mere addition of more free time change them into efficacious performers?

Even so I didn't give up on traditional approaches to helping PBers. I wondered, next, if I might do better to adopt a middle ground between the passive interventions usually favored by traditionalists and one closer to my own leanings toward direct intervention. As a compromise, I conducted studies that still relied heavily on PBer's self-reports but on far more systematic inquiries of their experiences. In this way, I hoped, I might learn more of value about the cognitions and feelings underlying PB and even stimulate PBers to think more about their dilatoriness and inhibitions. (Such endeavors were once called consciousness-raising experiences; I hoped they might induce self-correcting acts among problematic PBers.)

A Test to See If Making PBers Aware of Their Bad Habits Would Help

In this study I combined direct-observational methods with systematic interviews of PBers in trouble as new professors (that is, they had done no substantial writing for at least a year). One of my goals was to gather practical information about where and when crucial acts of PB occur in the early careers of professors. The other, about inducing self-change in PBers, has already been stated.

New faculty (total N = 17) were followed over the course of their first two years on campus and repeatedly interviewed to learn how they interpreted things that I had seen happen to them. So while the emphasis remained on what I observed firsthand and how those patterns related to PB, I also encouraged new faculty to share their interpretations of the most crucial events that happened to them.

In the original article (Boice, 1993a) I describe the lengthy procedure of training new faculty to be good reporters of their PB experiences, mostly by way of repeated trials of recalling thoughts and feelings at the time of the crucial incident but with increased focus on the process as opposed to the product:

Typical pretraining comments were interpretive: "I knew I had failed in a big way." With training, reports were less interpretative: "What I was actually thinking was about how I was in too much a hurry to do a proper job on the writing. Then I thought to myself, 'I'll write later, when I'm in a better mood, when I have more time.' I felt a wave of relief so vivid that I can feel it again now."

Sometimes these participants wondered something along with me, quite spontaneously. Would the mere act of helping them notice and reflect on negative turning points rooted in habits of PBing (that is, events with obviously high costs) help them move toward more efficacious patterns? I hoped so. Then I could back off from some of my harsh criticisms about the methods of traditionalists who study PB.

Results of the Self-Report Strategy

The records of PBers in this recollective-thinking-aloud technique proved to be unusually informative about the nature of vitally important instances of PB (for example, missing a deadline for submitting a grant proposal or for mailing in an abstract for a conference program). Reports of thoughts and feelings experienced during turning points in careers, with origins in habitual patterns of PBing, were especially fascinating.

Consider, first, the case of chronic, imperiled PBers who experienced clear turning points that seemed irreversible (for example, an angry argument with the department chair that had grown innocently from a series of overdue reports and student complaints of late arrivals to classes). These PBers seemed particularly unable to translate the insights gleaned from reflective recalls into everyday action.

I still don't see where I went wrong, if I did, and I'm tempted to think that events conspired against me. . . . You have yet to convince me that all this digging into my old thoughts at the time is worth while. Anyway, it's too late now to benefit. Maybe we should be talking about where my next job is coming from.

Then consider the chronic, troubled new faculty who had not yet reached a point of no return. They showed small but promising changes in response to the recollective-thinking-aloud procedure.

I *have* noticed how often I recalled being and feeling hurried when we looked over my thinking patterns. So I've decided I will combat that mood, or whatever it is, with deliberate instructions to myself to be less hurried, more patient when I'm trying to do important writing. . . . When I look back to those thinking patterns I can see how stupid and wasteful they are. They don't seem like they will be all that hard to change.

But even this extensive practice at consciousness-raising did not alleviate PBing for long. Within a month or two after the formal participation of these "reformed PBers" (as some of them called themselves), mentions of attempts to continue in these acts of self-management disappeared from my records of follow-up interviews.

Nonetheless, this extension of PBers' self-reports suggests a promising topic of inquiry. There may be points, particularly in careers or academic experiences, before which habits of PB may be most modifiable. Tendencies to PB evidently undergo a honeymoon period when we enter new work settings, an interval where we are more conscientious about planning and timeliness, one where our colleagues and supervisors are more tolerant of our untimely acts. But once a new opportunity seems wasted by having procrastinated and blocked for too long, instances of PB seem to occur more and more often, almost reflexively. After that point, in my observations, PB seemed implanted deeply, hopelessly, almost irreversibly. This may mean that timely interventions should occur early in the experiences of these new faculty, during the period when they can more easily set an efficacious course.

Common Patterns Leading to Turning Points

Earlier I suggested we can profit in learning more about the typical actions of PBers that seem to undermine their efficacy. Since then we have seen some examples: PBers tend to binge on and rush their writing. PBers work at immediately pressing things, like teaching preparation, excessively and to the point where they evidence diminished returns. Here, then, we have a chance to appreciate the mechanisms behind costly, decisive downturns.

There were four typical patterns—four predictable stages—in which promising beginners seemed to get mired in PBing beyond the point of easy return:

1. These chronic PBers failed to arrange for mentors and other collegial supports at least until after year 2 on their new campus (usually the point when they noticed the benefits that accrued to peers who had found good mentors and collaborators). How did PBers reportedly react to earlier offers of would-be mentors? Either they pessimistically assumed that accepting a mentor would be too great an imposition on any colleague worth working with or they took the elitist stance that they needed no help to survive the tenure process.

2. They put off collegial socializing until they reacted to departmental colleagues as adversaries who did not like them and who, presumably, did not care if they survived the tenure process.

3. They presented themselves in written reactions to student ratings of their classes as too busy to interact with undergraduates (whom they clearly regarded as nuisances).

4. They talked and acted as though marginalized from their campus (for example, spending little time in their offices, rarely attending campus events like concerts and fairs, referring often to the superiority of their former campuses).

By knowing these tendencies of PBers, it seems to me, we could aim our interventions at crucial kinds of PBing at critical times.

A Preview of Results from More Interventive Studies

Once the kinds of PBers depicted above were actively coached to emulate the skills of efficacy seen in quick starters (and were given ongoing feedback about their progress toward reasonable goals in emulating efficacious habits and attitudes), several dramatic improvements were recorded. First, the PBers given coaching *and* practice became more objective, useful observers of their own PBing than when they had been practicing recollective thinking aloud on their own. Second, the points of no return already considered, all of them unmistakable results of PBing (that is, not knowing how to work), were generally reversed in a year or two of regular practice; evidently, PB can be derailed or redirected in time to salvage careers. (My initial impressions about the modifiability of PB past the turning points proved to be overly pessimistic.) Even some novices who had received warning from tenure committees that they would probably fail the process were able to make impressive turnarounds. Their doubtful evaluators noticed the changes in how former PBers worked and socialized, and they could hardly overlook emerging evidence of increasing success at writing, at eliciting favorable responses from students, and at interacting with and learning from colleagues.

But these preliminary studies of interventions were just that, preliminary. I next moved to more thoroughgoing tests to see how enduring such effects of interventions for PB might be. Here again, there were no useful precedents in the literature; I had to work by trial and error—but only to the extent that I needed to sort out what, from the strategies I had already developed, would prove most effective in the long run.

PB TREATED IN ENDURING, ASSESSED FASHION

More Beginnings

Here too some of the approximations to meaningful interventions in the literature merit another look. Taken together, these studies provide a sense of what strategies are promising.

Earlier this book discussed the efforts of Malott and his colleagues to provide thesis writers with task specifications, weekly subgoals, and regular feedback on progress. The outcome, as far it went, was impressive. Ninety-three percent of those graduate students stayed on task, and nearly as many said they liked the strong structure and contingencies of the program. The cognitively oriented treatment study by P. Salovey and M. D. Haar (1990) helped almost two-thirds of its blocked writers move quickly to passing scores on laboratory tests of fluency. Other such reports (for example, Rosenberg & Lah, 1982) demonstrate immediate and consistent increases, not only in time spent writing but in spending the time efficiently. And there are, here and there in this little-known literature, accounts of effective interventions such as the use of daily quizzes to move students beyond usual problems of PBing in college courses (Wesp, 1986). One of the best of these usually overlooked studies was also born of a practical need— students who put off required paperwork as they proceeded through a graduate program. It merits the closer look that follows.

Burgar's Study

The first intervention that occurred to colleagues in a graduate program is the traditional approach taken once PB is publicly recognized: they wanted to rush to solutions before examining the problem; they wanted to implement punishments for violations of the established rule for meeting deadlines on paperwork. But P. Burgar's (1994) more patient analysis of the difficulty revealed that the fault lay more with the situation than with the students.

One problem was the remote location of the place where students would routinely make their applications for "continuation status." Another problem was that direct advising and feedback about timely paperwork were uncommon, so students had remained vague about what to do (and, predictably, had opted for inaction while taking care of other things). Once Burgar arranged a better location and more direct feedback from a faculty adviser, and once students had convenient opportunities to practice efficacy, the problems disappeared. Skills of efficacy depend on convenient opportunities to practice them. Too often we are put in situations where we are most likely to practice habits that undermine efficacy.

Limitations of Most Extant Studies

Despite the existence of a few interventions like the one just overviewed, studies of treatment of PB with quantitative, meaningful assessments of outcomes remain as uncommon as if suppressed by a powerful prohibition. Even interventions like the one just described are usually one-shot enterprises where their researchers published no significant continuations. In fact, though, there is nothing particularly difficult or unusual about conducting such intercessions in long-term, replicable ways.

Other, More Systematically Experimental Interventions with PBers

The rationale for the best-conducted of the more systematically experimental interventions, Sternberg's program for coaching students in tacit knowledge about how to succeed in school (Sternberg, Okagaki & Jackson, 1990), has already been presented. After one semester, the experimental group (who had been taught strategies for self-management, task management, and social management) showed gains on the Survey of Study Habits and Attitudes, notably on scales of Delay Avoidance, Work Methods, Teacher Approval, and Education and Acceptance. Specifically, these students displayed improvement in attitudes, motivation, and ways of working at things like information processing. So, Sternberg concluded, we *can* teach the usually unspoken knowledge crucial to practical intelligence for school. Looking at his work, I conclude that we can just as easily coach the usually tacit information about how to moderate PB.

Sternberg also offers informed cautions about attempting such interventions; his warnings go beyond reluctance to confront embarrassing failures amongst students. Teaching practical intelligence is not inherently easy. To do it teachers need to manage a fundamental reorientation of attitudes and of teaching styles. They must suddenly teach knowledge they usually do not try to impart, knowledge they have expected students to learn on their own (see Tobias, 1990 for a similar conclusion). And teachers may need to listen more closely to students for confirmations that such unconventional methods can work. Sternberg and his colleagues quote reassurances they collected, including this one: "Now I take my time with it. . . . Now I believe I can improve by working hard" (pp. 38–39).

Next, I summarize two quite different approaches to direct and prolonged interventions of my own.

Study 1: Making the Best of Historically Common Interventions

I designed this lengthy project to sort out effects of the four little-known curatives for PB reviewed earlier. I recruited a sample of fifty blocked writers, who all volunteered to schedule daily writing sessions for at least an academic year, and divided them into five treatment groups (Boice, 1992a). Interventions were applied in even-numbered months, with odd-numbered months serving as control conditions for (1) *free writing* (during the first ten to fifteen minutes of each writing session; (2) *contingency management* (with rewards earned by completing a preset number of pages per session, usually one or two); (3) *cognitive therapy* (where writers began sessions by listing maladaptive self-talk and disputing it with rational-emotive strategies); (4) *social supports and skills* (including a structured plan for soliciting regular feedback on formative drafts of manuscripts, imaginary rehearsal of audience reactions to writing, and habitual checks for clarity of writing); and (5) *combined treatments* (where ten writers, throughout the first year, experienced a combination of the four treatments just listed).

Thirty-seven of the forty participants in singular treatments took advantage of a second-year program with the combined treatment.

Before I reached the round number of fifty subjects, twelve dropped out. The program seemed grueling and constraining to some participants, especially in the first two treatment groups (where the most quitting occurred). Dropouts were nearly nonexistent with combined interventions, apparently because writers there felt they were making enough progress to stick with the discipline.

Most single treatments, compared to combined treatments, generated only modest productivity, not enough to meet the realistic goals of participants. The exception came with contingency management where writers wrote the most, albeit not with the most happiness or resilience. Writers given combined treatment wrote at a moderate but adequate pace (for example, they were meeting daily goals for output during 72 percent of their sessions toward the end of the program), and they, far more than writers given single treatment, maintained some of their stability during odd-numbered months where interventions were not formally in effect.

Writers given single treatment who moved, during the second year, into combined treatment showed similar benefits: more sessions with easy starts and without negative talk about themselves, more collegial discussion of and support for writing, and completion of at least one manuscript per year (with more willingness to revise rejected papers and with more editorial acceptances in refereed outlets). But success in the combined-treatment program did not relate to personality typologies of writers as, say, perfectionistic or phobic, not even to the kinds of writing they did (for example, the compressed manuscripts that mathematical theorists sometimes write versus the wordier prose of humanists).

The important message in this long-term study, I think, is this: while traditional, single treatments such as free writing help PBers, they fall far short of providing the enduring efficacy that the broad combination of treatments offers. (PB, so far as I can tell, is rarely limited to one problem or one domain; PBers can learn general strategies in order to moderate any kind of PBing.) Do lesser mixes offer fewer benefits? Other combinations do

somewhat better than single treatments. But whatever the combination, regular practice is most essential to the acquisition of
efficacious habits (see Ericsson & Charness, 1994). Still, regular
practice alone (as in the contingency-management group) can
leave writers irritable and inclined to drop out. Overall, efficaciousness included three allied skills in this study:

• automaticity for generating momentum or ideas.

• cognitive restructuring for ensuring more comfort, clarity, and economy

• social-skills training for finding support, sense of audience, and ways of
coping with disappointment

Studies 2 and 3: Models of Exemplary, Efficacious
Habits as Interventions for PB

The next two intervention projects began more inductively. Before beginning them, I made prolonged observations of how exemplary new faculty worked at scholarly writing. These novices
proved reliably different from chronic PBers in the ways already
outlined in this book.

Study 2 provided a simple regimen to helped teach busy, inefficient PBers to imitate the habits of exemplars. In particular, this
imitation meant slowing down and doing most of their important
work economically (in brief, daily sessions). In general, it helped
to produce dramatic, lasting increases in productivity (for example, pages written per year and manuscripts accepted in refereed
outlets) and to decrease exhibitions of busyness. The most vocal
beneficiaries of this change from PBing and its busyness were the
students of these faculty (Boice, 1989).

Study 3, an extended version of the project begun in Study 2
(Boice, 1995a), confirmed a difficulty of intervening in PB that
was portended in the study on combined treatments. Properly
done, interventions need to be broader and longer than might be
supposed. The realization came to me serindipitously, while I conducted separate programs for improving the writing productivity
and the teaching skills of junior faculty. (I had been accustomed,
like many of us, to seeing the two activities as essentially unrelated

[Feldman, 1987].) New faculty themselves appreciated the connection first.

Perhaps because the writing program lent itself to readier identification of basic skills that produce documented improvements, the resulting "writerly rules" were seen sooner by participants who moved next to the teaching program than by those who moved from teaching to writing. When they informally transformed the writerly rules into everyday practices related to teaching, they came to a uniform conclusion: the same efficacious ways of working at writing could just as well apply to teaching. Writerly rules were obviously similar to the basics we were experimentally adducing for teaching; better yet, they suggested some ways of working at teaching that might not have occurred to us while our concept remained narrow.

The long-term outcomes were remarkably strong. The writerly rules, all of them about working efficaciously, helped new faculty members find slow but sure success as writers and as teachers. These rules worked even more impressively and durably when novice professors were exposed to both programs. But in telling you these things, I am getting ahead of my story. First I want to acquaint you with the rules of efficacy (a.k.a. writerly rules) as we winnowed them from a larger list and tell you how they work.

Basic Principles of Efficacy

Following are the ten fundamental rules of efficacy that proved most effective in helping chronic, problem PBers manage comfort and fluency compared to matched controls. Each rule was accompanied in the study with detailed strategies for practice and assessment (Boice, 1995a; 1995b); here I greatly abbreviate the rules.

1. *Wait.* Waiting helps writers (and teachers) develop patience and direction for writing by tempering rushing. Its exercises include methods for calming, slowing, and noticing before and during starts. At first glance, this rule seems at odds with the second.

2. *Begin before feeling ready.* The second rule coaches writers in systematic ways of finding imagination and confidence; writers practice regular bouts of collecting, filing, rearranging, and outlining ideas while

making sure they solve the right problem and have the right materials and plans at hand. Neither efficacy nor its rewards, including happiness, just happen; they must be prepared for and cultivated (Csikszentmihalyi, 1994). The second rule, incidentally, is often mastered before the first; there is no necessary chronology or separation in these admonitions.

3. *Work in brief, daily sessions.* Writers are advised to work regularly at prewriting, at writing, and at additional things easily PBed. But the rule also means maintaining a regular habit of brief sessions that will persist because it does not supplant other important activities. Its strategies include contingency management (but only in the short run, until a habit of regular work is established; writers perform better with intrinsic motivation). A distinctive quality of productive, creative people is that each day they return to their desks (Gardner, 1993).

4. *Stop.* Stopping means halting in timely fashion, when breaks are needed or when enough has been done for the day. It means moving on from writing to other things including rest. This most difficult rule is practiced by means of planned breaks, by stopping early (often in the midst of tasks), and with external reminders (for example, social cues, such as a prearranged phone call from a friend about when to stop.

5. *Balance preliminaries with writing.* Writers practice the balance rule by scheduling periods of delay before moving from preliminaries to actual writing. They make clear, manageable plans for collecting, organizing, and conceptual outlining—in a way that ensures as much time spent on these preliminaries as on writing.

6. *Supplant self-defeating thinking and habits.* The sixth rule is about moderating the pessimistic, self-denigrating thoughts that lead to depression and inaction or overreaction (Seligman, 1991). It is also about changing habits that otherwise incline writers to shyness, suspiciousness, and related self-defeating behaviors (Baumeister & Scher, 1988). At its most complex, it teaches ways of making the private bets that discourage impulsiveness, by requiring a price for impetuous acts of PBing. When these bets are made well, they recast the penalty for defaulting as too expensive to permit indulgence in escape behaviors—those immediately rewarding acts that tempt us to be disobedient and self-defeating (Ainslie, 1975; Logue, 1994). Other exercises include (a) habitual monitoring for negative talk about the self and for maladaptive styles of working and (b) practice of rational-emotive therapies to defuse and redirect irrational thinking in and around sessions.

7. *Manage emotions.* The seventh rule, like the sixth, is about self-control but more about the emotional side of writing. In particular it means monitoring for and moderating the hypomania that can make writing rushed and superficial. It means working at a moderate pace punctuated by occasional bursts of excitement and accent that energize but do not prevent returning to unhurried gaits of working, that do not induce enduring depression (Boice, 1994). The resulting patterns of variability in pacing and emotional emphasis resemble what Carl Rogers identified as "focused voice" in his pioneering observations of expert therapists (Hill & Corbett, 1993).

8. *Moderate attachments and reactions.* The rule about moderation reflects the finding, in composition research, that successful writers tend to be less attached to their writing, especially in its formative stages. Their detachment allows more revision and more benefit from critics; it makes inevitable criticism less devastating. Writers in the treatment program are coached to notice when they are reluctant to stop during sessions, when they feel their early plans and drafts are already brilliant, when they are unwilling to share unfinished work because its ideas may be stolen.

9. *Let others, even critics, do some of the work.* The penultimate rule requires even more letting go, delegating, collaborating. It leads to regularly scheduled sharing of work and soliciting constructive praise and criticism. It engages writers in role-played approximations to socially skilled ways of handling and learning from criticism (for example, "Yes, I can see how someone might react that way . . .").

10. *Limit wasted effort.* Because this last rule, about not wasting efforts, comes late in the year-long program, when writers are beginning to work on their own, its practices are somewhat idiosyncratic. It nonetheless has a common theme, one originating in the finding that resilience in writing relies most heavily on ways of working with minimal wasted effort. Its exercises focus on monitoring for inefficiencies, notably impatience (for example, rushing work until fatigue sets in) and intolerance (for example, overreacting to an interruption or criticism).

Results of Applying These Rules of Efficacy to Writers

New faculty in the program profited compared to matched controls (whose involvement was limited to occasional assessments of experiences and progress). Participants benefited even more, as writers, when they extended their training to a second year of similar exercises in efficacious ways of teaching. The rules and strategies stayed much the same for teaching as for writing (Boice, 1995b).

Consider these samples of improved comfort, timeliness, and success in just the first year: (1) more completions of at least one scholarly manuscript (75 percent vs. 19 percent for controls); (2) more acceptances in refereed outlets (38 percent vs. 6 percent); (3) higher scores on a campus-wide rating instrument of their teaching by students ($\overline{X}$ = 2.4 vs. 2.0, where 4.0 was the maximum); and (4) more explicit assurances that retention and tenure were likely from departmental committees (38 percent vs. 13 percent).

Combined Results for Writers and Teachers

By the second year, when the program focus had switched to teaching, the results were far better in *both* teaching and writing domains (and reliably better than for matched controls now also in their second years on campus). For example, the percentages of subjects receiving combined treatment who completed manuscripts in the second year rose (to 94 percent vs. 25 percent for controls) as did acceptances (63 percent vs. 25 percent). Teaching ratings showed equally impressive gains (to $\overline{X}$ = 3.0 vs. 2.2).

New faculty who spent the first year concentrating on the teaching program and the second year on writing showed similar, somewhat more slowly achieved benefits (both as teachers and as writers). Why was the reversed pattern somewhat less effective? The junior faculty in this paradigm were unenthusiastic about mastering teaching while struggling with writing. The former activity offers few rewards beyond self-satisfaction and student approval on campuses I have studied.

Why did the combined and broadened program for moderating PB work better than either single treatment? First, acts of transferring efficacies to the other domain evidently forced new faculty to express the rules and to conduct their strategies more clearly, to notice what aspects of each made the most difference. Second, acts of generalization quickly grew beyond the bounds of the program. As the same basic principles proved helpful in other aspects of PB (for example, insomnia or failures to stick with plans for exercise) the rules seemed more obviously credible. (Again, PB and its curatives seemed to be domain-general.) Third, repeated trials with the writerly rules made each remastery easier and more thorough.

Once practicing these efficacies, new faculty enjoyed discovering new information in the literature about ways of overcoming PB. They helped me not only to see more of this rich store of knowledge but to sense where study and treatment of PB, once liberated from its ban, might go next. The structure and credibility provided by bringing these adjunctive literatures into the PB arena may help ease that bold move as discussed in chapter 5.

5

Procrastination and Blocking Seen in Close Parallels to Other Maladaptive Behaviors

To begin to see procrastination and blocking in broader perspective requires only a simple realization. Much of the literature about human behavior that could link maladaptive behavior patterns to PB usually does not do so. If it did, PB would be much better understood, perhaps even less embarrassing or difficult to study. To illustrate how easily we can see a substantial role for PB in a diversity of areas that we already may know better, I begin with the area that seems most obviously relevant to PB.

TIME USE

Some research on use of time has already been noted. It has been found that reasonable organization and routine improve a person's health, optimism, self-esteem, and study habits (Bond & Feather, 1988). It has been found that the overinvestment of time in short-term emotional relief sacrifices long-term benefits and promotes self-defeating patterns (Baumeister & Scher, 1988). Also discovered is the fact that broadly intelligent, efficacious people are more flexible and selective in allocating their resources, including time, better at allocating time among tasks, and better at automating some operations as a way of saving effort and time (Sternberg, 1988). Deficiencies in the same skills incur PB.

Other findings in nearby fields augment these insights about how efficacy differs from PB. People who do more than one thing at a time are better able to tolerate moderate imprecision and flexible scheduling while working; they usually do not react to unplanned events as problematic interruptions. This means that they are less concerned with promptness but more likely to achieve it. As a result, these polychronics work with less role overload and more sociability than do monochronics (Bluedorn, Kaufman, & Lane, 1992). Productive and eminent scholars work in highly structured patterns and carry out several projects at once (Fox, 1985). PBers, in contrast, fall short of such efficacy for reasons that include poor use of time. They delay use of problem-solving strategies until well after the need is apparent (Perkins, 1981), and they do not know how to arrange time and conditions to minimize fatigue and maximize the right kinds of practice (Ericsson & Charness, 1994).

Use of Time as a Skill

Clearly, time is central to PB in ways that go beyond dilatoriness. Individuals unskilled at estimating time and at distracting themselves while waiting tend to impulsiveness (Logue, 1994). Impulsivity, in turn, brings hostility, hurrying, and overvalued goals (Frese, Stewart, & Hannover, 1987). At their worst, the exaggerated oscillations of mood that follow can take on the qualities of manic-depression (Jamison, 1993). At best, the time urgency triggered by impulsivity means nervous tension, self-absorption, and sensitivity (Wessman, 1993). People obsessed by time aren't just hard on themselves but also on co-workers, whom they see impatiently, as slow-moving obstacles (Landy, Rastegary, Thayer, & Colvin, 1991). Even when impulsive people do finish things, they tend to do them so quickly that the rewards do not repay the costs of setting them up (Ainslie, 1975). When, in contrast, people develop a reasonable appreciation of time, they benefit in orderliness and confidence (Wessman, 1993), in reduced role overload and tensions (Macan, Shahani, Dipboye, & Phillips, 1990), and even in more sleep (Ericsson & Charness, 1994). Individuals skilled at using time report feeling more in charge of their time, better able to say no to requests, and better able to stop unprofitable routines and activities. Up close, then, time skills resemble self-efficacy (Britton & Tesser, 1991). Consistent with that finding, recent work on the personality correlates of PB suggests that only low self-efficacy predicts putting off important activities (Ferrari, Parker, & Ware, 1992).

A Historical Perspective on Time

Some of the best insights about time use and timeliness are the oldest. Historians note that close consciousness of time is a recent invention; for some 99 percent of human evolution we have reveled in the primal laziness that allows slow recovery from battle, chase, or harvest. Regular work (and its occasional resentment) awaited two things: routine tillage and the organization of labor; the most excessive routines were first perfected in slavery and kindred conditions (Durant, 1954). Only with the Industrial Revolution (and with the psychology of work that accompanied it) did employers fully appreciate the benefits of efficacy. Still, most of its lessons have been incompletely learned: One is that attentiveness (for example, as required in most scholarly writing) is abnormal, transient, exhausting; "primitives" knew better than people today how to use rhythms and resting to sustain it. Another is that the longer the workday, the greater the need for some unproductive work; waste in work comes primarily by way of fatigue and what best reduces waste, as indexed by errors, is a slower pace and a proportional amount of rest. The best way to reduce errors (including PB) is to work in shorter, more manageable segments (Rabinbach, 1990).

These historical accounts also offer a striking explanation for the seeming proscription against direct treatments for PB. Early psychologists and sociologists noticed that wasted energy and poor use of time differentiated people of low socioeconomic status from those of higher classes. By the point where Marxists adopted this discomfiting idea, it seemed even clearer that if we could use technology to increase the productivity and (more important) decrease the wasted energy of the lower classes, workers might be emancipated from competition, classism, even excessive PB. The democratic inclinations of the psychology of work have yet to find tolerance among American scholars (for example, Banta, 1993). Why? The reason is that to expose someone else's PBing may be to reveal that person's lower-class status. To offer effective help that enhances the practical intelligence of people on the margins violates one of psychology's least discussed, least understood prohibitions (Kipnis, 1994).

In the main, again, lack of time is not the problem in PB. Instead, it is more a matter of knowing how to use it efficaciously *and* of deciding who should be helped in so doing.

DISTINCTIONS BETWEEN PRODUCT AND PROCESS ORIENTATIONS

Some of the basic differences between product and process orientation have also been foreseen. Monochronics, because they are excessively task oriented and busy (that is, product oriented), do not know how to combine tasks and flexibly modify priorities (Bluedorn, Kaufman, & Lane, 1992). Effective organization and persistence depend largely on a present (that is, process) orientation, not on worrying about past mistakes or future rejections (Bond & Feather, 1988). Expert writers, because they work largely in the moment, from elaborate plans, are better at developing their own knowledge, identifying audiences, and spotting problems (Hayes & Flower, 1986).

That is, they are mainly process oriented, using a work style that is the essence of mindfulness, planning, and competence (Langer & Park, 1990).

Economies of Mindfulness

A *process orientation* also helps draw attention to what decisions and acts matter in the moment, to habits of thinking, feeling, and working and how they influence our efficacy (Tremmel, 1993). The unhurried, immersing flow of activity in mindfulness is an enjoyable end in itself (Csikszentmihalyi, 1990). It helps rein in a consciousness that otherwise may run out of control and head toward the fear, anxiety, and mindlessness that encourage PB (Field, 1936). Its present orientation fosters more patience for time spent en route in summarizing, questioning, and clarifying. Its more reflective and planned processing generates the imaginativeness and confidence necessary to social conversations and other involvements that impel decisive, public actions (Flower & Hayes, 1980). Further, immersion in a process orientation not only encourages the intrinsic motivation critical to optimal performance (Amibile, 1983); it also disinclines us to proceed in the least-effortful style that may be dictated by the extrinsic motivators common to a product orientation (Lepper, 1988). Put another way, in a process mode we display a learning orientation where we react to obstacles by increasing effort selectively and by varying strategies (Dweck, 1986).

How can we know, by contrast, that a *product orientation* wastes time and energy? Consider this bit of evidence: J. D. Williams (1985) measured electrical potentials in the articulatory musculature to identify writers who limited most of their covert talking to pauses in comparison to those who talked covertly throughout their writing sessions. Covert talking limited to pauses was directed to reviewing and planning, and it helped produce the best-quality writing. Writers who talked to themselves less discriminately while working were seemingly product oriented and apparently spent too much time worrying about possible mistakes and likely rejections.

Economies of Effort and Confidence

A process orientation (that is, living largely in the moment and attending to ongoing activities) also helps by encouraging more awareness of wasted time and effort. Skinner (1983), reflecting on his career, noted a crucial turning point when he realized that he was not using his time efficaciously: "When I am not working, I must relax—not work on something else!" (p. 79). P. G. Wodehouse paid particular attention to efficacy in the way he planned and wrote his seemingly spontaneous prose. He designed crisp dialog and carefully timed the exits and entrances of his characters as though in a stage play; he wrote with little waste (Jasen, 1981).

Other writers help demonstrate why planning does not limit creativity when it is done early, with room for flexibility. Of Dickens it was said: "He had the architectural plans drawn up, as it were, but he needed to build freely and instinctively" (Ackroyd, 1990, p. 560). Experts rehearse the whole process of important things they will do, including the solution, beforehand; then as they work, they can concentrate on process. This freedom to keep on noticing alternatives leaves them more predisposed to invent new concepts and schemata to improve an already understandable process (Carey, 1986). And it leaves them more inclined to build self-efficacy. The deeper the processing (for example, ability to store and recall), the more calm and confident the mode of working (Meier, McCarthy, & Schmeck, 1984).

Economies of Motivation

Process orientations promote the motivation and momentum that PBers struggle to find. Habitual acts of collecting and formulating ideas stimulate imagination, and they push, slowly and almost imperceptibly, for action (Mills, 1959: Murray, 1978). States of high consciousness or mindfulness elicit statements that control attention, that positively evaluate abilities, that set a positive emotion for proceeding (Glass & Arnkoff, 1986). Motivation and fluency not only require regular habits of paying attention but also the flexibility of a deliberate alternation between different mental postures such as generating or reviewing (Perl, 1978).

Once initiated in this process mode, motivation is perpetuated by reflective awareness and long processing (for example, by matching or assimilating novel or complex information with established schemata). Why? The flow of serene success in figuring things out slows reactivity, overreaction, and disappointment. The sense of control over input helps maintain an emotional stance of interest and joy (Singer, 1988). Efficacy is, in the final analysis, defined by resilience that depends on moderated arousal, lowered levels of perceived stress, and tolerated disruptions (Bandura, 1990; Landino & Owen, 1988; Rosenbaum, 1980).

Without this calm and confidence, the right risks are not taken, the right supports are not accessed, the right problems are not solved, and the right skills are not mastered (London, 1993). A painful example can be seen in the tendency of new women faculty who, when harried by work demands, react suspiciously or pessimistically to offers from would-be mentors (Boice, 1993a).

Economies in Understanding and Dealing with Resistance

Other parallels in the literature explain why PBers do not easily give up their maladaptive inclinations to work in product orientations. One of the most powerful instances occurs in one of the most venerated of activities: traditional teaching. Its guidebooks and experts fall shamefully short of helping people learn to work in a process fashion that would minimize PBing.

Consider some of the usual, well-intentioned failings of traditional teachers. They typically come to class fully prepared and so do not demonstrate how they themselves really think out and solve the problems they pose (Zoellner, 1969). Teachers and writers often trivialize the role of the audience and the process of helping its varied members grasp the essence of what is conveyed (Reddy, 1993). And only infrequently do teachers impart the process skills that moderate PB (for example, learning to attribute failures to efforts or strategy, not to ability [Dweck, 1986]). Student writers, for instance, learn best by way of a process orientation that allows them to work like efficacious writers: by taking intellectual control of a subject, discovering something worth saying, noticing relationships among ideas, and working regularly (Tremmel, 1989). That is, they need to learn the process, not just the product, of expert workers. When they do not, they more often become PBers.

Where might we best begin to change this aspect of traditional teaching? Perhaps in the training of teachers themselves.

Economies of Teaching

In the brief study I overview next, I looked specifically at new faculty struggling as teachers. I wondered: Could their slow starts in the classroom result from PBing (much as it did for novice writers)? Would their PBing reflect deficiencies in process orientation akin to those of dilatory, anxious writers? Could struggling teachers benefit by modeling the styles and habits of expert teachers? I'll explain more as we move along.

Introduction

Suppose, first, that you were chosen to observe these novices. How would you judge their prowess as teachers? You might look at the literature, where you would find thousands of articles and books about instructional development, most of them in education, but only a handful with hard evidence for improving teaching (Boice, 1996e). You would find lots of conjecture; experts on improving teaching commonly shun empiricism (Weimer & Lenze, 1991) while depicting teaching as an art that can only be undermined by scientists (Eble, 1985). So it is that psychologists writing on this topic emphasize admonitions over facts (for example, "To nurture good teaching, departments should offer encouragement." [Murray, 1995, p. 40]). (Traditional attitudes towards improving teaching are much like those for helping PBers.)

Then suppose, having decided to collect your own information, that you observed your junior colleagues to see how novices learn to teach. What would you find? (1) teachers learning by trial and error, too often by way of misinformation (for example, good content equals good teaching) than by way of proven efficiencies (Boice, 1992b); (2) senior faculty generally unaccustomed to reflecting on the basic skills of teaching and just as unlikely to guide apprentices in this realm; (3) probably an overall picture where the majority of faculty (and their students) find teaching disappointing (McGaughey, 1993).

Given those harsh realities, where would you go next? Perhaps you would assume that in watching struggling novices (compared to expert teachers) you might find some clues about which behavioral patterns make for success in the classroom. You might even select novices already designated as PBing writers—who had already evidenced poor ratings as teachers, even for novices. That, at least, is what I did.

The idea of what, exactly, to look for came to me when I studied cohorts of newcomers to professorial teaching careers for over a decade (Boice, 1992b). One thing stood out about good beginnings as teachers: clearly, new faculty with the best starts showed the lowest general levels of classroom incivilities. That is, the undergraduate courses taught by "intelligent novices," as we might call them in psychology, were far less marked by students coming late and leaving early, noisily. Far fewer students carried on their own conversations while the professor was talking. There was far less rudeness such as catcalls and groans. (Most of this was pointed out already, in chapter 1.)

There are obscure hints in the literature that classroom incivilities often make or break teachers (see Boice 1996c, for a review). There is even a suggestion of the central failings behind disruptive, demoralizing incivilities: too few teachers' immediacies such as smiling, open postures, and eye contact; not enough positive social motivators such as praising students' approximations to correct answers (Plax & Kearney, 1992). Along with that, there was a general *un*awareness of the processes of teaching, including checks for student reactions and comprehension (Boice, 1992b). Said simply, the slowest starters as teachers displayed the least "teaching awareness." Later, as I worked more closely with individual new faculty as both teachers and writers, I began to suspect that tendencies to PB in one domain were also found in the other.

In this summary of that study, I describe two related experiments derived from those beginning observations. One experiment determines whether high levels of classroom incivilities do in fact distinguish unsuccessful from successful teachers (and whether PB plays a significant role in these failures) and if they also reflect a lack of process orientation in teachers. The second experiment shows how training in immediacies and providing positive motivators (hereafter simply called immediacies) reduces classroom incivilities (of both teachers and their students), enhances student performance, raises student ratings of teaching, and, not least, improves teaching awareness of ongoing processes. It's not nearly as complicated as it sounds.

Experiment 1

1. *Participants.* To discern clear differences between struggling novices and consensus experts, I compared two groups of teachers in two large, public universities. One group consisted of fourteen newcomers to tenure-track positions in their second or third semesters of teaching (none had taught a class of their own before coming to campus). All fourteen had, in the prior semester, scored

in the bottom quartile on a campus-wide student evaluation of their teaching; all were considered by their chairs and/or deans to be in trouble as teachers; all had been encouraged by departmental colleagues to seek help. All fourteen also were procrastinating and blocking as writers in the sense of averaging less than one page of scholarly prose per week; none had yet completed a manuscript on campus and had it accepted by a refereed outlet. In other words, these newcomers' careers were off to generally troubling starts in ways that seemed to relate to PBing.

The comparison group of fourteen teachers was selected from faculty who had been on their campus at least five years and who had won teaching awards at the departmental level or above. All fourteen "experts" had garnered student evaluations in the top quartile of campus norms for the preceding semester. And all had published in steady fashion since coming to campus, at rates of at least .80 manuscripts in refereed outlets per year.

All 28 participants volunteered. There was another important commonality: all were teachers, at least once a year, of undergraduate survey classes of more than fifty students in a large lecture hall. I matched novices and experts within the social sciences or the hard sciences and for kinds of courses taught (for example, mathematical, statistical; survey and conceptual; lecture and discussion; or laboratory oriented).

2. *Methods.* I visited the classrooms of participants unobtrusively ten times distributed over the course of a semester (including the first three classes). In each such visit I made four distributed ratings during a class and used a scoring system described in detail elsewhere (Boice, 1996b); these categories of classroom incivilities become clearer here as I move to the results of this experiment. In this first of two experiments, my intent was to compare levels of classroom incivilities between the two groups of teachers (slow starters versus fast starters) and to compare those teachers' awareness of what precipitated those incivilities. Directly observed distinctions between the skills of accomplished and struggling teachers have rarely been attempted in college settings (just as they haven't for PB).

In Experiment 1, I also attempted to index the extent to which students paid a price for classes with high levels of classroom incivility. Because there are no widely accepted measures of student learning (for example, usual reliance on students' exam scores is problematic for a variety of reasons), I opted for two relatively unconfounded indices that fit the study situation nicely. One was a simple rating based on examination of the class notes from a random sample of four students after each class. Based on earlier research (Boice, 1996c), I set the following as a criterion of inadequate notetaking: only half as much writing as had been presented on the board or on overhead transparencies during class. To collect a second index of cost or benefit from a class meeting, I asked the same four students, individually, to explain for me what I deemed a focal concept (usually a list) delivered by the teacher in that day's class. I scored the student's oral response as inadequate if it represented less than half of what, in essence, had been presented and emphasized that day.

To gain a sense of a teacher's awareness of classroom processes, I used a form of the recollective-thinking-aloud procedure noted earlier to help the teacher reconstruct classroom experiences, particularly those associated with classroom incivilities that I had observed during my last visit. The actual procedures are described in detail elsewhere (Boice, 1996b). Briefly, I coached teachers, during each of these ten sessions in their offices, to report their thoughts and feelings as classroom incivilities occurred.

Experiment 2

The second experiment was an extension of the first. This time I coached struggling novices in the skills of immediacy to see if such an intervention would lessen classroom incivilities, raise student ratings, increase student benefit, and heighten process awareness of teaching.

1. *Participants.* One group comprised ten of the fourteen novices from Experiment 1 who here volunteered to participate in (*a*) a second semester, where I coached them in the kinds of immediacy skills that expert veterans had displayed in Study 1, and (*b*) a third semester, where I again charted the occurrence of classroom incivilities and of student benefits during ten sessions of large undergraduate courses.

The control group in Experiment 2 consisted of ten second- or third-semester novices who had evidenced similarly poor teaching ratings and writing habits (compared to the struggling novices of

Study 1) during their prior semester on campus. Controls were *not* formally coached in immediacy skills. Each of the control subjects was picked to match an experimental participant in terms of general discipline and type of course taught.

2. *Methods.* The scheme for visiting and rating classes remained essentially the same as in Experiment 1 except for two differences of note: I combined the two measures of student notetaking and comprehension into one (because students in Experiment 1 who fared poorly in one sphere almost always performed similarly in the other—that is, students who took few if any notes consistently failed to demonstrate their abilities to remember the central points). And I took a general measure of students' classroom incivilities, one that combined the categories outlined in Experiment 1 (that is, students in Experiment 2 had to score on all three dimensions in at least two of four observation intervals during a class to qualify as uncivil for the day).

The coaching scheme consisted of ten individual sessions before classes in the second semester of participation, usually of no more than ten minutes, where I modeled two simple skills of immediacy (for example, open postures with forward leans and smiles directed at students and positive comments given in response to potentially annoying student questions). I also mimicked the responses of students to such actions (for example, forward leans and eye contact). After such modeling, the novice teacher rehearsed the posture or movement, restated the verbal response, and predicted student responses to immediacies (and to their absence). Then, during the class session that followed, I rated the success of each novice in enacting the practices and shared that information with them afterward (always in terms of what they did well and then as suggestions of how they could improve on their approximations to effective immediacies). Here, as in Experiment 1, I elicited reflective recalls of process awareness from these teachers.

These immediacies, despite their seeming simplicity and ease of practice before class, were mastered slowly in classroom use, with many regressions under duress. So too, was attending to the moment-by-moment process of teaching during times that classroom incivilities occurred. Not until the end of this semester of practice were the novices and I pleased with their progress.

Figure 5.1
Classroom Observations

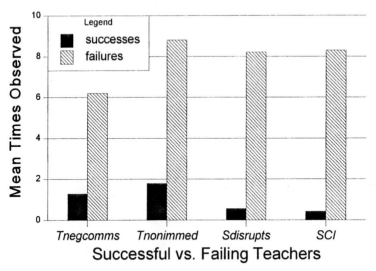

Successful teachers (with more than five years experience and with teaching awards) compared to struggling novices in terms of four dimensions of failure at "immediacies": teachers' negative communications (Tnegcomms) to students (e.g., threats); teachers' nonimmediate (Tnonimmed) nonverbal expressions (e.g., immobile, unfriendly postures); student disruptions (Sdisrupts) (e.g., coming late and leaving early, noisily); and, strong student incivilities (SCI) (e.g., cat calls). Counts on the Y-axis are based on 10 visits to a classroom per semester and four spaced observations per class meeting; I scored a dimension as uncivil when its count per class meeting was recorded in two intervals or more.

In the next (and third) semester of participation, I stopped the coaching sessions and reverted to classroom visits and recollective interviews like those of Experiment 1 in order to judge the enduring results of my intervention.

Results of Experiment 1

1. *Kinds of classroom incivilities*. Figure 5.1 depicts the dramatically different levels of classroom incivilities for the struggling novices compared to the expert teachers. In every category of incivility that had been established in earlier research as distracting and aversive by both teachers and students (Boice, 1996c), the

beginners and their classes performed at clearly poorer levels. (For purposes of analysis, I scored a class meeting as "uncivil" in each of the domains when I observed instances in at least two of my four, five-minute recording periods per class visit.)

2. *The primacy of classroom incivility.* Something not apparent in Figure 5.1 is that problems of classroom incivility were the first to appear in the spontaneous complaints of students to me, and they dominated student comments over semesters (in contrast to other common difficulties such as unclear presentations, rapid rates of presenting, lack of enthusiasm from the teacher, and deficiently clear examples of concepts). Classroom incivility may be the first crucial place for interventions.

3. *The product orientation of struggling novices.* As expected, the unskilled beginners were far less likely to reconstruct an ongoing-process awareness of how they taught. They, in contrast to expert teachers, were five times more likely to "draw blanks" when asked to recall what they thought or felt about student reactions during four specific moments I had selected from the prior class. This was the typical sort of response given by novices, even after repeated reconstructions:

Hmm. [long pause] What did I think of how the students were reacting to what I was doing? Don't know. What I can sort of recall was being very wrapped up in what I wanted to say, in making sure I was saying all the things on my notes, and, yes, I was working hard to get things written on the board. So I can't say I was doing much other thinking. I was just doing, you know? I probably wasn't paying much attention to the students. [in response to my question:] How did I feel? *That* I can recall. Tense, in a hurry. I wanted, more than anything, to get all the material covered.

Recollections of experts were far more direct and process oriented:

Yes, this is what I recall. I was thinking that the students were looking away from me and from their notes. I thought I should slow down and get them to ask some questions.

4. *Struggling novices and signs of PBing.* How, in addition to showing an inability to get past product orientations, did the trou-

bled beginners show signs of incorporating tendencies to PB into their reflective reconstructions? They, in almost complete contrast to experts, procrastinated and blocked in recognizing and dealing with classroom incivilities.

Sure, I noticed that, kind of. [I had just read my notes of a few students yelling rude complaints after she had assigned a reading for the next class]. But I pretty much ignored it. I went on to something else. [in response to my next question] Oh, it made me feel very nervous, like I was failing at teaching. It was one of those times when I hated teaching.

I hadn't thought much about it [a period of over three minutes where he had seemingly frozen in class], it makes me uncomfortable. It was when I was disrupted so rudely [a student had yelled, "You can't teach; no one understands what's going on here"]. I lost my place in the notes and I sort of panicked. I wasn't thinking much of anything, just trying to get going again.

5. *Why failures to recognize and act on the need for immediacies mattered.* Figure 5.1 suggests reasons why failures to exhibit immediacies so quickly became problems. Struggling novices far more often made negative comments in class that I, in accord with definitions of other researchers, deemed as off-putting and discouraging to students (for example, demeaning the question or response of a student or using threats or making students feel guilty to get their cooperation [Plax & Kearney, 1992]). And these same poorly rated teachers displayed far more of the postures, movements, and other nonverbal signs (for example, lack of eye contact with students) already linked to classroom incivility in simulated study conditions (Kearney & Plax, 1992). In Figure 5.1, these two dimensions of problematic teacher behavior are displayed as "Tnegcomms" (for "teachers' negative communications") and "Tnonimmeds" (for "teachers' nonimmediacies").

6. *More general difference between expert and novice teachers across the other three measures of classroom incivility.* There were differences for levels of student noise ("Snoise") that made the lecturer inaudible toward the back of the room. There were differences for student disruptions ("Sdisrupts") that actually halted teaching and for rude comments or noises or other forms of strong classroom incivility ("SCI"). The reliability of this difference be-

tween struggling beginners and exemplary veterans can be seen in the MANOVA (multiple analysis of variance) of the data in Figure 5.1: $F(5, 22) = 188.69, p > 001$.

Said simply, then, classrooms of the expert teachers were comparatively quiet and their students appeared to be more positively involved. Students in these exemplary classrooms were far less likely to create the noisy din and other distractions that made student involvement difficult in the courses taught by struggling novice teachers.

The other distinctive difference between the two kinds of classrooms reflects something that surprised the beginning teachers. Few of them, in contrast to the expert teachers, had imagined beforehand that they, themselves, could be significant contributors to classroom incivility. Figure 5.1, again, displays the matter graphically: The levels of negative comments for novice teachers ("Tnegcomms") were much higher; so too incidences of the non-immediacies ("Tnonimmeds") that seem to distance students. Few of the novices were aware of the classroom processes surrounding incivility (including their own and students' actions that led to them and exacerbated them); instead, they overlooked and put off the need to deal with these crucial incidents. Said simply, they acted like PBers.

7. *Students' costs.* Figure 5.2 helps answer one question posed by what has just been shown: Did the higher levels of incivility in the classrooms of struggling novices relate to the apparent costs or benefits to their students? The graphed results indicate predictable differences in student note taking (depicted as observed instances of "few notes") and in student ability to explain central concepts (observed instances where students could "not explain"). So does the MANOVA for these two kinds of student cost: $F(2, 25) = 45.03, p > .001$.

In other words, students in classrooms of struggling novices were far less likely to take useful notes or to comprehend central concepts. In contrast, students in the courses of expert teachers, were incivility was less prominent and where teachers were more immediate seemed better off in terms of note taking and comprehension. The most curious outcome in this comparison is only a suggestion, but it might be called "induced PBing." Students in the classes of PBing teachers not only put off note taking, but

Figure 5.2
Classes of Two Kinds of Teachers

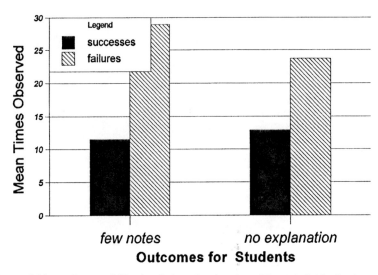

Successful (expert) versus failing (novice) teachers' students (N = 4 individually observed/queried after each of 10 class meetings) compared in terms of failures to take minimal notes or to recite and explain half of a list of concepts emphasized in class.

they far more often told me they felt unmotivated to study for these classes until the last minute than did students in the classes of expert, nonPBing teachers.

Results of Experiment 2

1. *Lowered levels of classroom incivility*. Figure 5.3 suggests that a semester of coaching in simple skills of immediacy led to lower levels of problem behaviors in the classrooms of novice teachers who had previously been associated with high levels of these negative and disruptive incidents. Compared to matched controls, these coached novices displayed fewer negative communications and off-putting nonverbal expressions in their classrooms. Their classrooms had fewer instances of problem noise levels. Their students engaged in more note taking ("SNT") and were more likely to comprehend essential points after class; their students were more commonly seen as involved (that is, most class members

Figure 5.3
Results of Interventions

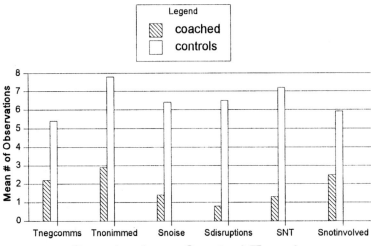

Coached vs. Control Teachers

Two groups of struggling novices, coached versus uncoached in skills of immediacy, compared in terms of five measures of outcome during a semester of observations. The Y-axis represents means of total scored numbers of problems with immediacies during each of my 10 classroom visits in the first four domains: my observations of teachers' negative communications (Tnegcomms); of teachers' nonimmediate (Tnonimmed) postures or gestures; of student noise (Snoise) that interfered with hearing the main speaker; and, of student disruptions (Sdisruptions) that halted classroom presentations. The fifth and sixth outcomes represent mean instances, after each observed class, where less than minimal notes were taken by students (SNT) and instances where students paid little obvious attention (Snotinvolved) to the teacher by engaging in questions or discussions with him or her.

were obviously oriented, attending, listening, answering questions, and engaging in discussion—indexed in Figure 5.3, in the opposite view, as "Snotinvolved").

In contrast, student disruptions were far more frequent in the classrooms of novice teachers. The MANOVA for the data represented in Figure 5.3 suggests a reliable effect of coaching: $F(6, 13) = 38.53 \ p > .001$.

2. *Increased student ratings.* Another, more indirect, measure proved consistent. Student evaluations of these courses on a cam-

pus-wide instrument: $\overline{X}$ = 1.98 (SD = .50) for coached novices; $\overline{X}$ = 3.58 (SD = .57) for uncoached novices (on a scale where 1 = excellent and 5 = poor; where there was one global score per teacher [based on the item, "likely to recommend this class to a close friend"]); in a one-way ANOVA $F(1, 18)$ = 44.31, $p < 001$.

3. *Heightened awareness of teaching (and lessened PBing).* After only a semester of practice at noticing classroom incivilities (their own and their students'), coached novices showed improvement, by about a factor of two, in reporting awareness of the classroom events around the time of incivilities. So while they had only begun to approach the teaching awareness of the experts, these beginners made clear progress, particularly towards recognizing the thoughts and feeling that warn of impending incivilities. The following is a typical recollection:

As soon as I heard myself using guilt induction (I was starting to remind them that they were disappointing me by not coming to class prepared), I thought: "No, you're being negative; say something more positive." I did.

There were also consistent signs that coached beginners were beginning to deal more efficaciously with situations where they once might have procrastinated and blocked. That is, they did better in terms of recollecting times when they were tempted to do so, at recognizing the events leading up to that hesitation, and at supplanting the temptation with more direct action. For example:

I know myself well enough now to have recognized the sign. I noticed the dour faces and I thought: "OK, what am I doing?" But at the same time, almost, I thought something quite different: "Forget it and just get through this." Just hearing myself say both things, helped me actually tell myself to pause and figure things out. So I stopped and asked, "Am I getting ahead of you?"

General Discussion

These simple methodologies, of the sort we rarely use in taboo and near-taboo areas such as discussions of PBing and teaching, produced useful information about a specific role of PB in teaching improvement. It is one of the first experimental demonstrations I know of to demonstrate PB in the act of teaching. These results support contentions made earlier that PB is domain-general, perhaps even to areas that have not, heretofore, been considered.

In the first experiment, observation of a telling difference between struggling novices and expert teachers suggested two crucial patterns of skills for involving students and producing higher ratings of classes by students: (1) teachers' postures, gestures, and statements of immediacy that temper classroom incivilities, and (2) teachers' awareness of ongoing events surrounding incivilities. This finding, in turn, prompted a second experiment that modeled a way of coaching struggling novices in "immediacies" as a means of lowering classroom incivilities, of raising student benefits, of enhancing ratings by students, and of heightening awareness of the teaching process. The result of that intervention is an uncommon demonstration that professorial teaching can be improved in reliable, meaningful, and durable ways. And it includes the more unusual suggestion that at least one fundamental failing of novice teachers struggling in the classroom is related to habitual patterns of PBing (including deficiencies in process orientation and excesses in product orientation).

This inquiry also produced other benefits. One is a clearer sense of why classroom incivility (as a seeming relative of PB) undermines the attempts of many new teachers to find comfort and success (for example, like PB, it is unwittingly initiated by teachers, for the most part). Another is an understanding of how classroom incivility (and its roots in PB) affects student performance: it distances and alienates students from the teacher, even to the point of discouraging them as note takers. A third benefit is the suggestion of a practical way to help novice teachers make better beginnings (by teaching them the simple skills of immediacies, much as we might teach efficacies to PBers).

These results run counter to traditional expectations, one dating at least to William James's assumption, in *Talks to Teachers* (1898), that teaching is more an inborn talent than a learnable skill. The present study disputes the belief that teachers must be born and it belies the supposition that good teaching requires little more than good content. Just as important, it opposes the widely held notion that there are no fundamental rules for teaching well, that each of us must learn to teach in idiosyncratic ways, and that empirical study and systematic intervention must be incompatible with excellence in college teaching. If we accept teaching as just another set of behaviors to be systematically studied and remedied, as a congeries of skills without mysterious qualities, we can counter the growing pessimism about improving college teaching. We might also learn surprising new things about PB.

If such a venture into teaching seems too far afield, reconsider the sort of theme dominant in this chapter, one that looks for useful, comforting parallels. The strategies and assumptions I employed in this study resemble those of already popular movements in psychology. We could apply to research on teaching many of the emerging ideas and techniques now common in studies of expertise, a field that suggests a central role for the regular practice of simple skills and for coaching (Ericsson and Charness, 1994; Simonton, 1994). So, too, the growing fascination with failures we call self-handicapping (Baumeister & Scher, 1988; Baumeister, Heatherton, & Tice, 1994) and pessimism (Seligman, 1991). We might even harken back to older, forgotten traditions such as Pierre Janet's emphasis on learning to work at tasks more economically by not annoying the people around us, even students (Ellenberger, 1970). The question that remains is why scholars do not more often apply perspectives such as these to something so central to our profession as teaching.

To return now to the major argument of the chapter, if a process orientation promotes knowing how to work, what promotes efficacy? One possibility has just been presented: heightened awareness of process. The next section of this chapter will consider another parallel possibility—one still a bit foreign to traditional research in PB: problem solving.

PROBLEM SOLVING

To the extent that PBing is *not* knowing how to work efficiently, efficaciously (even of not knowing how to translate insights and advice into performance), it is a failing of problem-solving skills. The considerable information about studies on problem solving expands what little we know about PB. It also specifically illuminates the cognitive, emotional, and work components of PB. This is an enormous literature, one I only sample here as a prelude to the last chapters of this book.

Expertise

We respond to the problems we pose (Flower, 1990). When we fail to plan clearly, reasonably, what happens? Without concentrated directedness, we risk PBing. Writers who lack clear demands, assignments, and resources reserve their best efforts for other tasks (Hayes, 1988). How do experts find optimal structures? They re-see problems via playfulness (Stack, 1980). They attentively notice and plan while getting ready, instead of waiting passively. They patiently find the ideal pace for each task (Perkins, 1981). They concentrate deeply and take risks (Amibile, 1983). Once more, they practice, practice, practice (Ericsson & Charness, 1994).

Emotions

Expert writers, perhaps because they find more success in their work, report experiencing more positive emotions, fewer signs of negativity such as boredom, anxiety, and confusion while working (Brand, 1986). One reason may be familiar: a state of moderate happiness broadens awareness and flexibility in making decisions (Oatley & Jenkins, 1992). As an example of that principle, consider Lewis Terman's gifted subjects, who turned out to be most successful by their seventies. They showed the highest levels of contentment and self-confidence, of openness and spontaneity, and of freedom from pervasive hostility, irritability, and dissatisfaction (Schneidman, 1984). Emotions may be as important to PB as thinking.

Cognitions

When we try to work with performance (that is, product) goals in mind, perceptions of our ability must be high before we undertake a challenging task. So it is that PBers unwittingly handicap themselves with perfectionistic and unrealistic expectations. The predictable result of *not* adopting the opposite orientation, a learning (process) stance, is a combination of defensive strategies (for example, withdrawal or debilitation in the face of obstacles) and poorer learning (Dweck, 1986).

The dimensions just reviewed (on expertise, emotions, and cognitions) converge to make much the same point, one central to this book: success is largely a matter of knowing how to work (and PB is basically not knowing how to work). Still, to illumine the traditionally shadowy, amiably indistinct notions of PB, we need to do more. The next chapter illustrates a radical way to do so.

6

Procrastination and Blocking Seen Interconnectedly with Other Disorders

I've chosen just a trio of instances to begin to show how psychology already employs concepts and findings that could interconnect with PB. The first is about eating disorders, the second and third about mental illness. Together, they require even more patience and tolerance than ever; at first glance they may seem entirely out of bounds in a consideration of procrastination and blocking. Ultimately, I hope you'll agree, they lead to new vistas on PB.

BINGE EATING AND PROCRASTINATION AND BLOCKING

T. F. Heatherton and R. F. Baumeister (1991) provide an acclaimed interpretation of binge eating as a major kind of eating disorder. Their perspective could do as much for PBing as for other forms of disorder.

Consider, first of all, the parallels between their notion of bingeing and what has already been said about PB. Binge eaters suffer from high standards and demanding expectations, especially in terms of public appearances. They overreact to the demands of others as threats to their self-esteem.

To escape these discomforts, binge eaters narrow their attention away from broad, meaningful thought to focus on the self and lowered levels of awareness (overall, to what we might label a product orientation). This narrowing disengages normal inhibitions against eating by fostering uncritical, mindless acceptance of irrational beliefs (most of them probably about outcomes, few about learning better ways of controlling food intake). Curiously, dieters often use bingeing as a means of self-regulation; it is how they, as overcontrolled people, let go to experience pleasurable feelings and magical thinking.

How Can This Knowledge About Binge Eating Be Applied to PB?

Knowledge about bingeing on food apparently identifies the crucial turning point where we commit to PBing: the moment where we narrow our attention and logic in order to escape short-term discomforts. It also suggests the central weaknesses in PBers: they, like dieters, feel chronically restrained and anxious from overconcern with a product orientation. (Perhaps PBers too are overcontrolled.) Once they experience discomfort, PBers habitually turn to narrowing and the products of low-level thinking—the easy, the relieving, the immediately enjoyable, even blocking. Blockers often come to portray PB as a convenient way of experiencing pleasure, at least in the short run.

What, by contrast, can studies of PB offer researchers and practitioners who work with binge eaters? What we have seen about PB and its opposite, efficacy, suggests unusual ways of combating the perfectionism and overreaction that lead to bingeing. Ultimately the proven strategies for moderating them come down to building efficacy: (1) the process orientation of reflective awareness, of slowing down and calming and finding the ideal pace and the right problem to solve; (2) the attribution of failures and imperfections to external, variable, and sporadic things like lack of good strategy or effort (and not to inherent failings of character); and (3) the habit of regular, deliberate practice at basic skills such as waiting, planning, and building successes.

Experts on blocking even offer useful insights about that moment where control is lost. R. T. Kellogg's (1994) analysis of how writers slip may be as profound as the account of the transition to bingeing just seen: Fluent writers work holistically, with broad phrases and meanings and intentions and, so, coherently. But when a particular thought proves difficult, all the resources of short-term memory are concentrated on a few words. This is the point when writers lose track, misconnect, blunder, and block.

So it may be parsimonious to consider binge eating as a kind of PBing. Researchers on obesity and other eating disorders might profit by seeing more of the importance of moderation, balance, and practice in the impulsivity they seek to understand and control. Eating pathologies, after all, are only a part of the complex of self-confidence problems in most sufferers (Striegel-Moore, Silberstein, & Rodin, 1993).

MENTAL HEALTH, CREATIVITY, AND PROCRASTINATION AND BLOCKING

The second example of speculation and research intersecting with PB helps illuminate the latter in a very different way. Here I use the traditional misunderstanding of creative madness to explain further the taboo against serious study of PB. Such explanation brings a deeper understanding of PB itself.

The topic of creative madness is a long-time favorite in psychiatry and psychology. Its message about PB is covert but imaginatively powerful—in ways, I believe, that help ensure its unquestioned popularity. Notions of creative madness imply that healthy efficaciousness actually stands in the way of creative productivity. In this customary view, creativity depends on madness and its disarray (including the untimeliness of PB).

Where does the notion of creative madness originate? To an extent, creative artists themselves contribute to the image that success depends on mental illness and disorganization. Writers, for instance, often portray writing as maddening (Didion, 1981), themselves as unsociable (Theroux, 1980), one another as embittered and psychotic (Ellenberger, 1970). More often, they like to emphasize the suffering necessary to creative achievement, much of it sounding like procrastination and blocking. The nineteenth-century novelist Joseph Conrad, for instance, bemoaned his difficulty in writing to anyone who would listen: at times this great writer of seagoing tales was so distracted or blocked that he wrote only a line per day over several successive days (Meyers, 1991). Over time, Conrad's misery as a writer took a heavy, then fatal toll in mental and physical problems. Still he, like many famous artists, supposed this suffering to be the price of creativity.

This odd image—of creative productivity as necessarily un-healthy—persists for a variety of reasons. For one thing, writers, like the rest of us, enjoy complaining at times. For another, its conservative, undemocratic message fits all too nicely with tradi-tional views of things like PB.

The Nature of Notions About Creativity and Mental Illness

Concerns about unhealthiness in creative productivity date back to at least the mid-nineteenth to early twentieth century, when automatic writers worked in marathons and Surrealists immersed themselves in spontaneous bouts of euphoric work (Boice & My-ers, 1986). Both groups experienced distress, depression, and su-icidal tendencies. One implicit conclusion of these old accounts is that creativity, if carried beyond the mundane, is accompanied by madness. A related implication is that creativity begins with mad-ness. Nowhere, except in the shunned psychologies of work (recall Pierre Janet), did anyone suppose that mania (and its partner, depression) was itself the product of long, unsupervised bouts of automaticity, in particular its excessively narrowed and prolonged, uninterrupted ways of working. Janet, if asked, would have attrib-uted the strain and madness to extended sessions of unrelenting, tense work. Moreover, he probably would have noted that re-search in the psychology of work indicated diminishing returns in working to the point of mania: carried to excess, the rushed su-perficiality of such work and its ensuing fatigue and depression could only interfere with creative productivity (Ellenberger, 1970; Rabinbach, 1990).

For all its initial promise as a topic of study, widespread interest in this presumed link between creativity and madness or disarray is recent. Discussions of creative madness now focus on mood disorders (depression and mania) as afflictions of successful writ-ers and other creative people. This is the general argument: manic-depression occurs at uncommonly high rates amongst creatively productive writers; therefore, creativity somehow depends on this emotional disorder. C. Holden (1987), for example, lists writers, especially poets, who displayed unmistakable signs of manic-depression (for example, Robert Lowell and Randall Jarrell) and who committed suicide (for example, Sylvia Plath and Anne Sexton). But in such anecdotal accounts we cannot know how selective the samples are. Exponents of creative madness do not draw out comparable numbers for maladies in other stressful, often criticized kinds of work. If, for instance, public officials proved just as depressive and suicidal as writers, we might be more inclined to attribute the costs of both careers to poor working conditions and frequent exposures to disapproval.

To provide a better feel for contemporary beliefs about creative madness, I turn first to the acknowledged leader in the field, Kay R. Jamison. This psychologist, who works in psychiatric and medical settings, offers the most objective, systematic account of the arena (Jamison, 1993). Yet her presentation is traditional and, so, has its romantic side:

That impassioned moods, shattered reason, and the artistic temperament can be welded into a "fine madness" remains a fiercely controversial belief. (p. 3)

Who would *not* want an illness that has among its symptoms elevated and expansive mood, inflated self-esteem, abundance of energy, less need for sleep, intensified sexuality . . . and sharpened unusually creative thinking and increased productivity? (p. 103)

Specifically, Jamison supposes that the cycle of mania and depression, as it moves from its fiery side to its judgmental side, results in creative productivity of singular, almost magical power. (If you think of her defense of "fine madness" from the point of view that has been taken with PB, Jamison emphasizes PB's short-term benefits and downplays its long-range costs. She also, like other traditionalists, favors hereditary causes.) Manic-depression, in Jamison's view, carries the divine (or at least biologically implanted) gift of "multiple selves." The evidence for her view is circumstantial at best.

Consider the data Jamison calls up to support her enthusiastically received claims. She cites the studies of others such as A. M. Ludwig's (1992) computation that 18 percent of poets reviewed in the *New York Times* had committed suicide and that of all writers so mentioned the rate of hospitalization was six to seven times that of nonartists. She pays especial homage to the pioneering studies of N. C. Andreasen (1987), the first investigator to use modern psychiatric diagnostic criteria to determine the relationship between mental illness and creativity (for example, of her fifteen creative writers, 80 percent reported treatment for mood disorders; 43 percent some degree of manic-depression). Better yet are Jamison's own connections drawn between madness and creative productivity: Of forty-seven eminent, award-winning British writers and artists, 38 percent reported treatment for mood disorder, most for poets and playwrights. One-third of those recalled histories of severe mood swings cyclothymic in nature, one-fourth had periods of extended elation, nine-tenths had intense, highly creative and productive episodes, one-half had sharp increases in manic mood just prior to an intensely creative period.

Add to these relationships another. Manic-depressive disorders are most common amongst the professional or upper classes (Jamison, 1993), the very locus of productive genius reserved by tradition (see Simonton, 1994, for a more egalitarian view).

Why Reports of Creative Madness Are So Popular and Persistent

Why do accounts of creative madness glamorize a seemingly maladaptive way of behaving (for example, Kohn, 1988)? They amiably excuse (and even encourage) artists in their eccentricities and foibles, especially in the area of creative productivity (much as traditionally amiable characterizations forgive PBers). Notions of creative madness seemingly explain why so much important work comes at the expense of suffering and wasted effort. Creative madness even associates depression and mania, also outcomes of chronic bingeing and PBing, with genius.

Traditional conclusions seem so consonant with personal experience and common sense that you might wonder why they should be questioned.

Problems with Claims for Creative Madness

Examinations of this sacred belief in creative madness have come slowly, hesitantly. A. Rothenberg (1990) was one of the first to point out its methodological and logical shortcomings. Andreasen, for example, was the sole interviewer and diagnostician of the writers, all of them from the Iowa Writers Workshop. Moreover, her definition of creativity was membership in that workshop. In her study and in Jamison's, the only criteria for emotional illness were the subjects' own reports of treatment (and those reports also came from people in a work culture where creative madness is apparently prized).

Rothenberg also reminds us of a related set of cautions: Writers are better able to understand and share mental experiences than are other people. And, eminent people may enjoy exaggerating their own aberrations, especially those with a noble, mysterious aspect (Ocshe, 1990). We, in recounting the genius of geniuses, might like to imagine their eccentricities (not their hard work) contributing to their accomplishments. If what it took was mainly hard work (Simonton, 1994), not just hereditary genius, the whole enterprise might become common.

But what if creativity *did* depend largely on the genius of working efficaciously? The mere possibility opens the way to other views.

An Alternative, More Frugal Explanation

We could, I contend, just as well attribute creative productivity to learned skills like persistence. Dickens, among other great writers, often wrote amid weariness and discouragement. Indeed, he often found a "special genius" of working to help dispel these and other moods (Ackroyd, 1990). Expertise, a close kin of creative genius, in fact depends largely on regular, efficient habits of working (Ericsson & Charness, 1994). Despite the growing evidence, tradition has overlooked skills-based interpretations of creativity, interpretations that could discredit creative illness.

Related Reasons for Questioning This Tradition of Amiability

Notions of creative madness ignore the conclusions of esteemed researchers in creativity. Frank Barron, in his book *Creativity and Psychological Health* (1963), related the following qualities of creativity: strength of ego, independence of judgment, personal soundness, ability to rally from setback, and combined complexity

and simplicity in personality. In a recollection of writing that classic, in 1986 he emphasized his disagreement with romantic notions
of creativity and poor mental health:

> The creative person is at once both naive and knowledgeable, destructive
> and constructive, occasionally crazier yet adamantly saner. . . . More pos-
> itively: Without knowledge, no creation; without stability, no flexibility;
> without discipline, no freedom. (p. 18)

Dean K. Simonton (1994) offers another balanced view: While
creative productivity seems to depend on "weirdness" (usually
some mixture of psychoticism and mania), its level must be moderate enough to allow work. The somewhat odd individuals who
achieve greatness, many of them from families with members who
show immoderate degrees of mental illness, are at risk of becoming unstable themselves when they lose their balance.

What, then, could move them past the essential autonomy and
perserverence that permit success and into the emotional and cognitive extremes that undermine creative productivity? In my view,
the problem of not knowing how to work with patience and tolerance can push weirdness above that threshold—when conditions
are optimal.

The Nature of Manic-Depression

Another oversight in traditional, romantic accounts concerns
the nature of manic-depression itself. Viewed objectively, creative
work is healthy and adaptive; strong neurotic and emotional
symptoms are maladaptive (Ochse, 1990). Even a milder state of
mania, hypomania, disables writers far more than it helps.

Consider what my own direct-observational studies of usually
blocked writers show. Working under a state of extended hypomania (in marathon sessions over days) typically engenders
rushed, unreflective, and unrevised work. Soon after, as a rule,
these bouts of bingeing lead to periods of increased scores on the
Beck Depression Inventory, which indicate moderate or higher
levels of depression. In the longer run they lead to markedly lowered output of written pages (Boice, 1994). Conversely, writers

who write more efficaciously, without the impulsivity and wild mood swings of bingeing, write more and write better over time. The aftermath of excessive binges of writing (of the sort necessary to produce the symptoms of hypomania depicted above from Jamison) goes beyond diminished productivity in the longer run to fatigue, insomnia, misery, social strife, PBing, and momentary promises not to work in binges again. Eventually, working in the sort of emotional cycle glamorized by elitist champions of creative madness leads to less quality and creativity and to less editorial acceptance of writing (compare, again, writers who work without bingeing and PBing, with generally mild emotions and brief sessions [Boice, 1993b]). What psychiatry and psychology have assumed is a basis for creativity is more likely the symptom of working at it inefficaciously.

Another Illustration of How Creative Madness and Efficacy Affect Creativity

Even when I present data like those just above, many listeners doubt their meaningfulness. They imagine that while bingeing and mania might hinder the writing of the academic types I usually study, true artists really do need the whole benefits of creative madness—the vicissitudes of manic-depression, the other kinds of wasteful maladies including PB, and, of course, the pitiable suffering, in order to do their best work. To convince them otherwise, I have found, I fare better with personal case histories.

Consider, first, the case of Dickens (Ackroyd, 1990). He typically wrote in great binges that lasted well into the night. Then, too manic to sleep, he walked at great length, often twenty-five miles, to relax. The next day he often suffered dysphoria and difficulty in resuming writing; in the long run, Dickens's hypomania led to frequent depressions and blocks. Eventually, his lifestyle seemed to contribute to the diseases that killed him prematurely. All that, of course, does not prove that the hypomania, bingeing, depression, and blocking that commonly accompanied Dickens as a writer undermined his creative productivity. It remains only a possibility.

Case histories that show writers working, alternatively, with madness and blocking and with efficacy and fluency are less common but more conclusive. Conrad provides one of the best demonstrations (Meyers, 1991). Early in his career, including the period during which he established his lasting fame, Conrad wrote slowly, painfully; he often procrastinated, blocked, and suffered at writing. When he was stuck, which was often, he was afflicted with crippling neurasthenia, which further prevented him from writing: PB usually builds in a vicious circle.

"My nervous disorder tortures me, makes me wretched, and paralyses action, thought, everything! I ask myself why I exist. It is a frightful condition. Even in the intervals, when I am supposed to be well, I live in fear of the return of this tormenting malady . . . before the pen falls from my hand in the depression of a complete discouragement." (Meyers, 1991, p. 119)

That sounds like a typical case of creative illness, one where Conrad's depression and other agonies somehow helped him find brilliance. But could his wild swings between euphoria and dysphoria have been more the symptom of his problematic PBing? Consider the evidence that his main problem was not knowing how to work. For example, even though he always began his work days at exactly the same time each morning, he spent most days struggling to get started. As a rule, he did little or no writing until evening and then he binge-wrote until late into the night. The usual result was slow and painstaking writing—and utter exhaustion; during this period of his career, he typically wrote no more than three hundred words a day (as a full-time writer!). His editors constantly chafed at his dilatoriness, and Conrad described his own experience as exquisite torture, one that required crisis and frenzy to complete his work.

In the middle stage of his career, Conrad was forced, more or less, into an efficacious style of working. His close friend, the novelist Ford Madox Ford, became a kind of mentor and amanuensis who provided him with remarkable support and structure. For starters, he gave the impoverished Conrad his house and financial aid. He listened to Conrad reading aloud his work and suggested words and phrases, even forgotten incidents.

Ford's more direct help was even more significant. He proofread and corrected Conrad's manuscripts. He even took dictation as Conrad talked about what he would like to write. Ford offered him several good ideas and had the uncanny ability to stimulate him to write when he would other otherwise have been overcome by illness, exhaustion, and despair. He also helped structure Conrad's writing days with planning. The result of this regular, relaxed work style was a remarkable increase in Conrad's productivity. Conrad could, dictating to Ford, write a thousand or more words a day. During this period, he made significant progress on *Nostromo* and finished *One Day More*.

Ford was so effective in inducing efficacy that it vanquished most of the madness (and PBing) from Conrad's writing. Nonetheless, Conrad eventually had a falling-out with Ford (whose help he never really appreciated). Thereafter, Conrad resumed his old ways of slow, tormented, and often PBed writing. His productivity lessened, and so, according to his chroniclers (for example, Meyers, 1991), did the quality of his writing. The creative madness he experienced with *Under Western Eyes* was so intense that it led to his complete nervous breakdown. The results included recurring pain from chronic gout and the ever present anxiety about money. As in the old days, he usually started his novels without a clear plan and so had no idea where the book might end, or when. By the summer of 1909, his publisher was so dissatisfied with Conrad's failure to deliver the long-awaited manuscript that he wanted to sever their business connection. When the publisher refused to advance any more funds, Conrad threatened to throw the manuscript into the fire. It was eventually finished, but it was one of his last.

Clearly, Conrad's old habit of PBing was more costly than his temporary diversion into efficacy (and its absence of creative madness). His return to PBing not only slowed and then halted his deteriorating work, but the strains it induced brought him misery and an early death.

So the point in all this discussion is that efficacy can work better than madness, suffering, and PB. We can, with another great mental stretch, see a crucial role for inefficacy in most, perhaps all, mental illnesses. Such an examination, I trust, will help you revise your notions about PB even further from the traditional stance.

HOW KNOWLEDGE OF MENTAL DISORDERS CAN BE APPLIED TO PROCRASTINATION AND BLOCKING

Psychiatry and clinical psychology may mislead in their claims about creative madness, but they do better elsewhere. For instance, they offer striking but usually neglected parallels to PB in their accounts of personality disorders (American Psychiatric Association, 1994). Why look into this dark corner? Here, we see PB in its most pathological, little-known extremes. Here we can behold procrastination and blocking in crystalline form.

Not until I reached this rarified vantage point did I discern what I conclude are the three basic components of PB (previewed in the previous chapter and to be reencountered here). As I did so, I realized something else. There is a predictable price in taking an uncomfortable topic to its limits. Whatever perseverance you have mustered for examining PB is put to test here.

In what follows, I survey the seven personality disorders most clearly connected to PB.

Obsessive-Compulsive Personality Disorder

The essential features of obsessive-compulsive personality disorder (OCPD) include recurrent obsessions severe enough to be time-consuming or to cause marked distress that impairs functioning. Its usually impulsive and driven thinking leads to repetitive behaviors that help relieve the discomfort of intrusive thoughts and feelings—in the short run (much like the narrowing that Heatherton and Baumeister depict for binge eaters). OCPD means that time is poorly allocated, that deadlines are missed, that other people are annoyed.

When people with OCPD cannot control their physical or interpersonal environments, they "act-out" passively, indirectly. Their high levels of anger, inflexibility, and perfectionism bring an intensity to work that makes relaxation and hobbies unlikely. Even the worries that drive these tensions and their compulsive acts of relief are aimed in maladaptive directions; this disorder is often associated with depression, anxiety, and eating problems. How similar is PB to OCPD? Their fundamentals (but not their intensities and pathologies) are identical for many kinds of chronic PBers I have studied.

Dependent Personality Disorder

The essential features of dependent personality disorder—submissiveness and clinging—might sound remote from PB. But underneath those primary symptoms are commonalities. The "dependency" of this disorder can be seen in difficulties with everyday decisions, with initiating projects, and with self-confidence. It even appears in reliance on others or deadlines to make decisions.

Victims of personality disorders tend to belittle their abilities, to equate disapproval with worthlessness, to risk mood, anxiety, and adjustment disorders. They appear to be primed for PBing.

Avoidant Personality Disorder

The chief features of avoidant personality disorder (APD) sound immediately familiar to someone interested in PB: a pattern of social inhibition, feelings of inadequacy, and hypersensitivity to negative evaluation. People with APD avoid work or social activities that elicit fears of rejection; they assume other people are critical and disapproving until they themselves pass stringent tests. Not only do such people handicap themselves by feeling extremely hurt by the faintest of signs of rejection, but their tentative demeanor elicits ridicule and derision (which in turn confirm their self-doubts).

Narcissistic Personality Disorder

This malady of narcissistic personality disorder sounds no more relevant to PB than the dependent personality disorder, at first consideration. Its signal qualities include grandiosity and need for admiration. Yet its roots call up images of PB: impatience, rumination about overdue success, expectations that one's acts must match those of the most brilliant individuals, and dismissal of corrective feedback as rudeness and stupidity. (Earlier in this book this pattern could have been labeled as a product orientation.)

One predictable result of narcissism is poor vocational functioning, especially where competitive risks and public evaluations can arise. Another result is working in spurts that alternate between social withdrawal and hypomanic bursts of grandiosity. This disorder may be associated with eating problems and with substance abuse.

Histrionic Personality Disorder

What has histrionic personality disorder, this pattern of excessive emotionality and seeking for attention, have to do with PB? Its sufferers, like most problem PBers, crave excitement; they cannot tolerate delayed gratification (or a process orientation). They often initiate projects with great enthusiasm and then lose interest. And they are likely to make suicidal gestures.

Borderline Personality Disorder

People with borderline personality disorder show an impulsive instability of personality, of relationships, and of work. The usual outcomes of such instability include binge eating, overreactions to stressful events, and periods of dysphoria punctuated by bouts of anger or panic. Its intensely episodic nature undermines almost every aspect of everyday living (as does the episodic bingeing considered earlier).

Antisocial Personality Disorder

People with antisocial personality disorder deceive and manipulate others for personal profit and pleasure. They often do so inefficaciously, though, because they fail to plan ahead or to show enough signs of public responsibility (for example, regular attendance at work) to find social acceptance. So they suffer dysphoria marked by tension, intolerance for boredom, and depression.

What Personality Disorders Can Teach Us

Taken together, what do these seven personality disorders tell us about PB that might not have been apparent before? They

portray PB in a more complex, interrelated way than has traditional literature. Each disorder reveals a fascinating mechanism of
PB taken to its extreme. By assembling the personality disorders
in the context of this book, it is possible to show the common
roots of seemingly different kinds of PB (for example, dependent
or avoidant). Personality disorders show so much interrelationship
that, like PB, they are often diagnostically nonspecific (Emerson,
Pankratz, Joos, & Smith, 1994).

There are, it seems to me, several advantages in looking for
those links:

First Advantage

Personality disorders reveal first-order principles of PB. The
first-order principles, as I think of them, that emerged here might
have remained unnoticed in less concentrated and less costly manifestations of PB. Still, this analysis takes us back to the same
intriguing, interconnected triad of basic PB factors that we already
know, more or less (see if you agree about the following as common to the personality disorders I just described):

- compulsions and impulsivity utilized to relieve tension owing to perfectionism and impatience
- a readiness, once there is narrowing and disinhibition, to move into
habitual patterns of easy, mindless acts (even though these tend to undermine progress toward perfectionist goals) including withdrawal from
the confusion
- an aftermath of disappointment, lowered self-confidence, disapproval
by others, depression, and uncertainty about abilities (The problems set
in motion by this third stage persist: indecision and delays, more indignant anger in response to attempts by others to help, less inclination to
learn how to work efficaciously.)

These interrelated factors of personality disorders and PBing
suggest the beginnings of a working model of PB, one I elaborate
in the next chapter.

Personality researchers have also started looking into links between personality disorders and PB. We might wonder: Do they
too find suggestions of first-order factors? They do, in a preliminary way.

Ferrari, Johnson, & McCown (1995) conclude that only the most awkward, eccentric types of personality disorders (including narcissistic and antisocial disorders) may relate to procrastination. Although they can report correlational outcomes to support this connection, they cannot explain them, except to suppose that their favorite cause, conscientiousness, must be involved. They do, though, suppose that one other personality disorder, passive-aggressiveness, relates to procrastination in basic, behavioral ways. Support for this assumption comes in J. T. McCann's (1988) finding that passive-aggressive people stubbornly resist fulfilling the expectations of others, are inconsistent and inefficient in their work, and often feel gloomy and despondent.

Second Advantage

Personality disorders suggest more reasons why PB has been a neglected topic. This is the telling point: personality disorders are considered pervasive. Yet, psychiatry and clinical psychology pay little attention to them, usually supposing them fixed and difficult to change. T. Millon (1981), the consensus expert, summarizes treatment prospects with phrases such as "not inclined to seek therapy. . . . many of these personalities are unable to change because they possess deeply rooted habits that are highly resistant to conscious reasoning. . . . these personalities will challenge therapists and seek to outwit them. . . . the behavioral style of the compulsive personality is unlikely to change. . . . relieved of tension, many will lose their incentive to continue treatment" (pp. 179, 199, 213, 242, 272). If the fundamental qualities of personality disorders seem characterological and irreversible, why wouldn't clinicians respond in like fashion to similar symptoms in PBers? Apparently they do.

The DSM-IV (*Diagnostic and Statistical Manual of Mental Disorders*, Volume IV), like the field it represents, gives personality disorders brief coverage. It comes closest to openly acknowledging PB in a more congenial, delimited section—on adjustment disorders. These consist of emotional or behavioral symptoms in response to psychosocial stressors. Technically, they (1) occur soon after the occasion of stress, (2) involve excessive distress and impairment in social or occupational functioning, and (3) are resolved within six months. One of its subtypes is "unspecified" and includes interrupted occupational or academic functioning.

The problem with "adjustment disorder" as a label is that it has led to little progress in understanding or treating maladies such as grief or PB. It is, whatever else, amiable. But it does remind us that many instances of PB occur in response to occasional, focal events; only more chronic, costly PBing, presumably, shares worrisome links with personality disorders.

Third Advantage

Once we look at personality disorders, we are cued to scan other established views of mental disorders to look for more elucidation of procrastination and blocking. The few examples that follow illustrate the possibility ubiquitous role of PB in problem behaviors.

Self-Defeating Behaviors

The core failings of people who exhibit these self-destructive tendencies remind us of the three themes of PB in personality disorders that we just saw:

1. impatience in the face of constraining and perfectionistic pressures
2. impulsive relief in mindless and irrational activities
3. aftermaths of lowered efficacy (for example, never completely processing the event to change future behavior)

R. F. Baumeister and S. J. Scher (1988) characterize self-defeating behaviors as poor choices elicited by aversive states and by prospects of short-term relief. The irrational tradeoffs include self-handicapping (for example, creating obstacles that carry the blame for anticipated failures), substance abuse (to replace the aversive short-term state with pleasant sensations and lowered self-awareness), face work (where tangible rewards are sacrificed to save embarrassment), and shyness (a protective self-presentation style that relieves the risk of rejection by making no social impression at all).

These impulsive, excessively self-focused acts (that is, self-defeating behaviors) lead to predictable problems of perseveration, of choking under pressure, of learned helplessness, of poor bargaining strategies, and of ineffective ingratiation. Together, the basic elements of self-defeat closely resemble those of PB (and, perhaps, of personality disorders). The pattern I suggested above (impatience, impulsiveness, and regretful outcomes) appears more clearly in more recent work by Baumeister and his colleagues.

In that view taken from research on dieting failures and similar problems, these are the five reasons why self-regulation fails (Baumeister, Heatherton, & Tice, 1994):

1. When *standards* are vague, unrealistic, or inappropriate, then conflicting tendencies to act can confuse, delay, and frustrate. Irrational, impatient thinking takes over (for example, anxiety induces a preference for speed over accuracy). Why? The quickened pace and results provide the relief of busyness and of suppressed ruminations. But as we try to control our emotions rather than solve external problems, we tend to drift away from our usual attentiveness and self-control.

2. Next, *reduction of monitoring* occurs as the discomforts of self-awareness and of evaluation are put out of mind and impulses usually held in check rise to the surface. Without immediate, process-oriented thinking, thought patterns that ordinarily help control impulses are displaced, and if mistakes occur, choking under pressure (that is, blocking) is likely.

3. Focus on trying to control emotions may result in *inadequate strength.* Weak self-regulation arises with fatigue and lack of regular practice at self-control, especially if the impulse and its emotional arousal are strong. The outcome of this weakness is seen most dramatically in failures to stop the behavior and the extremes that follow.

4. *Lapse-activated causal patterns* appear once failures at stopping become obvious to the person. Then, as lack of control snowballs, the conditions for further lapsing are set. The longer the impulse is freed, the more its motivation (for example, to escape guilt) grows. The longer the sequence of events in the impulsive act, the harder to stop or redirect it. In extreme cases, called zero-tolerance thinking, the mere slip into an impulse brings complete release of self-control. Immersion in immediate sensory pleasure can take both excitement and distress to extremes.

While Baumeister and his colleagues are speaking of problems of impatient inattention, impulsive opting for emotional relief, and regretful inefficiencies that follow in terms of failures of self-regulation, they could just as well be talking about PB. More import, their basic principles of failure in self-regulation suggest a model much like that developed here in a PB framework.

Attributional Styles That Commonly Accompany Depression

With attributional styles again, we already know the idea: When we attribute failures to internal, stable, and universal causes, we dispose ourselves to depression (for example, Seligman, 1991). But when we make external, variable, and specific (EVS) attributions, we moderate depression and display an ideal, healthy, excuse-making pattern (Snyder & Higgins, 1988).

If indeed, as C. R. Snyder and R. L. Higgins point out, this EVS pattern relates to superior athletic performance, selling, problem solving, high academic performance, and psychotherapeutic outcomes, why would it do less for PB? (Recall that exemplary new faculty characteristically displayed realistic EVS patterns associated with their efficacy.) Or why not expect that learning this cognitive style of making attributions could help temper general problems of self-control, including tendencies to PB? (Recall too, that new faculty in treatment programs with careful coaching quickly learned to generalize their efficacy to treat a variety of PBing including insomnia and postponed medical exams.)

Are there limitations in such a proposal? On the one hand, a pessimist might respond by mentioning two things mentioned earlier in the book that suggest PBers are unlikely to learn the EVS style: (1) the poor observational skills of PBers, who see each new problem as unlike its precedents and (2) tendencies of PBers, like those of borderline and narcissistic personality types, to practice improvement with inconstancy. On the other hand, an optimist, could argue that these too are mere failings of industrial society to teach learnable skills.

Self-Control

In self-control the problem is one of discounting events or rewards that are delayed (Logue, 1994) and of failing to establish broad, rewarding patterns that make acts of impulsivity undesirable (Rachlin, 1994). Getting past this impetuousness requires learning how to wait and when to wait. (Binge eating, stealing, substance abuse, suicide attempts—and PBing—are impulsive acts.) It needs practice at timely stopping (Baumeister, Heatherton, & Tice, 1994).

What might help counter that impatient impulsivity? First, deliberate practice at delaying rewards while carrying out more and more effortful tasks would be helpful. A second aid would be more learned associations of this industriousness with rewards: by arranging satisfaction in doing good work (Eisenberger, 1992) and close but not excessive emotional ties to working (Gardner, 1993). Third would be more awareness of cues that portend troublesome impulses and more prior commitment to ways of avoiding disobedience (for example, choosing to see the task as a long series of small challenges, arranging sufficient rewards to encourage obedience along the way, and setting the terms of the private bet against impulsivity so that they are unambiguous but flexibly realistic [Ainslie, 1975]). A fourth aid would be regular noticing of what reinforces impulsivity and whether preventive measures as precommitments work reliably to help build healthier patterns of action that resist impulsive disruptions (Rachlin, 1995). Fifth, it would help to make precommitments designed with loopholes for unusually strong impulses, safety valves that exact a price for disobedience but permit it (and still keep exceptions exceptional). Without such loopholes for exceptional temptations, single, strong incidents of PB can destroy entire programs of precommitments.

Here, with problems of self-control, there is more promise of interventions. Why? Excess that inconveniences and endangers society by, say, stealing and drug abuse, demands action (Logue, 1994). When impulsivity, mindlessness, and lowered self-efficacy reach that disruptive level, we no longer call them PBing or even self-defeat. Moreover, we less often joke about them.

What, to turn the analysis around, does PB tell us about self-control? It can be seen more interrelatedly, as a problem of impatience, narrowing, depressive attributions, and poor habits of working. Self-control, like PB, can be linked to already wide perspectives of behavior disorders: the excessive self-focus that accompanies most behavioral pathologies (Ingram, 1990); the poor management that comes from vague goals, lack of commitment to learning, and weak feedback (Locke & Latham, 1990); the lack of sustained, deliberate practice that keeps performers from expertise (Ericsson & Charness, 1994); and the constricted social contacts that limit successful ways of working (Simonton, 1994).

With these and earlier considerations in mind, the scene is set for a more formal look at the model of PB that has been abuilding and that has been conspicuously absent from the field until now.

7

A Model of Procrastination and Blocking

The circle of interrelatedness presented in chapter 6 clarifies the notion that PB and its kin can be seen concisely: as not knowing how to work, think, and emote efficiently and as predispositions to act, instead, in impulsive, narrow, and immediately relieving ways. A helpful way of grasping this elementary pattern aligns Sternberg's three modes of learning how to work with the three elements of PB seen earlier in personality disorders. Together the triads depict what may be the most basic problems to be solved if PBers, of any variety, are to find efficacy. Here again, there are the three main points:

THE BASIC PROBLEMS

Impulsivity

Impulsivity is born of self-imposed constraints and impatient demands for relief from pressures to undertake high-priority, difficult tasks; it reflects deficits in tacit knowledge about *self-management*. (PBers are impulsive in escaping and avoiding difficult priorities, in quickly and mindlessly turning to easy, low-priority tasks that afford emotional control—in the short run.)

Already effective treatments for self-control aim at patience (for example, by calming, slowing, and active waiting) and at tolerance (for example, by way of playful experience at handling agitated impatience). These interventions often begin at the simplest level, of building steady involvement via assignments to do nothing more than monitoring one's daily habits. The kind of attention involved, to the immediate moment, is the very mindfulness often missing among PBers.

Mindlessness

The problem of mindlessness emerges from a product (as contrasted to process) orientation and is a difficulty of *task management,* notably of solving the wrong problem (because reactions to distress and narrowing tend to be fixed and self-defeating). Interventions reviewed earlier include coaching PBers to work in the following ways:

1. in a process mode (for example, by emulating the pauses for reflection and planning displayed more spontaneously by exemplary workers [Boice, 1994]);
2. in small, regular, and timely bits of difficult chores that ensure timely starting, momentum, and stopping;
3. with clear learning goals that provide direction and feedback (for example, Locke & Latham, 1990);
4. with the help of coaching and supports that promote self-instructions for coping with failures and for finding self-satisfaction (Meichenbaum, 1985).

Without these interventions, the next result is predictable.

Pessimism and Low Efficacy

The problem of intertwined pessimism and low efficacy reflects not knowing how to socialize, externalize thoughts and actions, and attribute blame in optimistic, rewarding ways. Together the deficits mean poor *social management.* Treatments include teaching the following social skills:

1. cooperating (for example, via co-teaching)
2. being able to imagine oneself in the place of another (and so, to move outward from a narrow focus on oneself)

3. finding ways to agree with and learn from disapproval
4. treating one's own and others' failings tolerantly, by generally attributing them to a realistic EVS pattern

THE THREE-PART MODEL

The three-part general model just suggested, which explains causes in hard-hearted fashion and lists proven interventions for alleviating those causes, is unique in the field of PB. Still, no single element in it is new, except in applying it to PB.

Has the Model Any Usefulness?

I think the model is useful for the following reasons. First, the model suggests a clear definition of PB with three parts:

- PB is a sequential, interconnected problem of impulsivity, mindlessness, and pessimism that delays and hinders action (particularly the sort that could lead to long-term rewards).
- PB's postponements and anxieties persist well beyond the time of diminishing returns (with low-priority, inefficient behaviors dominating in the meanwhile).
- The eventual, impulsive results of PBing (usually bingeing or avoidance) further lower the probability of timely, confident actions in the future.

Said more simply, PB is a problem of not knowing how to work patiently, mindfully, and optimistically.

Second, the model is useful in showing how procrastination and blocking are simply related parts of the same general process (that is, P is more the impulsivity of putting off the difficult in favor of short-term, predisposed relief; B is more the eventual result of struggling, silence, and discouragement). In everyday experience, then, P and B are inseparable.

Third, the model usefully suggests how PB could relate to other problems of self-regulation (that is, the same three factors of impulsivity, narrowing, and pessimism may be basic to most psychopathologies). Fourth, the model implies that prevention and treatment of PB, whatever the seeming variety, require interventions aimed at all three components (self-management, task management, and social management).

The Easily Memorized Components of the PB Model

The components of the model are impulsivity, mindlessness, and pessimism (IMP).

How the PB Model Relates to Contemporary Notions in Psychology

Relatively new insights and strategies for each of these three components are proliferating in psychology. *Self-management* may begin, as A. Bandura (1986) suggests, with tempering the high arousal that usually debilitates and narrows performance. Managed in moderation, arousal can facilitate deployment of skills. *Task management* might revolve around emulating what experts do by allocating time among tasks, by organizing knowledge into stored problem solutions, and by defining problems in ways that render them soluble (Sternberg, 1988). Task management overlaps with social management in its reliance on doing things outside our heads—on keeping some of memory externalized in notes and prompts, on knowing how to consult references and friends (Bruner, 1990). *Social management*, at least as it concerns PB, may depend heavily on retraining in attributing blame and on experience at social success. Optimistic attributional styles predict a clear, unique cause that affects coping, depression, and physical symptoms (Schrier & Carver, 1992). Such optimism affords ways of reinterpreting criticism and disapproval, of shifting the blame away from overconcern with the self (and toward a realistic EVS pattern), of approaching others more openly and acceptingly (Seligman, 1991). Optimism means working more publicly, in ways that presume more public acceptance.

Contemporary psychotherapies help patients reframe stressful perspectives by breaking large overwhelming problems into more specific, more positive modes of problem solving, by normalizing reactions to social situations, and by fostering new assumptive worlds (for example, Meichenbaum, 1993). Less common are approaches that address all three problems of PBing (impulsivity, mindlessness, and pessimism), although, arguably, changing any one of them may mean changing them all.

How the PB Model Might Help Lift the Traditional Taboo

The problem behind the taboo against studying and intervening in PB is simple. Psychologists and other social scientists generally resist anything more than descriptions of problem behaviors. (They also may prefer explanations of problems that cast little onus on the sufferers.) They do theorize about what causes PB, self-defeat, and other dysfunctions, but they subtly, amiably delay and avoid addressing direct interventions that modify the behaviors of intact, adult humans (Kipnis, 1994).

The similarities in this problem and in old difficulties of dealing with PB may be evident: in both there is a reticence to leap from polite, dismissable description to interventions that induce people in trouble to make real changes. The wariness of many researchers, even therapists and teachers, about seeming directive, about appearing to impose on others, is more pervasive and powerful than we ordinarily admit. Customarily, we like to suppose that merely giving patients and students information about inefficacies somehow suffices. The evidence, however, says otherwise.

But what we now know about PB may prime an unusually clear way of conceptualizing and facilitating the move to interventions. Consider this metaphor: The instant where we cease planning and then look ahead to formal writing is where we most often procrastinate and block (if the transition is too impulsively abrupt and narrow; if habits of coping operate mindlessly and self-defeatingly; if expectations are pessimistic). The prospect of moving from description to intervention may elicit a similar reaction of impatient mindlessness and short-term avoidance (unless we recognize the importance of preparing for the transition).

What might help psychologists make these related transitions to more open consideration of PB and to more frequent interventions? In the end, we may need to recognize that amiable, ineffective approaches have made us well-meaning but irresponsible

PBers in understanding and treating common maladies like PB. Even in that optimistic stance, though, there are problems to be recognized and dealt with. The most telling of these is the topic of the next chapter.

8

Why the Taboo May Persist

The taboo against direct examination and effective intervention in procrastination and blocking, like any other taboo worth its salt, is self-perpetuating. How so? It acts to discourage and punish those who break it. (I can attest to its discouraging effects when my manuscripts face traditional editors and reviewers.) It embarrasses people if psychologists openly notice PBing that is serious, if we do not keep a customary and polite distance. The mere labeling of an individual as a PBer brings indignation (one prominent editor recently said to me, "You're blaming the victim; these people can't help procrastinating").

Conforming to the taboo, by contrast, keeps things amiable, humorous, and less painful—at least in the short run. Implicit acceptance of this proscription brings mysterious credit to PBers by way of the attractive misbelief that PBing is the combined curse and blessing of a gifted few. Conformity even offers benefits to the efficacious: the minority of us who succeed and find fulfilment may suppose that those who fail deserve to or are destined to.

To emphasize the powers of this taboo, I develop two themes in this final chapter. The first is taking a closer look at the literature on how well patients comply with medical advice and prescriptions. Here, even with PB at its most costly, levels of medical adherence remain disastrously low. The taboo is as broad as it is strong. The second theme is describing the prices paid by four

prominent psychologists who dared to break the taboo by intervening in everyday PBing with strategies for increasing efficiency.
The prices they paid were so large that their work was misrepresented and their health imperiled.

WHAT MEDICAL NONCOMPLIANCE HAS TO DO WITH PROCRASTINATION AND BLOCKING

Traditional articles in scholarly journals about PB number in
the low hundreds, but articles about medical compliance (increasingly known as medical adherence) number in the thousands.
Hundreds (not tens) of articles and books about noncompliance
now appear each year in the fields of medicine, nursing, social
work and medical sociology, health psychology, and elsewhere.
Here, in contrast to almost all the PB literature, the costs of dilatoriness and inhibition are presented as unmistakably high, often
fatal.

So in this domain, called noncompliance or nonadherence, do
we at last see PBing taken seriously? It is valued only to the extent
that noncompliance is more often reported and lamented. Just as
in the traditional coverage of PB, accounts of nonadhering patients are almost always descriptive and theoretical. Only a handful of practical interventions for noncompliance have been
published, and these do not appear to be well known or widely
emulated. In most medical settings, evidently, noncompliance is
accepted as an occupational given. Even here the taboo holds.

I begin this inquiry into medical noncompliance with an overview. It will present patterns that too closely resemble those of
traditionally conceived PB to suppose that noncompliance is a
completely separate area of study. Noncompliance makes for interesting reading, particularly in its frequent summaries (for example, Clayton & Efron, 1994). From this gargantuan literature
I gleaned the following constants:

- For most kinds of medical prescriptions, behavioral and chemical, noncompliance ranges from 30 to 60 percent.
- Only a few, but nonetheless convincing, studies provide evidence that
compliant behavior is adaptive (for example, adherence to exercise regimens leads to reliably greater success on dietary regimens, in after-care
programs for new mothers, in preventive screenings for cancer).

- There is universal agreement (in contrast to the traditional PB literature) that noncompliance is a serious problem, one for which there are
  few practical solutions. Nowhere do these researchers and practitioners
  seem to joke about noncompliance or suppose it somehow adaptive.

Much more is written about causes of nonadherence, supposed
and proven.

Reasons for Noncompliance and Compliance

Thorough coverage of the reasons for following or not following
medical advice would require a book of its own. Instead, I represent the field in terms of five of its most important findings: (1)
Noncompliance is greatest amongst patients who are least interested in health, least motivated to follow recommendations, and
least inclined to believe treatment (or prevention) will be worth-
while. (2) The more chronic the disorder and the longer the need
for treatment, the greater the noncompliance. (3) Treatments that
bring the most immediate and obvious symptom relief elicit the
most compliance. (4) Treatments that require the most change in
personal habits produce the least compliance. (5) The most effective solutions for noncompliance are direct and behavioral (for
example, objective monitoring, prompting of correct responses,
performance feedback, and reinforcements for compliant behaviors).

Some articles about noncompliance seem to have particularly
direct relevance for psychological study of PB. For example,
merely imparting knowledge about a disorder and the benefits of
compliance (a traditional favorite), in itself, does little to improve
adherence (Clayton & Efron, 1994).

What These and Related Reports About
Noncompliance Tell Us About PB

Consider just some of the parallels and extensions of reports
about noncompliance.

- *Interest and involvement.* PBers and noncompliers show less interest in
  health and compliance than do efficacious counterparts. PBers seen
  more traditionally, as in earlier chapters, display curiously kindred ten-

dencies: lower general awareness of time (for example, they less often have clocks and calendars around them) and more resistance to reading or talking about PB. They are, in short, generally unaware of time until it is a problem, and they remain disinterested or dismissive of PB until forced to notice it. The role of involvement has rarely been mentioned in publications about noncompliance or PB, even though its role in the success of students has been well documented (Pascarella & Terenzini, 1991). The opposite of involvement, passivity, may be an important behavioral and cognitive component of PB. So too may be pessimism (Seligman, 1991).

• *Broad, relatively uninterruptible patterns.* The more the treatment for noncompliance requires patients to interrupt established, personal habits, the greater their resistance to change. This realization may help move researchers and practitioners in the field of PB to consider dilatoriness and anxious inhibition as broad patterns that discourage changes in any one part (Baumeister, Heatherton, & Tice, 1994; Rachlin, 1994). Said more simply, we probably cannot expect to reduce noncompliance or PBing without extensive, related changes in habit patterns. Indeed, recent behavioral research with PBers confirms that notion: the most successful cure for delaying and blocking at writing involved a variety of changes in writing habits including session lengths and pace of working that generalized to other everyday patterns including sleep and exercise (Boice, 1995a).

• *The importance of environment.* Surroundings, including clinic settings and practitioners' styles, are as responsible for noncompliance as are patients themselves. Compliance goes up demonstrably as clinics are more accessible, affordable, and friendly. Compliance benefits from clearly structured appointment and reminder systems, most of all when rewards are provided for timely involvement. Consider why this clear demonstration was less likely to occur to traditionalists who study PB than to researchers in medical fields. Psychologists, far more than medical people, look to personality typologies for explanations. And traditionalist psychologists object more readily to attributions of blame to environmentalist or behavioral determinants. Medical researchers, to their credit, are less constrained by the politics of research, at least as psychologists practice them, and more concerned with practical results.

• *The probable identity of medical noncompliance and PBing.* One apparent difference in the two areas is in the labels, but they mean pretty much the same thing (especially when we consider that contemporary researchers on noncompliance no longer assume it is always intentional). Another obvious difference may be no more substantial. Psychology and medicine do have different cultures, but they might profit in considering the similarities between the fields.

After all, I would argue, research about both noncompliants in medicine and PBers is already beginning to demonstrate the patterns suggested in the PB model. My own preliminary studies of general noncompliants who delay and block on dental examinations suggest the same three, intertwined steps as before: First comes *impatience* at facing the discomfort of pressures to seek timely treatment, and with that come narrowing and impulsivity that begin to turn prospective patients away from the threatening act to something more immediately comforting. Second come *mindless, irrational, self-defeating acts* in predictable patterns for individual procrastinators ("You see, when I get tense about those things, I calm myself by eating chocolate ice cream"). If tensions remain high, and they may, even these temporary diversions can be blocked by an overwhelming sense of anxiety and paralyzation. Third come the *aftereffects in lowered self-efficacy*, often as soon as a vague awareness of depression or irresponsibility sets in. Chief among the cues of an ambivalent reaction is the statement that the delayed task was unimportant for the moment (for example, "I don't have time for that right now; I've got other things that must be done first; it won't matter to put off what is only going to be root-canal anyway").

With these general findings of researchers on noncompliance in place, I repeat my purposes. I hoped to show that even in the realm of medical noncompliance, the taboo against understanding and treating PB holds fast and that (just as with traditionally labeled PB) noncompliance and compliance are based at least in part on simple, learnable, or changeable factors.

Examples of Recent Progress in the Compliance Literature

Involvement is nicely demonstrated in M. G. Wilson and J. Edmunson's (1993) finding that patients with problems of high cholesterol who regularly update their knowledge in that area not only adhere to advice better but have fewer health problems. Strong habits of impulsivity may play an even larger role in the opposite direction. Patients who enter exercise programs for smokers and the obese comply far less with prescriptions for work-outs, and ultimately they evidence more myocardial infarctions (Tooth, McKenna, & Colquhoun, 1993). To manage their exercise regimens, these patients may need to manage other tendencies related to PBing, including binge eating and smoking. What actually helps most patients make one or more changes in compliance? One help is interventions such as frequent prompts and prods.

Are such interventions justifiable? In one study, they led to timely compliance, and that, in turn, resulted in higher survival rates for compliers (46 percent) than for noncompliers (13 percent [Lombard, Lombard & Winett, 1995]).

There are also indications of what patient characteristics predict nonadherence. Depression can be a strong indicator, especially in elderly patients (Carney, Freedland, Eisen & Rich, 1995). So too, anxiety-prone, addictive, controlling patterns (Kayloe, 1993), and what practitioners call oppositionalism in patients (Stine, 1994) also suggest the likelihood of nonadherence. Even the literature on compliance occasionally includes personality traits as explanations. Failures of adherence are attributed to deficiencies in such traits as self-esteem (Taal, Rasker, Seydel & Wiegman, 1993). Some researchers point out more observable and useful correlates: general anxiety as a predictor of noncompliance amongst asthmatics (Mahwhinney, 1993) or low socioeconomic status of families as likely to lower compliance in after-care programs for children with cancer. Perhaps the most promising predictors combine personality characteristics with environmental variables (particularly where the latter can be changed): for instance, compliance with treatment may be best when patients test well for high self-esteem *and* demonstrate good relationships with their doctors (Viinamaki, Niskanen, Korhonen & Tahka, 1993).

What, in the end, does this enormous area of study, one perhaps a hundredfold larger than research on PB in psychology, tell us about interventions that work? It tells us even less than accounts of PB. Consider the usual train of logic and usefulness. First, where systematic interventions have been attempted, they are generally indirect and superficial. In one of the best of these (Boardway, Delamater, & Tomakowsky, 1993), adolescent diabetics were taught stress-management techniques (for example, relaxation). Compared to controls without the intervention, these patients reported less diabetic-specific stress but showed no greater improvements (1) in compliance with treatments in general, (2) in self-reported self-efficacy regarding their diabetes, or (3) most telling, in metabolic control. So, commonly preferred treatments (notably relaxation and cognitive restructuring) only confirm suspicions that little can be done for noncompliers.

Second, even more discouraging is the fact that patients exposed to strong behavioral strategies such as reinforcements for compliance actually ended up as even less compliant later, after the contingencies were dropped (Finney et al., 1993). From this result is drawn the implication that direct interventions are likely to backfire (but without any recognition of usual strategies of behaviorists, that is, more gradual withdrawal from the contingencies in ways that could have circumvented the disastrous results reported by Finney et al.).

Third, the very best studies of interventions for noncompliants still lack essential controls and follow-ups. G. A. Hamilton et al. (1993) devised what might be an exemplary program for patients with primary hypertension: a systematic, understandable plan of care that kept them involved and prompted and written and video materials that educated them. The outcomes are impressive: more appointments kept, greater drops in systolic blood pressure, and higher physician ratings of patient compliance. But the tragic shortcoming is that we cannot know how the results compared to patients in a similar but untreated comparison group. Nor does that article reveal how durable the effects of the intervention were, once formal treatments stopped. (Controlled analyses of other postprogram compliance show an almost complete failure in continuation of thoroughgoing treatment programs [McCaul, Glasgow, & O'Neill, 1992].)

How the Literatures on Noncompliance and PB Compare

The literatures compare all too well. Both rely almost entirely on descriptive accounts that imply helplessness in correcting the problem. Both noncompliance and PB almost always involve clear elements of dilatoriness and anxious inhibitions (for example, appointments or exercises missed in favor of other, more immediately rewarding tasks; preventive examinations, say for cancer screening, put off out of anxiety and insufficient information about how best to arrange help without embarrassment [Lauver & Ho, 1993; Bazargan, Barbre, & Hamm, 1993]). Neither noncompliance nor PB is well understood. That is, different observers attribute them to different factors, often in conflicting fashion (for example, some to a lack of self-esteem, some to generally bad habits such as smoking and obesity, some to poor patient-doctor interactions). Of course all the attributions could be correct to a degree, perhaps even interactive. But to the reader just encountering either literature, the appearance is one of confusion and superficiality.

Neither area, again, has produced enough well-tested interventions to influence psychologists or doctors. (Psychology, probably because of its emphasis on methodology, can boast of about ten such studies in print; medical compliance has none.) Just as problematic, both arenas prefer amiably indirect, inconclusive measures of PBing. So noncompliants, like other PBers, are depicted in terms of personality traits that seem forgivable (for example, poor self-esteem) and unchangeable. Even in research on compliance, though, someone has been brave enough to point out the reason why this custom is problematic: the more objective and direct the assessment, the lower the estimate of compliance (Stone, 1979). In other words, the less direct the measure of noncompliance by researchers, the less serious the problem appears to be.

What, in the final analysis, can we learn from studies of medical compliance? They suggest that here too there are powerful and usually unmentioned pressures against close, interventive examination of PBing. The taboo is effective regardless of its high costs. To complete my case about its force, I turn to accounts where the individual costs of defying the taboo are matters of record.

CASE STUDIES OF FOUR PSYCHOLOGISTS WHO DEFIED THE TABOO

Only one of the following four great psychologists, the last, has an enduring fame commensurate with his contributions: (1) *Pierre Janet* was perhaps the greatest pioneer of psychotherapy, but his insights were commandeered by Freud; psychoanalysts despised his interventive approach into things like PB, and they discredited him in lastingly effective ways. (2) *Alfred Adler,* also one of the most inventive of all psychotherapists, was disparaged and excommunicated by the Freudians, who disliked his practical, interventive bent for turning patients into more efficient, effective individuals. (3) *Frederick Taylor* was the primary mover in the psychology of work, a successful effort to transform workplaces, tools, timing, and motion of the work itself, into more productive, less fatiguing situations for workers. Taylor was abhorred and misunderstood to an irrational extent for his interventions to economize work and minimize PB, probably to the extent that should be expected for such a blatant violation of the taboo. (4) *B. F. Skinner* was, and still is, hated, reviled, and misrepresented more than any other psychologist. He took the boldest steps in identifying and manipulating the simple environmental pressures and rewards that can replace PBing with efficiency. Skinner is not detested and distorted because his methods failed to help PBers—but because they did help, so obviously and so effectively.

Pierre Janet

Janet (1859–1947) was bright and delightful. But he did not fit the mold, in a psychology trying to be a science, of a great scientist. He did not feel driven to obtain fame, and he did not display the customary period of madness that led to self-discovery and certainty about possessing a sure truth—the seemingly requisite form of creative illness for great pioneers in psychology (see Ellenberger, 1970). Instead, Janet never took himself too seriously; he put a premium on having fun and helping people with his psychology. He was interested in practical results, not in impressive theorizing.

Formative Years

In graduate school Janet taught philosophy, but he grew more interested in hypnosis (perhaps because his hero, the pioneer neurologist Jean Charcot, had just rehabilitated it from one of its taboo periods). Janet's initial experiments showed that the "suggestion" of a trance state or its manifestation such as paralysis could work from a distance, and his reports created a sensation. As a consultant to a local hospital, he was assigned a ward of hysterical women and he began scouring the old writings of Franz Mesmer and other "magnetists" for treatment ideas related to his discovery. This practical side of his interests seemed to him to be related to his religious leanings and somewhat at odds with high science. (Religion, like hypnosis, is generally a taboo subject amongst scientists.)

I was very religious, and I have always retained mystical tendencies which I have succeeded in controlling. It was a question of conciliating scientific tastes and religious sentiments, which was not an easy task. (Janet, 1930, p. 123)

Not long after Janet completed his doctorate with Charcot, the master died in disgrace. His fall came not because his treatments were ineffective but because they offended influential people. The result was that some of Janet's best work would be ignored:

These studies have been somewhat forgotten today because of the discredit thrown on observations relative to hysteria since the death of Charcot in 1895. Hysteria patients seemed to disappear because they were now designated by other names. It was said that their tendency toward dissimulation [feigning] and suggestibility made an examination dangerous and interpretations doubtful. I believe these criticisms to be grossly exaggerated and based on prejudice and misapprehension. (Janet, 1930, p. 127)

Janet's Research

As a graduate student Janet used the technique of automatic writing to uncover the unconscious causes of hysterical terror in patients; for him, hysterical paralyses were a kind of blocking (often with components of procrastination). In typically imaginative and thoroughgoing fashion, he discovered that the hypnosis underlying automatic writing was more complex than it first appeared. The more manifest side of automaticity produced a "public role" and materials aimed to please the hypnotist; its more latent side was a hidden set of patterns rooted in habits of childhood.

Janet drew heavily on his experiments with four hysterical women to write his first book, *L'Automatisme psychologique* (1889), a forgotten classic. Among his insights were these: hysteria (like hypnosis and PBing) involves a narrowing of the field of consciousness; rapport (that is, communication with the therapist) too is a distortion in how the world is perceived, one that fits the scheme of the hypnotist; and, hysterical symptoms have roots in subconscious, fixed ideas, with an autonomous and impulsive life of their own (unless uncovered by the therapist).

Eventually Janet noticed that the mere suggestion of a release from patterns like PBing would work only briefly and only with superficial, inconsequential habits. What worked better, he discovered, were repeated ventures into hypnosis (often by way of automatic writing). As deeper crises were released, their origins proved to be older and older and liberation from them kept the mind clear for longer and longer periods. The essential change involved in all this, it seemed obvious at last, was the slow, accepting breakdown of the hallucinatory schemata held by the patient. Here, Janet came up with one of his greatest discoveries, one still generally unappreciated in clinical psychology: insight by the patient about the nature of the problem and then a feeling of release are not enough; to keep the symptom pattern away, the picture behind it must be replaced by substituting a new picture or schemata, bit by bit.

Janet was, then, a pragmatist and interventionist. He drew the ire of leading psychologists who interpreted science to mean description but not intervention. Even so, he persisted in his innovations. One was an applied concept of psychological energy and of its uneconomical expenditure by neurotics (individuals that readers of this book might label PBers). These are people who overreact and tire easily, often becoming depressed; who chronically invest most of their energy in anxiety and so cannot enjoy happiness or pleasure; who avoid publicly evaluated efforts including social relationships; and who spend lots of time and energy solving problems that most people would consider insignificant. Janet's psychotherapies, not surprisingly, focused around what he called psychological economies. In these he helped change the ways in which patients worked (in terms of pacing and timing) and the conditions of work (such as noise levels and other dis-

tractions) at their occupations. All this too has been largely rejected or ignored by clinical psychology.

Janet's Influence

By 1900, Janet's friends and patients expected him to become
the founder of a great school. Obviously, he did not. Some of the
reasons, including the fall of Charcot, were external to him. Some
related to his personality, a rather sane and unpretentious one.
Janet was content to write at his own steady pace, without much
reliance on style. He did not sacrifice accuracy and usefulness for
speed or impressiveness. And, he tended to see things, including
his own work, with some perspective and humor. He didn't even
show much indignation at the theft of his ideas (Ellenberger,
1970)—a matter that takes us to the third reason for his obscurity.
Freud, in particular, appropriated many of Janet's ideas and made
them seem his own (not an unusual act, according to Ellenberger,
for someone whose creative illness was so important to his career).
The pattern in which Freud did so is interesting in itself because
it typifies a sequence found throughout history; it is a clever way
of punishing the violator of a taboo and, simultaneously, augmenting one's own welfare: First, Freud summarily acknowledged
Janet's discoveries. Second, he became more and more critical of
Janet's work and even accused him of plagiarizing his own. Third,
he simply stopped mentioning Janet, and the world soon forgot
him. Henri Ellenberger (1970), a historian who tried to resurrect
Janet, recounts one example:

Though Freud had summarily acknowledged Janet's previous research in
1893 and 1895, he became increasingly critical of him. Janet's report on
psychoanalysis at the London Congress in 1913, at which he claimed priority for the discovery of subconscious fixed ideas and cathartic therapy,
was the signal for violent attacks against Janet by certain psychoanalysts.
Ernest Jones [Freud's official biographer and a member of his inner cir-
cle] publicly and expressly accused him of dishonesty, asserting that
Freud's discoveries owed nothing to Janet. In 1945, the French psycho-
analyst Madeline Cave, in defiance of chronology, accused Janet of hurried plagiarism upon the publication of Breuer and Freud's paper of 1893
[Janet's appeared in 1889]. (p. 408)

Janet's death in 1947 went largely unnoticed, except to his old
friends and patients. By the end, it was clear that he had paid a

dear price for his unconventional approach. What was so objectionable about his approach? I believe he was punished and forgotten most of all for his direct exposure of and effective treatment of PBing.

Alfred Adler

Adler (1870–1937), too, was bright, objective, and innovative; he may have started more influential movements in psychology than anyone else. Yet, he is remembered and valued today, for the most part, only by a small group of disciples.

One good way to picture Adler is as the opposite of Freud. Adler was as homely and unassuming as Freud was handsome and charismatic. Freud grew up in a comfortable home with doting parents and all the comforts of life; Adler was raised in a ghetto and spent far more time with his rough peers than with his parents. Freud had a distinguished university career, lived in a prestigious neighborhood, collected the finest art treasures, and served only the choicest clientele; Adler had or did none of those things. Nor did he want to.

Not surprisingly, Adler's psychology is about peer relationships, about overcoming inferiorities and gaining social ascension, about health and school psychologies as ways of improving the lot of the disadvantaged, and about the inefficiencies of neurotic patients. I believe that these were callings more important in psychology as Freud's.

Early Beginnings in Social Medicine

Adler began his career by trying to treat the everyday problems that occurred outside his office. His first book, *Gesundheitsbuch für das Schneidergewerbe* [*Health Book for the Tailor Trade*] (1898), was a pioneering effort in what is now called health psychology. It was one of the earliest demonstrations of the relationship between economic situations and disease within a given trade. It focused on a ghetto activity, the tailor trade, and its crowded, unhealthy conditions of work. Tailors' hours were long and their businesses often relied on family to help meet deadlines. Tailors worked, hunched over, on sewing machines and breathed the dust of cloth that fostered respiratory infections, pulmonary tuberculosis, circulatory disturbances, intestinal diseases, and short-sightedness. They used scissors and needles in ways that caused repetitive strain injuries and abscesses on fingers. And, among other things, tailors held threads in their mouths that caused gum infections and alimentary ailments. Most telling in all this accumulation, Adler concluded, was the fact that tailors evidenced the lowest life expectancy of all trades.

In this and in later publications, Adler pointed out the discrepancy between scientific medicine and social medicine. Scientific medicine was making rapid progress, but for some reason (perhaps having to do with its disdain for patients who seemed unwilling or unsuited to help themselves) it was not applying its advances where they were needed most. Adler's assumption, in contrast, was *not* that tailors procrastinated and blocked in arranging better working conditions and care for themselves because of ingrained personality traits. Instead, he supposed that their working conditions and habits demanded direct examination and exposure, even humane interventions.

Adler's studies helped reinforce the general movement to improve working conditions and to educate workers about healthier ways of working. That effort, in turn, led him to the educational system, particularly the primary grades, as a place to induce social change (that is, intervention) most efficiently. In 1904 he published an article, "Physician as Educator," in which he developed another facet of helping people from low socioeconomic backgrounds where efficiencies are less commonly learned. Weak, sickly, underprivileged children, Adler noted, too often experience school as a setting that further undermines their confidence and courage. To help, parents and then teachers should be trained in ways of instilling self-confidence (for example, by striking a balance between pampering and punishing) and themselves behaving more effectively. Adler's later, individual therapies would be modeled after excellent methods of teaching (where, for instance, the therapist does not take a superior position to the patient).

Adler as a Freudian

Adler was already a success in social and educational medicine before joining the psychoanalysts. It was to be a tenuous relationship. From the outset, Adler (somewhat like Carl Jung) rebelled against Freud's mythology of sexuality in infants, particularly his basing it on pampered, selfish children. Put simply, Adler regarded Freud as too esoteric, theoretical, and impractical. Adler's lasting contributions were simpler and more pragmatic—notions of inferiority and of neurotic overcompensation. His work marked the beginnings of studies about self-esteem in psychology, a research area that continues to grow. Adler saw that one of the problems of neurotic overcompensation was overreaction to even the smallest setback.

Adler After Freud

In Adler's next major book, *Uber den nervosen charakter* [*The Nervous Character*] (1912), he elaborated on his ideas and the clinical facts about neurosis. What matters most, he concluded, is how patients perceive themselves. Neurotics not only live with constant fictions and fantasies but they come to believe them. Adler relied on a broad range of experts to help shape and support his conclusions: physicians, pediatricians, university psychiatrists such as Emil Kraepelin, psychotherapists such as Janet, writers such as Goethe and Shakespeare, and philosophers including Nietzsche.

In *Understanding Human Nature* (1927), Adler extended his notions about compensation. He made clear the impact of educational errors, especially in exposing poor children to humiliation, that reinforced the sense of social inferiority of the poor. Among the neurotic results of this pattern for the victims are jealousy and hatred, retreat and helplessness, shyness and anxiety, even tyranny when given the opportunity. What, besides balanced treatment by primary teachers, would help? Adler thought that education, even at the lowest levels, should emphasize social relationships as efficiencies and teach ways of limiting the wastefulness of social deceit. He was emphatic in assuming that people need to be alerted to fictitious life goals (which is why his therapeutic method puts great diagnostic value on patient's first memories, then on dreams, then on ways of playing that reveal lifestyles). Goals for his patients included abandoning fictitious life goals in favor of realistic ones and building courage combined with "community feeling." In his view, neuroses and other kinds of misbehavior including criminality, were deviations from community involvement. So while some of the corrective lies in uncovering fictions, some also lies in finding community support in the form of group therapies, educational interventions, and social medicine. Adler's approach was, more than any other analytically related therapy, practical, common-sensical, and interventive. It had little of the appearance of classical science, and so the Freudians dismissed it as superficial.

The Price Adler Paid

Did it matter in the long run that the establishment rejected and then suppressed his innovations for being both unscientific and interventive? While he was not so personally devastated as other interventionists excommunicated from the Society, such as Otto Rank, Adler's ideas and techniques were to go uncredited in mainstream psychology. PBers and other patients he would have labeled as neurotic are still unlikely to find a therapist with his practical, skills-oriented approach.

Frederick Taylor

By the 1880s and 1890s, many leading psychologists in Europe and then America were involved in a major movement to study the role of fatigue and will in work. The mood for the study of efficiency had been ripe since the mid 1800s; materialism (a philosophy that leads to the notion that humans and other animals can be seen profitably as machines) was a revolt against religion, and it brought an interest in the laws of energy behind labor. Early psychologists (including Janet) supposed that mental illness often results from an unwise expenditure of energy that leads to constant exhaustion, busyness, and vulnerability to overreaction. "Productivism" was already in vogue when Karl Marx promoted the idea of emancipating the lower classes by making them more efficient. Marx wanted to redesign work settings and educate workers to free them from the low levels of productivity that kept them chained to lower socioeconomic status. Marx thought, and many psychologists agreed, that the major failing of capitalist industry was the fatigue and wasted effort to which it exposed its lowest-level workers.

As early as the 1860s French physiologists were conducting time and motion studies the better to understand ways of decreasing fatigue and enhancing efficiency. Cinematography helped break motions into discrete movements, and it showed how efficient actions vary from the inefficient kind. It led to training for more efficient movements that reduced fatigue and increased output. It revealed the distinctive aspects of inefficient, fatiguing work: impulsive excessiveness, irregularity, and poor organization. These discoveries, it turned out, extended even to ways of eating, sleeping, and thinking. Productivists showed that efficiency matters as much for intellectual and creative efforts as for factory work. In all these domains, the efficient way to efficiency was clearly established: a slower pace, increased periods of rest, and simple, rhythmic movements. Rest cures helped patients not to avoid work but to limit tense, irregular, inefficient work. The sign of an efficient and healthy person, in that view, was an economy of action and a modicum of PBing.

An obvious place to apply the psychology of work was industry. In the late 1800s, workers often labored twelve hours a day, six days a week, with poor work conditions and little time for rest.

Taylorism

Frederick Winslow Taylor (1856–1919) built a system of research and demonstration to advance "scientific methods" for industrial use. Taylorism was based on time-and-motion studies; Taylor aimed, often by way of observing exemplary workers, at devising more efficient tools, more economical movements in using them, more divisions of tasks into simple components, and the least-fatiguing patterns of resting and pacing. Taylorism was attractive to employers because it allowed new workers to be trained quickly and effectively at a time when factories were hiring unskilled people; by definition, it increased the productivity of individuals and plants. Workers generally liked it too; when they worked efficaciously they earned far more while reporting less fatigue and more enjoyment in their jobs. In short, Taylorism was cost-effective and generally humane. Moreover, Taylorism was so simple it could be exported anywhere, with demonstrable results:

By discovering the most efficient method of executing a given task through precise observation and measurements, Taylor also discovered the optimal conditions of work. "He doubled and tripled the efficiency of machine-tools, and he increased in the same proportion, the daily output of workers. . . . even in crafts, each task required a complexity of organization that surpassed the capacity of the worker." As Taylor had found in his example of a pig-iron monger named Schmidt, "The alteration of rest and work, the speed of the movements, the weight lifted in each effort, considerably modified the fatigue for the same amount of work." (Rabinbach, 1990, pp. 244–345)

Inevitably, defenders of the taboo against observing inefficiencies (and intervening to correct them) took after Taylor. Unions were among the first opponents; in 1913, for example, the workers at a Renault plant went on strike until the "time and motion man" was taken off the floor. Academics too, many of them laboratory researchers, objected to Taylor's supposed view of workers as machines whose only value was to produce more and more output. Leading psychologists criticized Taylorism for attending only to acts and behaviors, not to the subjective experiences of workers. Taylorism became the whipping boy of both humanists and scientists, many of whom apparently knew little about its specifics. It became the subject of novels in which workers were treated inhumanely; mistruths and rumors about it were commonly spread. As a result, Taylor, one of the great innovators and researchers, is either unknown or reflexively disparaged in psychology today. True, there are vestiges of his methods and ideas in modern industrial-organizational psychology (for example, human factors research, human resource management, and ergonomics) but such psychology is now an applied field that rarely measures the effects of its interventions carefully (and so avoids the objections against serious interventionism).

In the main, Taylorism comes up today only when writers recount its ostensible evils as a safeguard against its revival. One example can be seen in Martha Banta's (1993) book, *Taylored Lives*. She not only condemns Taylor as an unprincipled liar (he supposed, after all, that scientific rationality would reign supreme over time) but also as a demeaner of people (because he concluded that nearly everyone needed to learn the disciplines of efficiency). Banta particularly objects to a central theme in Taylor's most famous book, *Principles of Scientific Management* (1913), the notion that you cannot effect change in workers by merely talking to them, that workers must experience to learn. (This idea, in Banta's view, means that Taylor had a condescending view of factory workers.) She depicts Taylor as an anxious neurotic because of his concerns for discipline and order; the more so because he eventually admitted feeling lonely and isolated in his efforts. In the end, she simply dismisses Taylorism as unworkable (despite the facts to the contrary):

It is unlikely, however, that even the most innovative of the industrial engineers and product designers will offset the passivity diagramed into a Joe or a Josephine; the schematic measurements of these representations eliminated moral and immoral qualities, and with them eliminate emotional needs and intellectual doubts. (p. 292)

In other words, who would want to live and work in a world where everyone is automatically good or productive? where PBing is moderated to noninjurious status?

Banta's vitriolic attitude toward Taylor and productivism is typical of things written by Taylor's colleagues and ours. Moreover, these condemnations serve the taboo: they constantly warn against a revival of productivism by portraying it as the inherently evil enemy of all good causes—including human rights and feminism—always without presenting its advantages.

The Price Taylor Paid

Throughout his career, Taylor's well-intentioned interventions elicited opposition from colleagues in management; effective politicians usually outmaneuver effective researchers (Nelson, 1980). The reason seems clear in retrospect. Taylorism not only threatened the status quo but also imperiled the jobs of traditional managers:

It is well-known to all executives that it is one thing to give employees instructions and quite another to get them to follow the instructions faithfully. And these instructions of Taylor's called for exceptional work—and not only for greater continuity of effort but also for a higher order of attention and watchfulness. They thus ran counter to the average man's very human disposition to take things easy. They, in fact, called for marked and *permanent* changes in his habits. (Copely, 1969, p. 260)

How, specifically, did Taylor's critics deal with him? At best, they claimed they could not understand him (despite his clear specification of jobs and of performance standards). More often, they claimed his only goal was to speed up workers. At worst, they found ways to terminate his consultantships in companies and even generally to ban his methods. For a long time, Taylor cheerfully adapted himself to obstacles, but when the U.S. Commission on Industrial Relations carried out a long, agonizing examination that led to the prohibition of stop watches and bonus payments in government facilities, he was heartbroken. He died, not long after, at age fifty-nine, in 1915.

His critics had won. While the firms that introduced his methods during his lifetime had been the most meticulously organized factories, his strategies for managing tools, materials, machines, supervisors, and workers declined in popularity. Fewer and fewer companies created formal planning departments or issued detailed instructions to employees. Taylor's attempts to move industry away from centralized management would lie fallow in America for a long time (D. Nelson, 1980).

Only one other psychologist, so far as I know, suffered even more than Taylor at the hands of taboo enforcers.

B. F. Skinner

B. F. Skinner (1904–1990) may have been the most imaginative, innovative psychologist of his century or any other. He is also the most misunderstood of psychologists, largely over matters of interventionism. When his career reached the point where he applied his interventionism to obviously effective ways of controlling and improving human behaviors, especially of intact adults, there was no stemming the flood of distortion and dislike that came his way.

Young Skinner

Skinner's childhood was highlighted by a happy self-discipline. From an early age, he showed remarkable tendencies to devise apparatus to make himself behave as he should, just as he would when adult and famous:

> We subscribed to the *Philadelphia Inquirer*, a good Republican paper [Skinner's father was a lawyer], which carried Rube Goldberg's cartoons with his outrageous contraptions and his Foolish Questions. Goldberg's influence can be detected in a gadget I built to solve a personal problem having to do with hanging up my pajamas. I had a bedroom of my own, and in the morning I often left my pajamas lying on my bed. While I was eating breakfast, my mother would go upstairs to check, and when she came found them there, she would call to me, and I would have to stop eating, go upstairs, and hang them up. She continued this for weeks. It did not make me any more inclined to hang them up before coming down to breakfast, but it was nonetheless aversive, and I escaped in the following way. The clothes closet in my room was near the door, and in it I fastened a hook on the end of a string which passed over a nail and along the wall to a nail above the center of the door. A sign reading "Hang up your pajamas" hung over the other end. When the pajamas were in place, the sign was up out of the way, but when I took them off the hook at night, the sign dropped to the middle of the door where I would bump into it on the way out. (Skinner, 1976, pp. 122–123)

In that amusing and amazing portrayal of the young Skinnerian we can learn more about him than his ingenuity. He had a strong dislike for aversive controls (none more than the nagging of his mother): his mature psychology, then, would emphasize nonaversive ways of inducing people to change their behavior. Moreover, he was already behaving as if he had no free will. When I describe this anecdote in my history-of-psychology classes, it un-failingly divides students into two general groups of arguers. The first immediately complain that Skinner should have "willed him-self" to hang up his pajamas and avoided the whole silliness of building a contraption to make him do what he should. (These students believe in will and conscientiousness as kinds of person-ality traits.) The second group is surprised at the complaint. It seems obvious to them that children (and adults, for that matter) often fail to remember to do things and that being hassled and told to "will" themselves to do the thing is a surefire route to unreliability. It is far better, the second group concludes, simply to arrange a painless reminder to make sure the thing gets done automatically. In most cases, the two groups do little to change each others' minds, almost as if each set of students had come to class preinclined to reject or accept Skinner's interventionism.

Skinner as a Graduate Student and Young Professor

In the early stages of his career, not surprisingly, Skinner opted for discipline and efficiency; he, like the successful executives mentioned earlier in this book, simply didn't procrastinate and block. As he started his first professorial job at the University of Minnesota, he continued to make all the right moves for launching a successful career. As a rule, new faculty are overwhelmed by the work required to prepare classes and the unenthusiastic response of undergraduate students. Not Skinner. He found ways to excel at teaching quickly, while also making the work easier. He had students do a lot of the work in his large introductory class; they collaborated in pairs with inexpensive apparatus and they loved it. Skinner's own classes influenced more students to go on to dissertations in psychology than any other introductory course I know of, perhaps the highest compliment a teacher of introductory psychology can garner.

His good start as a teacher helped him make an exemplary beginning as a researcher. Why? He didn't struggle at teaching, so he also had time and energy to devote to research and writing. His enthusiasm for teaching attracted students to work with him on his research, as unpaid assistants. And, he didn't hesitate to talk in class about what really interested him: his views of behaviorism and his own research. Doing so helped him clarify his ideas about research and taught him to be comfortable and competent while doing more than one thing at once. So, on the same day, he could move back and forth between his work at teaching, at writing, and at research, often thinking of connections between all of them. Over time, he taught courses even more directly helpful to himself, among them a class on literary writing. He was, in a word, efficient.

Eventually Skinner's research moved beyond studies of rats and pigeons. His bent for pragmatism, behavioral control, and gadge-

teering inevitably moved him to real-life problems. He didn't quite
know it yet, but trouble was just around the corner. He was beginning to violate psychology's great taboo.

Skinner as an Interventionist with Humans

The difficulty began innocently enough. Skinner wanted a second child and his wife objected to the work it would entail. So
Skinner, a devoted father, devised a gadget to make the job of
raising their second baby easier. It was the infamous, widely mis-
construed "baby box." Therein lies one of psychology's most fascinating tales. (And one of the clearest demonstrations about what
happens when a psychologist violates the unwritten taboo about
employing interventions to make humans more efficient.)

The outrage over the baby box resembles the sort usually saved
for the worst kinds of religious heretics. You can read about it in
his three-volume autobiography or rely, as I have done here, on
his account in *Psychology Today* (Skinner, 1979a).

He began with careful thought about a baby's needs and realized that during most of our evolutionary history, human infants
had been raised in a tropical climate, without benefit of clothing.
The Skinner's first child (Julie, who later became a prominent
psychologist), then five years old, had suffered through the usual,
excessive clothing and enclosing endured by babies at that time:
layers and layers, including a diaper, shirt and nightgown; a thick
mattress covered by pad and sheet; and, finally, being zipped into
a flannel blanket. With her arms in flipperlike sleeves and her
body encased in so much insulation, how could she have developed the strength and dexterity that could have come in a more
natural setting? The answer, for Skinner, at least, was a more
comfortable environment that would protect the new baby from
extremes of temperature and free it for easy movement (all without the usual danger that the baby would smother itself in the
bedding).

The gadget would, Skinner decided, be little more than an en-
closed crib (a place where the baby would ordinarily spend much
of its time when not being held and played with by other people).

For our second child, Deborah, I built a crib-sized living space that we
began to call the "baby tender." It had sound-absorbing walls and a large

picture window. Air entered through filters at the bottom and, after being warmed and moistened, moved by convection upward through and around the edges of a tightly stretched canvas, which served as a mattress. (A small fan blew the air if the room was hot.) A strip of sheeting 10 yards long passed over the canvas, a clean section of which could be cranked into place in a few seconds.

She wore only a diaper. Completely free to move about, she was soon pushing up, rolling over, and crawling. She breathed warm, moist filtered air, and her skin was never water-logged with sweat or urine. Loud noises were muffled though we could hear her from any part of the house. (p. 30)

Skinner resisted the temptation to do many experiments on Deborah, but he did make her special toys such as a music box she could activate by pulling on a ring. The gadgets and her freedom of movement appeared to encourage exceptional muscular strength; she stayed unusually clean and free of infections and colds. Moreover, as Skinner took pains to point out, Deborah was not socially isolated. She spent about the same amount of time that most babies would in a playpen, a teeter chair, and playing with her family; she showed no reluctance to be returned to the baby tender.

By 1945, with the project a success, Skinner couldn't resist sharing his gadget with the general public; he submitted an article to the *Ladies Home Journal*. Initially, the *Journal* delayed; the idea aroused great controversy among the staff. They wanted pictures of the baby tender; they wanted to know if the baby could really be heard from another part of the house; they worried about not giving the baby a bath every day; they asked if the roll of sheeting would have to wait a week for laundering even if it was badly soiled. With these questions answered, the article appeared with a title Skinner would not have chosen: "Baby in a Box." Other media picked up the story quickly.

From there, the trouble grew. The magazine article used the label "box" and inevitably people supposed it resembled the boxes Skinner used for operant conditioning with rats and pigeons. Criticism and gossip began to build. Skinner had not anticipated the objections to interventionism in the service of efficiency.

An article in *Life*, for example, described the baby tender as a menacing cage and pessimistically predicted that its isolation from viruses would leave the baby susceptible to respiratory infections as an adult (in the experience of Skinner and of others who raised their babies in tenders, the result was quite the opposite). Things got worse. Rumors spread, sometimes with the assistance of prominent psychologists and psychiatrists, that Skinner's daughter had become psychotic or suicidal (she hadn't). College teachers still tell the story, completely untrue, that the baby was raised in a box with shock grids to deliver punishments and with a lever to be pressed for food. In fact, Deborah grew up to be a successful artist who married a professor and lives in London. Deborah herself had to fire off a protest to the BBC over a program that depicted her as crazy.

Why do these irrationalities continue? It isn't that Skinner was an ill-intentioned, Machiavellian person. Instead, he openly and persistently violated a sacred taboo. He might as well have been the person who announced that the earth revolved around the sun.

Skinner as Classroom Interventionist

Undeterred, Skinner turned next to a topic that consumed the second half of his career, intervening to improve education in school settings. (And for this effort, what had been a mild protest would become a much louder chorus of misunderstanding and hatred.) He had already, as a teacher himself, noticed the usual failing of classrooms: students studied to avoid the consequences of not studying. In 1953, when he joined a group of fathers on Father's Day watching their children in a fourth-grade mathematics class, he became convinced that someone had to help solve the usual dilemma of classrooms: students who either worked too quickly and grew bored or else worked with frustration and strain.

The answer, of course, was a gadget; within days he had built a primitive teaching machine. Arithmetic problems were printed on cards and inserted in the machine; the student entered an answer (by moving levers) at the side. Correct answers produced a light. More sophisticated models soon followed: correct answers were not revealed until the student figured them out and only then a new frame appeared; the process of becoming competent in a topic like math could be divided into a great many small steps, and students could proceed, always successful, at their own pace. Eventually, the machines could take students who needed extra help into "branched programs" that added more clues.

A report to a governmental agency shows how sophisticated teaching machines had become by the late 1950s:

> The student is first asked about familiar things—for example, dots, lines, distances, angles, and so on—using his everyday vocabulary. He is led— much as a lawyer "leads" a witness—to discuss relations among these, many of which he has probably not previously noticed. Technical terms are then slowly inserted. For example, in geometry, the student first discusses dots; a dot then comes to indicate merely a point in space and the discussion proceeds in terms of points. Within a short time, and with little effort, the student finds himself discussing many of the materials of geometry or trigonometry in technical terms. His behavior may begin to "pay off" in the discovery and demonstration of unexpected properties or relations. (Skinner, 1983, pp. 119–120)

Of course, the teaching machines worked. Too well, perhaps. In Skinner's own classes, students paced themselves well and clearly learned and applied the principles. Better yet, they liked the machines and found the learning process self-reinforcing. (On average, undergraduates could learn the course material well in about fifteen hours, a fraction of the time required for conventional lecture classes and studying.) The teaching machines produced equally impressive results elsewhere. Eighth-graders in a Virginia school, for example, learned a full year of algebra in a single term and at a ninth-grade level. Retests a year later showed retention rates at over 90 percent (compared to a rate of 70 to 80 percent for students who learned in traditional classes). And so on.

Criticism was immediate. Many teachers assumed that programmed learning had to be superficial ("did they *really* learn algebra?"), despite the fact that many programs were specifically designed and tested to teach basic concepts and their broad applications. Even more teachers concluded the machines would put them out of work (despite Skinner's demonstrations that their time was better spent in individual coaching of students than in lecturing whole classes). Teachers claimed that the machines lacked the warmth and personality of an inspired teacher (despite the fact that students enjoyed programmed learning and preferred it to conventional teaching). Popular writers such as Joseph Krutch concluded that the machines could only degrade students. The humanistic psychologist Carl Rogers denounced Skinner's methodology and recommended setting up situations where students would *want* to learn, where they would have the power, where they would not need teaching. Real education, in Rogers's view, was something that would have to take place on top of the superficial things that Skinner was teaching.

The point in all this criticism may have been that most critics of a highly controlled, efficient learning environment objected most to how well it worked. It could only, they concluded, rob its victims of their freedom and dignity. Critics were not dissuaded by facts such as accelerated performance of ghetto school children. And they did not seem to be bothered, as Skinner was (and Adler too), about the general failings of traditional educational methods. Critics reacted most, apparently, to the violation of a great, unspoken taboo.

The Price Skinner Paid

Religious leaders, humanists, and many psychologists reacted to Skinner's best-selling book, *Beyond Freedom and Dignity* (1971), in ways that recalled objections to Darwin and *Origin of Species*. Numerous debates were organized, almost always overloaded in favor of the defenders of freedom, dignity, and PBing. Skinner eventually refused invitations to speak on programmed learning; he had finally admitted to himself that the truth does not always prevail. Moreover, he had grown tired of insistent claims that he wanted to take away people's freedom ("As a scientist I did not think of people as free initiating agents to be credited with their achievements, but I was proposing changes in social practices which should make them *feel* freer than ever before and *accomplish* more [1983, pp. 310–311]). One review of Skinner appeared with the face of a rat replacing his own (Darwin had been depicted similarly, except as part monkey). Threats against Skinner's life were made, some in so convincing a fashion that he walked to campus by unpredictable routes for years. The saddest moments for Skinner, though, were ones like this:

Last night Debbie and I went to the Gardner Coxes' for some music in their garden. A group of young people, mostly current Harvard and Radcliffe students, sang a mass by William Byrd. It was a capella and, for most of the singers, sight reading. Very well done. Ragged clouds moved across the sky, one of them dropping briefly a fine misty rain. Half a dozen lights burned among the green branches. Several kittens played on the grass. . . . the night was quiet and the music beautiful. . . . As I said goodnight, she [the hostess] motioned toward the young man who had conducted the music and said, "You know, he thinks you are a terrible man. Teaching machines, a Fascist . . ." (1983, pp. 246–247).

Skinner's Legacy

What remains today of Skinner's innovations and brave theorizing? Remarkably little. Teaching machines, even in the computer age, have had little impact on education; it is business as usual. Behaviorism and its interventionism have become passé and cognitive psychologists (who describe but usually do not intervene) commonly joke about Skinner as an anachronism. Even Skinner's *Beyond Freedom and Dignity* is out of print. The taboo has worked once again.

A Final Point About the Taboo Against Interventionism

We can distance ourselves from Skinner, Taylor, Adler, and Janet because psychology seems to get along without them. Somehow, they can be dismissed as radicals who were too insensitive to human values to leave a stronger impact. We *do* prefer our freedom and dignity to a system, like Skinner's or Taylor's, where the environment and the schedule are more responsible for our good work and efficiencies than we are. And where we are free to indulge in PB.

We are, most of us, more comfortable with a psychology that stays within the limits of amiable description and understanding; once we take up serious interventionism, it seems, we either become pawns of the controllers or evil controllers ourselves. Yes, we study critical social issues such as aggression and racism, but we analyze it, even manipulate it, under artificial laboratory conditions with freshmen as subjects; we do not venture actually to change society in efficient ways. Instead, like Martha Banta, we assume that we are so all so intelligent and rational that merely being informed about what might work better will solve problems such as pollution and warfare, even PBing.

Do we pay a price, in the long run, for preferring noninterventionism? Psychology, as we have seen, has accomplished virtually nothing to help increase the compliance of patients with medical programs and even less to induce them to initiate and maintain preventive treatments and tests. It essentially ignores the inefficiencies and inhumanities of situations like dissertation delays (mean time for completion now runs to more than seven years for projects that realistically require a year or two but can be delayed far longer). It overlooks the high rates of dropouts in our graduate programs (perhaps half of students at the dissertation stage do not finish, more for women and minorities). And it minimizes the role of procrastination and blocking in other spheres. PBing could well be, as I suggested earlier, basic to a variety of mental ailments, notably self-destructive behaviors.

So our tradition of neglect of procrastination and blocking is neither benign nor helpful. We might do well to ask questions like this one: Are we better off with our supposed freedom and dignity (and its costs like blindness and kidney failure for diabetics who put off treatments) or with more attention to things that embarrass and require interventions? The answer: it depends on whom you ask.

Summary

Consider what has been discussed in this unconventional account of procrastination and blocking.

AN ADMISSION OF COST

For one thing, the book unashamedly admits that PB is often costly—too costly to continue to ignore if we care about the plight of marginalized people. The cost is too exorbitant if we care about those of us who put off medical exams or neglect treatment regimens. It is too wasteful if we want life to be more efficient and joyful for ourselves and others.

THE REASONS FOR NEGLECT

For another thing, the book has considered why tradition has neglected and avoided PB. The reason, evidently, relates to tradition's intolerance of direct, effective interventions in general: close examination of PBing or questions of PBers' excuses is a social impropriety. Therefore, the literature on PB is mostly superficial and conjectural (it rarely deals in real-life, costly sorts of PB that demand serious interventions). The best-known mentions of PB are humorous and congenial.

In general, psychologists treat PB amiably, if at all. We assume, mistakenly but politely, that PBers are more likeable and free, probably even more creative, because of their PBing. While the reasons why society politely ignores occasional PB are fairly conspicuous (that is, minimization of embarrassment), those for the neglect of chronic, problematic procrastination and blocking are harder to justify.

Evidently, the short-term benefits of PB suffice, in part, to keep potential examiners at bay: PB, as noted, offers autonomy, excitement, retribution, and opportunities to do something easy and relieving—in the short run. It offers the magic of sudden inspiration; its worst effects are often delayed and discounted. And when we begin to see it in ourselves we shy away from what might seem its only corrective—the excesses of obsession-compulsion. Besides, PBers make particularly difficult patients and students when interventions are proposed. Given all these factors and the social discomfort of examining PB, no wonder we have attended to other, seemingly more pressing and immediate things.

We have, in the main, put off and blocked the study and treatment of PB. (Or, on the few occasions of study, we have depicted PB as characterological and irreversible, in terms of amiable explanations such as perfectionism.)

A USEFUL MASS OF INFORMATION

For a third thing, there is in fact a distillable, useful mass of information about PB. The scholarly literature follows four approaches to explanation and intervention. The earliest trend I called automaticity; its proponents assume that excessive self-consciousness delays and blocks action. Some of its most useful discoveries (for example, that hypnotic susceptibility predicts fluency in writing) are now lost from view; some of its most durable strategies (for example, free writing) have found overuse and little accountability. The next approach in that foursome is psychoanalytic and humanistic. Its deepest insights are old and about links between PB and problems of impulse control. The third approach, a spurt of behavioral interest in PB, proved the most promising and disappointing. Behaviorism's early objectivists advocated direct, unapologetic study of PB and of effective ways to work. Its recent practitioners have preferred overly simple and coercive interventions (for example, contingency management). The most recent approach relates PB to personality factors and is now the fastest growing. It relies almost exclusively on amiable explanations of PB offered by PBers themselves.

Together, these trends in the study and treatment of PB share the same limitations. Their scholarship and empiricism are occasional; their evidence for lasting effectiveness of admonitions is even rarer. That overview also considered reasons why the field needs more examination of traditional explanations for PB such as perfectionism, low tolerance of frustration, irrational thinking, and low self-esteem. The field may need a more integrative, less amiable explanation, perhaps one as simple as equating PB with not knowing how to work (including not knowing how to turn knowledge into performance).

A SIMPLE PATTERN OF DEFICIENT SKILLS

In the fourth main step of the book, I proposed a simple pattern of deficient skills as typical for PBers:

• They put off things that make them uncomfortable, particularly when they are unsure about how to do them efficaciously. With delays come anxiety, embarrassment, and inflated definitions of success—all in the absence of knowing how to work in a process mode and how to use waiting times to prepare.

• Then, when there can be no more waiting, actions are impulsively rushed (often binged or else blocked) and failure is risked compared to more reflective, informed ways of working at tasks like writing.

• Finally, the more the exposure to this vicious cycle, the lower the self-esteem and inclination to find new ways of working, the higher the socially prescribed perfectionism and time pressures, the greater the tendency to struggle and block the next time. Test anxieties, dilatory self-care, and their kind may be little more than the result of not having learned the usually tacit skills of efficacy. In this view, efficacy is a teachable, learnable skill (even its first step, of wanting to change).

LITERATURE NOT USUALLY ASSOCIATED WITH PROCRASTINATION AND BLOCKING

To support this jump from tradition, I took a fifth step: I extended my review to literatures not usually associated with PB. There are, it turns out, psychologists already attending to the real costs of mindlessness and self-defeating behaviors (for example, students who fail because they lack tacit knowledge about how to thrive in school). And there are researchers observing the distinctive habits of high-achieving students (for example, they rehearse, plan, and summarize), of productive scholarly writers (they carry on several projects simultaneously), of intelligent students (for example, they master time allocation by, among other things, wasting little time on inappropriate responses), of relatively expert student writers (for example, they revise by working less locally), and of renowned experts (they practice and improve their skills regularly). Together, these and other looks at exemplary performance clarified PB by specifying its opposite—what efficacious (that is, efficient, confident, resilient) people do.

Another specification of efficacy came from my own, direct-observational studies of quick starters in professorial careers: these exemplars worked more productively, happily, and successfully. Why? Apparently the reason is that they were distinctive in demonstrating efficacious problem-solving styles (for example, customarily attributing disappointments in an EVS—external, variable, specific—pattern). Also exemplars learned to work in intrinsically rewarding and healthy ways.

GOOD EXAMPLES OF INTERVENTIONS

The sixth and toughest step in extending the usual coverage of PB lay in finding good examples of interventions. Sternberg's project for teaching the tacit knowledge of success in school may be the most usefully directive. He and his colleagues coached students in three kinds of management (self-management and task and social management) and demonstrated gains in skills such as study habits, information processing, and motivation. His conclusion is germane to PB: the usually tacit unmentioned ways of working that characterize intelligent students can be taught.

COMPONENTS OF EFFICACY

Toward the end, I drew out other information about the likely skills components of efficacy, here too from literature that makes no direct mention of PB. Time use is a learnable skill, one that promotes health and optimism; even the rhythms and pacing that make intense work more productive and less fatiguing can be taught. Learnable too are (1) mindfulness that reins in a consciousness otherwise given to petty thoughts and counterproductive worries; (2) process (as distinct from product) orientations that allow discovery and pleasure while working calmly, patiently, and productively; and (3) efficient styles of problem solving. Expertise and efficacy rely on playfulness and risk taking, even more on brief, regular, and deliberate practice, some of it under the tuteledge of a master teacher or therapist. These ways of non-PBing also demand a balance of emotions that avoids sustained excursions into extremes of mood such as depression or mania.

POSSIBLE LINKAGE TO MENTAL DISORDERS

Two extensions of PB to the clinical literature helped confirm the tentative sense, here, that PB may be linked to a variety of mental disorders. One extension was about binge eating, the precipitants of which match those of PBers in most ways (for example, overresponding to discomfort by narrowing attention away from broad and meaningful thought to focusing on the self, unrealistic thinking, and impulsive acts). The other extension was taken from personality disorders that seem to be founded on problems we might label as extreme PBing. (The avoidant type, for example, suffers from social inhibition, feelings of inadequacy, and hypersensitivity to negative evaluation.) From these established and interrelated portrayals of PB, I condensed the three-part, descriptive model (above) of how PB operates: (1) *compulsions and impulsivity* (with origins in self-imposed constraints, socially prescribed perfectionism, and impatience) employed to relieve tension; (2) *predisposed patterns*, once tending toward mindless self-absorption, to act irrationally, to gain short-term rewards including emotional control; and (3) *an aftermath of disappointment*, indecision, anger, unsociability, pessimism, and blocking. All three, in the view taken here, are largely problems of not knowing how to work and think and emote.

This model has some possible advantages. It helps define PB: impulsivity (and its inconstancy), mindlessness, and misattribution act together to hinder important, delayable actions. It also helps define its opposite, efficacy: patience (and its regular practice of essential skills), planning, and optimism combine to produce sufficient, timely, and on-target action. It suggests that prevention and treatment of PB need to encompass all three factors. And it shows why procrastination and blocking are inseparable (one usually precedes and overlaps with the other in those three steps).

CLOSE STUDY SLOW TO COME

Still, there is a reason why close study and proven interventions for PB may be slow in coming. The taboo against exposing the real nature and costs of PBing has been noted. So too has the resentment directed to those who intervene to help PBers become more efficient and efficacious. The power of this traditional taboo was illustrated in a review of the literature on medical noncompliance: Too many patients self-destructively procrastinate and block by not carrying out their prescribed schedules for medications and exercising. Too few physicians and social scientists take the problem seriously or bravely enough to address it with practical, widely applicable interventions. The costs of violating that taboo were depicted in the careers of four innovative psychologists (Adler, Janet, Taylor, and Skinner) who dared to intervene in common, everyday problems like PBing. These four, and others (including Albert Ellis discussed early in this book), were severely criticized, misrepresented, and even suppressed. The four were all well-intentioned pragmatists who saw PB as serious problems underlying a variety of wasteful, unhealthy behaviors. None of them, so far as I know, set up interventions for PBers in self-aggrandizing, Machiavellian ways. But all of them were made to pay a considerable price for breaking the taboo.

WHAT NEXT FOR PROCRASTINATION AND BLOCKING?

Finally, what next for PB, if we take a more optimistic stance? More exposure of its real mechanisms and costs may help advance its study and treatment. More systematic and sustained attempts to prevent and moderate PB should sort out the insights and strategies that help most. A willingness to link PB with established phenomena such as self-defeating behaviors will help lessen the mystery and embarrassment surrounding it. In any case, the climate of acceptance may be extended to the study of PB; the untabooed study of such allied concepts such as impulsivity and bingeing puts PB in a better position for discovery.

In the end other things may prove just as powerful in the acceptance of the study of and intervention in PB. It is, again, a real and often terrible problem, one we must face as we make progress in areas such as improving compliance with medical treatment (Anderson, Kiecolt-Glaser, & Glaser, 1994) and helping marginalized people succeed (Exum, 1983). So, we might best (like experts at revising their own writing) work with a wide and patient perspective. In the long view, of the sort I have tried to take here, we can see that good advice about ways of alleviating PB has been available for centuries, particularly at times before the taboo took so firm a hold. Consider this conclusion from a venerable economist who knew about efficacy:

The man who works so moderately as to be able to work constantly, not only preserves his health the longest, but in the course of the year, executes the greatest quantity of work (Adam Smith, *The Wealth of Nations*, 1776).

References

Ackroyd, P. (1990). *Dickens.* New York: HarperCollins.

Adler, A. (1898). *Gesundheitsbuch für das Schneidergewerbe.* Berlin: Carl Heymanns.

Adler, A. (1912). *Uber den nervosen charakter.* Weisbaden: J. P. Bergmann.

Adler, A. (1927). *Understanding human nature.* New York: World.

Ainslie, G. (1975). Specious reward: A behavioral theory of impulsiveness and impulse control. *Psychological Bulletin, 82,* 463–496.

Amabile, T. M. (1983). *The social psychology of creativity.* New York: Springer-Verlag.

Amar, J. (1919). *The physiology of industrial organizations.* New York: Macmillan.

American Psychiatric Association. (1994). *Diagnostic and statistical manual of mental disorders* (4th ed.). Washington, DC: American Psychiatric Association.

Anderson, B. L., Kiecolt-Glaser, J. K., & Glaser, R. (1994). A biobehavioral model of cancer stress and disease course. *American Psychologist, 49,* 389–404.

Andreasen, N. C. (1987). Creativity and mental illness: Prevalence rates in writers and their first-degree relatives. *American Journal of Psychiatry, 144,* 1288–1292.

Asimov, A. (1979). *In memory yet green.* New York: Avon, 1979.

Bandura, A. (1986). *Social foundations of thought and action.* Englewood Cliffs, NJ: Prentice-Hall.

Bandura, A. (1990). Conclusion: Reflections on nonability determinants of competence. In R. J. Sternberg & J. Kolligan (Eds.), *Competence considered* (pp. 315–362). New Haven: Yale University Press.

Banta, M. (1993). *Taylored lives.* Chicago: University of Chicago Press.

Barlow, D. H. (1993). Effectiveness of behavior treatment for panic disorder with and without agoraphobia. In B. E. Wolfe & J. D. Maser (Eds.), *Treatment of panic disorders* (pp. 105–120). Washington, DC: American Psychiatric Press.

Barrios, M. V., & Singer, J. L. (1981). The treatment of creative blocks: A comparison of waking imagery, hypnotic dream, and rational discussion techniques. *Imagination, Cognition, and Personality, 1,* 89–101.

Barron, F. (1963). *Creativity and mental health.* Princeton, NJ: Van Nostrand.

Barron, F. (1986). This week's citation classic. *Current Contents,* No. 14 (April 17), 16.

Baumeister, R. F. (1991). *Meanings of life.* New York: Guilford.

Baumeister, R. F., Heatherton, T. R., & Tice, D. M. (1994). *Losing control.* New York: Academic Press.

Baumeister, R. F., & Scher, S. J. (1988). Self-defeating behavior patterns among normal individuals: Review and analysis of common self-destructive tendencies. *Psychological Bulletin, 104,* 3–22.

Bazargan, M., Barbre, A. R., & Hamm, V. (1993). Failure to have prescriptions filled among Black elderly. *Journal of Aging and Health,* 5(2), 264–282.

Bergler, E. (1950). *The writer and psychoanalysis.* Garden City, NY: Doubleday.

Beswick, G., Rothblum, E. D., & Mann, L. (1988). Psychological antecedents of student procrastination. *Australian Psychologist, 22,* 207–217.

Bird, C. (1983). Time: How not to put it off. *Working Woman,* May, pp. 61–62.

Birner, L. (1993). Procrastination: Its role in transference and countertransference. *Psychoanalytic Review, 80,* 541–558.

Blakeslee, S. (1994). Program to cut risks of diabetes surprisingly fails to lure patients. *New York Times,* Feb. 28, pp. A1 & B2.

Block, L. (1984). Fear of writing. *Writer's Digest,* August, pp. 52–54.

Bluedorn, A. C., Kaufman, C. F., & Lane, P. M. (1992). How many things do you like to do at once? An introduction to monochronic and polychronic time. *Academy of Management Executive, 6,* 17–26.

Boardway, R., Delamater, A. M., & Tomakowsky, J. G. (1993). Stress management training for adolescents with diabetes. *Journal of Pediatric Psychology, 18,* 29–45.

Boice, R. (1982). Increasing the productivity of blocked academicians. *Behaviour Research and Therapy, 20*, 197–207.

Boice, R. (1983a). Contingency management in writing and the appearance of creative ideas. *Behaviour Research and Therapy, 21*, 537–534.

Boice, R. (1983b). Experimental and clinical treatments of writing blocks. *Journal of Consulting and Clinical Psychology, 21*, 183–191.

Boice, R. (1983c). Observational skills. *Psychological Bulletin, 93*, 3–29.

Boice, R. (1985a). Cognitive components of blocking. *Written Communication, 2*, 91–104.

Boice, R. (1985b). Psychotherapies for writing blocks. In M. Rose (Ed.), *When a writer can't write* (pp. 182–218). New York: Guilford.

Boice, R. (1987). Is released time an effective device for faculty development? *Research in Higher Education, 26*, 311–326.

Boice, R. (1989). Procrastination, busyness, and bingeing. *Behaviour Research and Therapy, 27*, 605–611.

Boice, R. (1991). Quick starters. *New Directions for Teaching and Learning, 48*, 111–121.

Boice, R. (1992a). Combined treatments for writing blocks. *Behaviour Research and Therapy, 30*, 107–116.

Boice, R. (1992b). *The new faculty member.* San Francisco: Jossey-Bass.

Boice, R. (1993a). New faculty involvement of women and minorities. *Research in Higher Education, 34*, 291–341.

Boice, R. (1993b). Primal origins and later correctives for midcareer disillusionment. *New Directions for Teaching and Learning, 55*, 33–41.

Boice, R. (1993c). Writing blocks and tacit knowledge. *Journal of Higher Education, 64*, 19–54.

Boice, R. (1994). *How writers journey to comfort and fluency: A psychological adventure.* Westport, CT: Praeger.

Boice, R. (1995a). Developing teaching, then writing amongst new faculty. *Research in Higher Education, 36*, 415–456.

Boice, R. (1995b). Writerly rules for teachers. *Journal of Higher Education, 66*, 32–60.

Boice, R. (1996a). Bingeing and procrastination/blocking. Manuscript submitted for publication.

Boice, R. (1996b). Classroom immediacies improve college teaching. Manuscript submitted for publication.

Boice, R. (1996c). Classroom incivilities. *Research in Higher Education, 37*, 453–486.

Boice, R. (1996d). *First-order principles for college teachers.* Bolton, MA: Anker Press.

Boice, R. (1996e). What discourages research-practitioners in faculty development. In J. C. Smart (Ed.), *Higher education: Handbook of theory and research* (in press). New York: Agathon Press.

Boice, R., & Myers, P. E. (1986). Two parallel traditions: Automatic writing and free writing. *Written Communication, 3,* 471–490.

Boles, R. N. (1985). The pain of time. *Newsletter about Life/Work Planning,* No. 1, 1–4.

Bond, M. J, & Feather, N. T. (1988). Some coordinates of structure and purpose in the use of time. *Journal of Personality and Social Psychology, 55,* 321–329.

Borne, L. (1858). *Gesmmelte Schriften.* Milwaukee, WI: Bickler, 1858.

Boudin, H. M. (1972). Contingency contracting as a therapeutic tool in the deceleration of amphetamine use. *Behavior Therapy, 3,* 604–608.

Bowers, P. (1979). Hypnosis and creativity: The search for the missing link. *Journal of Abnormal Psychology, 88,* 564–572.

Boyle, P. (1995). *Socialization experiences of new graduate students.* Ph.D. diss., SUNY at Stony Brook.

Brand, A. G. (1986). *The psychology of writing: The affective experience.* Westport, CT: Greenwood.

Brande, D. (1934). *Becoming a writer.* New York: Harcourt, Brace.

Britton, B. K., & Tesser, A. (1991). Effects of time-management practices on college grades. *Journal of Educational Psychology, 83,* 405–410.

Brown, R. (1981). This week's citation classic. *Current Contents, 13,* (7), 16.

Bruner, J. (1990). *Acts of meaning.* Cambridge: Harvard University Press.

Buehler, R., Griffin, D., & Ross, M. (1994). Exploring the planning fallacy: Why people underestimate their task completion times. *Journal of Personality and Social Psychology, 67,* 366–381.

Burgar, P. (1994). Enforcing academic rules in higher education: A total quality management program. *Research in Higher Education, 38,* 43–53.

Burka, J. B., & Yuen, L. M. (1983). *Procrastination.* Reading, MA: Addison-Wesley.

Carey, S. (1986). Cognitive science and science education. *American Psychologist, 41,* 1123–1130.

Carney, R. M., Freedland, K. E., Eisen, S. A., & Rich, M. W., et al. (1995). Major depression and medication adherence in elderly patients with coronary artery disease. *Health Psychology, 14,* 88–90.

Clayton, B. E. & Efron, N. (1994). Noncompliance in general health care. *Ophthalmic & Physiological Optics, 14,* 257–264.

Cleary, T. (1993). *The essential Tao.* New York: HarperCollins.

Copely, F. B. (1969). *Frederick W. Taylor.* New York: Augustus M. Kelley.

Covey, S. R. (1989). *The seven habits of highly effective people.* New York: Simon & Schuster.

Csikszentmihalyi, M. (1990). *Flow: The psychology of optimal experience.* New York: Harper & Row.

Daly, J. A. (1985). Writing apprehension. In M. Rose (Ed.), *When a writer can't write* (pp. 43–82). New York: Guilford.

Daly, J., & Miller, M. D. (1975). The empirical development of an instrument to measure writing apprehension. *Research in the Teaching of English, 9,* 242–249.

Didion, J. (1981). *Slouching towards Bethlehem.* New York: Washington Square Press.

Dillon, M. J., Kent, H. M., & Malott, R. W. (1980). A supervisory system for accomplishing long-term projects. *Journal of Organizational Behavior Management, 2,* 213–237.

Domash, L. (1976). The therapeutic use of writing in the service of the ego. *Journal of the American Academy of Psychoanalysis, 4,* 261–269.

Downey, J. E. (1918). A program for a psychology of literature. *Journal of Applied Psychology, 2,* 366–377.

Durant, W. (1954). *Our Oriental heritage.* New York: Simon & Schuster.

Dweck, C. (1986). Motivational processes affecting learning. *American Psychologist, 41,* 1040–1048.

Eisenberger, R. (1992). Learned industriousness. *Psychological Review, 99,* 248–267.

Elbow, P. (1973). *Writing without teachers.* New York: Oxford University Press.

Ellenberger, H. (1970). *The discovery of the unconscious.* New York: Basic Books.

Ellis, A., & Knaus, W. J. (1977). *Overcoming procrastination.* New York: Institute for Rational Living.

Emerson, J., Pankratz, L., Joos, S., & Smith, S. (1994). Personality disorders in problematic medical patients. *Psychosomatics, 35,* 469–473.

Epel, N. (1993). *Writers dreaming.* New York: Carol Southern Books.

Erickson, M. H. (1937). The experimental demonstration of unconscious mentation by automatic writing. *Psychoanalytic Quarterly, 6,* 513–529.

Ericsson, K. A., & Charness, N. (1994). Expert performance: Its structure and acquisition. *American Psychologist, 49,* 725–747.

Erikson, E. H., & Kubie, L. S. (1940). The translation of the cryptic automatic writing of one hypnotic subject by another in a trance-like dissociated state. *Psychoanalytic Quarterly, 9,* 51–63.

Exum, W. M. (1983). Climbing the crystal stair: Values, affirmative action, and minority faculty. *Social Problems, 30,* 301–324.

Feldman, K. A. (1987). Research productivity and scholarly productivity of college teachers as related to their instructional effectiveness. *Research in Higher Education, 26,* 227–298.

Ferrari, J. R. (1991a). Compulsive procrastination: Some self-reported characteristics. *Psychological Reports, 68,* 455–458.

Ferrari, J. R. (1991b). Self-handicapping by procrastinators: Protecting self-esteem, social-esteem, or both? *Journal of Personality, 25,* 245–261.

Ferrari, J. R. (1991c). A preference for a favorable public impression by procrastinators. *Personality and Individual Differences, 12,* 1233–1237.

Ferrari, J. R. (1991d). Procrastination and project creation. *Journal of Social Behavior and Personality, 6,* 619–628.

Ferrari, J. R. (1992a). Procrastination and perfect behavior. *Journal of Research on Personality, 26,* 75–84.

Ferrari, J. R. (1992b). Procrastination in the workplace. *Personality and Individual Differences, 13,* 315–319.

Ferrari, J. R. (1993). Christmas and procrastination: Explaining lack of diligence at a "real-world" task deadline. *Personality and Individual Differences, 14,* 25–33.

Ferrari, J. R., Johnson, J. L., & McCown, W. (1995). *Procrastination and task avoidance.* New York: Plenum Press.

Ferrari, J. R., & Olivette, M. J. (1994). Parental authority and the development of female dysfunctional procrastination. *Journal of Research in Personality, 28,* 87–100.

Ferrari, J. R., Parker, J. T., & Ware, C. B. (1992). Academic procrastination: Personality correlates with Myers-Briggs types, self-efficacy, and academic locus of control. *Journal of Behavior and Personality, 7,* 495–502.

Field, J. [1936] (1981). *A life of one's own.* Los Angeles: J. P. Tarcher.

Finney, J. W., Hook, R. J., Friman, P. C., Rapoff, M. A., et al. (1993). The overestimation of adherence to pediatric medical regimens. *Children's Health Care, 22,* 297–304.

Flett, G. L., Blankenstein, K. R., Hewitt, P. L., & Koledin, S. (1992). Components of perfectionism and procrastination in college students. *Journal of Social Behavior and Personality, 20,* 85–94.

Flower, L. (1990). The role of task representation in reading-to-write. In L. Flower, V. Stein, J. Ackerman, M. J. Kantz, K. McCormick, & W. C. Peck. (Eds.), *Reading-to-write* (pp. 35–75). New York: Oxford University Press.

Flower, L. S., & Hayes, J. R. (1980). The cognition of discovery: Defining a rhetorical problem. *College Composition and Communication, 31,* 21–32.

Fox, M. F. (1985). Publication, performance, and reward in science and scholarship. In J. C. Smart (Ed.), *Higher Education: Handbook of theory and research,* vol. 1 (pp. 255–282). New York: Agathon Press.

Frese, M., Stewart, J., & Hannover, B. (1987). Goal orientation and planfulness: Action styles as personality concepts. *Journal of Personality and Social Psychology, 52,* 1182–1194.

Freud, S. (1900). *The interpretation of dreams.* (A. A. Brill, Trans.). New York: Macmillan.

Gardiner, N. H. (1908). The automatic writing of Mrs. Holland. *Journal of the American Society for Psychical Research, 2,* 595–626.

Gardner, H. (1993). *Creating minds.* New York: Basic Books.

George, J. M. (1991). Time-structure and purpose as a mediator of work-life linkages. *Journal of Applied Social Psychology, 21,* 296–314.

Glass, C. R., & Arnkoff, D. B. (1986). Think cognitively: Selected issues in cognitive assessment and therapy. *Advances in Cognitive Behavioral Research, 1,* 35–71.

Glendinning, V. (1993). *Anthony Trollope.* New York: A. A. Knopf.

Goodman, P. (1952). On writer's block. *Complex, 7,* 42–50.

Gurney, A. R. (1977). *Entertaining strangers.* Garden City, NY: Doubleday.

Hall, B. L., & Hursch, D. E. (1982). An evaluation of the effects of a time management program on work efficiency. *Journal of Organizational Behavior Management, 3,* 73–86.

Hamada, R. (1986). In defense of procrastination. *University Magazine, 8*(1), 28–29.

Hamilton, G. A., Roberts, S., Johnson, J. M., Tropp, J. R., et al. (1993). *Health Values: The Journal of Health Behavior, Education and Promotion, 17,* 3–11.

Harriman, P. L. (1951). Automatic writing as a means for investigating experimentally induced conflicts. *Personality, 1,* 264–271.

Hayes, J. R (1988). Comment in J. A. Langer (Ed.), Research on written communication: A response to Hillock's report. *Research in the Teaching of English, 22*, 89–111.

Hayes, J. R., & Flower, L. S. (1986). Writing research and the writer. *American Psychologist, 41*, 1106–1113.

Heatherton, T. F., & Baumeister, R. F. (1991). Binge eating as escape from self-awareness. *Psychological Bulletin, 110*, 86–108.

Hilgard, E. R. (1977). *Divided consciousness: Multiple controls in human thought and action.* New York: Wiley, 1977.

Hill, C. E., & Corbett, M. M. (1993). A perspective on the history of process and outcome research in counseling psychology. *Journal of Counseling Psychology, 40*, 3–24.

Holden, C. (1987). Creativity and the troubled mind. *Psychology Today, 21* (4), 9–10.

Holtzman, P. S. (1962). On procrastinating. *International Journal of Psychoanalysis, 45*, 98–109.

Ingram, R. (1990). Self-focused attention in clinical disorders: Review and conceptual model. *Psychological Bulletin, 107*, 156–176.

Jahoda, M. (1981). Work, employment, and unemployment. *American Psychologist, 36*, 184–191.

James, W. (1885–89). Notes on automatic writing. *Proceedings of the Society for Psychical Research, 1*, 548–563.

Jamison, K. R. (1993). *Touched with fire.* New York: Free Press.

Janet, P. (1889). *L'Automatisme psychologique.* Paris: Alcan.

Janet, P. (1930). Pierre Janet. In C. Murchison (Ed.), *History of Psychology in autobiography* (pp. 123–133). Worcester, MA: Clark University Press.

Jasen, D. A. (1981). *P. G. Wodehouse: A portrait of a master.* New York: Continuum.

Jensen, G. H., & DiTiberio, J. K. (1984). Personality and individual writing processes. *College Composition and Communication, 35*, 285–300.

Jones, A. C. (1975). Grandiosity blocks writing projects. *Transactional Analysis Journal, 5* (4), 415.

Kayloe, J. C. (1993). Food addiction. *Psychotherapy, 30*, 269–275.

Kearney, P., and Plax, T. G. (1992). Student resistance to control. In V. P. Richmond, and J. C. McCroskey (Eds.), *Power in the classroom.* (pp. 85–99). Hillsdale, NJ: Erlbaum.

Kellogg, R. T. (1994). *The psychology of writing.* New York: Oxford.

Kimble, G. A. (1979). *A department chairperson's survival manual.* New York: Wiley.

Kipnis, D. (1994). Accounting for the use of behavior technologies in social psychology. *American Psychologist, 49*, 165–172.

Koeske, G. F., Kirk, S. A., & Koeske, R. D. (1993). Coping with job stress: Which strategies work best? *Journal of Occupational and Organizational Psychology, 66,* 319–335.

Kohn, A. (1988). Madness of creativity. *Los Angeles Times,* Dec. 12, Pt. II, p. 3.

Kraus, S. J. (1993). A new look at new faculty members. *Contemporary Psychology, 38,* 543–544.

Kronsky, B. J. (1979). Freeing the creative process: The relevance of Gestalt. *Art Psychotherapy, 6,* 233–240.

Kubie, L. S. (1965). Blocks to creativity. *International Science and Creativity, 22,* 69–78.

Lakein, A. (1974). *How to get control of your time and your life.* New York: Signet.

Landino, R. A., & Owen, S. V. (1988). Self-efficacy in university faculty. *Journal of Vocational Behavior, 33,* 1–14.

Landy, F. J., Rastegary, H., Thayer, J., & Colvin, C. (1991). Time urgency: The construct and its measurement. *Journal of Applied Psychology, 76,* 644–657.

Langer, E. J. (1989). *Mindfulness.* Reading, MA: Addison-Wesley.

Langer, E. J., & Park, K. (1990). Incompetence: A conceptual reconsideration. In R. J. Sternberg & J. Kolligan (Eds.), *Competence considered* (pp. 149–166). New Haven: Yale University Press.

Lauver, D., & Ho, C. H. (1993). Explaining delay in care seeking for breast cancer symptoms. *Journal of Applied Psychology, 23,* 1806–1825.

Lay, C. H. (1986). At last, my research article on procrastination. *Journal of Research on Personality, 20,* 474–495.

Lay, C. H. (1988). The relationship of procrastination and optimism to judgments of time to complete an essay and anticipation of setbacks. *Journal of Social Behavior and Personality, 3,* 201–214.

Lay, C. H. (1989). An assessment of appraisal, anxiety, coping, and procrastination during an examination period. *European Journal of Personality, 3,* 195–208.

Lay, C. H. (1990). Working to schedule on personal projects: An assessment of person-project characteristics and trait procrastination. *Journal of Social Behavior and Personality, 5,* 91–103.

Lay, C. H. (1992). Trait procrastination and the perception of person-task characteristics. *Journal of Social Behavior and Personality, 7,* 483–494.

Lay, C. H., & Burns, P. (1991). Intentions and behavior in studying for an examination. *Journal of Social Behavior and Personality, 6,* 605–617.

Lay, C. H., Knish, S., & Zanatta, R. (1992). Self-handicappers and procrastinators: A comparison of their practice behavior prior to evaluation. *Journal of Research in Personality, 26*, 242–257.

Lay, C., & Schouwenburg, H. C. (1993). Trait procrastination, time management, and academic behavior. *Journal of Social Behavior and Personality, 8*, 647–662.

Leader, Z. (1991). *Writer's block.* Baltimore: Johns Hopkins University Press.

Lepper, M. (1988). Motivational considerations in the study of instruction. *Cognition and Instruction, 5*, 289–309.

Locke, E. A., & Latham, G. P. (1990). Work motivation and satisfaction: Light at the end of the tunnel. *Psychological Science, 1*, 240–246.

Logue, A. W. (1994). *Self-control.* Englewood-Cliffs, NJ: Prentice-Hall.

Lombard, D. N., Lombard, T. N., & Winett, R. A. (1995). Walking to meet health guidelines: The effect of prompting frequency and prompt structure. *Health Psychology, 14*, 164–170.

London, M. (1993). Relationships between career motivation, empowerment, and support for career development. *Journal of Occupational Development, 66*, 55–69.

Ludwig, A. M. (1992). Creative achievement and psychopathology: Comparisons among professions. *American Journal of Psychotherapy, 46*, 330–356.

Macan, T. H., Shahani, C., Dipboye, R. L., & Phillips, A. M. (1990). *Journal of Educational Psychology, 82*, 760–768.

Mack, K., & Skjei, E. (1979). *Overcoming writing blocks.* Los Angeles: J. P. Tarcher.

Martin, L. J. (1917). An experimental study of the subconscious. In J. E. Coover (Ed.), *Experiments in psychical research* (pp. 422–438). Stanford: Stanford University Press.

Mawhinney, H., Spector, S. L., Heitjan, D., Kinsman, R. A., et al. (1993). As-needed medication use in asthma usage patterns and patient characteristics. *Journal of Asthma, 30*, 61–71.

McCann, J. T. (1988). Passive-aggressive personality disorder: A review. *Journal of Personality Disorders, 2*, 170–179.

McCaul, K. D., Glasgow, R. E., & O'Neill, H. K. (1992). The problem of creating habits: Establishing health-protective dental behaviors. *Health Psychology, 11*, 101–111.

McCown, W. (1995). The relationship between venturesomeness, impulsivity, and procrastination in college students and adults. Radnor, PA: *Integral/Apogee Research Paper No. 95–08.*

McCown, W., & Ferrari, J. R. (1995). A meta-analysis of treatments for procrastination in high school and college students and adults. Unpublished manuscript, Northeast Louisiana University.

McCown, W., & Johnson, J. (1989a). Validation of an adult inventory of procrastination. Paper presented at the Society for Personality Assessment, New York.

McCown, W., & Johnson, J. (1989b). Differential arousal gradients in chronic procrastination. Paper presented at the American Psychological Society, Alexandria, VA.

McCown, W., & Johnson, J. (1991). Personality and chronic procrastination by university students during an academic examination period. *Personality and Individual Differences, 12*, 413–415.

McCown, W., Johnson, J., & Petzel, T. (1989). Procrastination: Principal components analysis. *Personality and Individual Differences, 10*, 197–202.

McCown, W., Petzel, T., & Rupert, P. (1987). Personality correlates and behaviors of chronic procrastinators. *Personality and Individual Differences, 11*, 71–79.

McGaughey, R. A. (1993). But can they teach? In praise of college teachers who publish. *Teachers College Record, 95*, 242–257.

Meichenbaum, D. (1985). Teaching thinking: A cognitive-behavioral perspective. In S. F. Chipman & J. W. Segal (Eds.), *Thinking and learning skills*, vol. 2 (pp. 407–426). Hillsdale, NJ: Erlbaum.

Meichenbaum, D. (1993). Changing conceptions of cognitive behavior modification: Retrospect and prospect. *Journal of Consulting and Clinical Psychology, 61*, 202–204.

Meier, S., McCarthy, P. R., & Schmeck, R. R. (1984). Validity of self-efficacy as a predictor of writing performance. *Cognitive Therapy and Research, 8*, 107–120.

Meyers, J. (1991). *Joseph Conrad*. New York: Charles Scribner's Sons.

Milgram, N. (1988). Procrastination in daily living. *Psychological Reports, 63*, 752–754.

Milgram, N., Batori, G., & Mowrer, D. (1993). Correlates of academic procrastination. *Journal of School Psychology, 31*, 487–500.

Milgram, N., Srolof, B., & Rosenbaum, M. (1988). The procrastination of everyday life. *Journal of Research in Personality, 22*, 197–212.

Millon, T. (1981). *Disorders of personality*. New York: Wiley.

Mills, C. W. (1959). *The sociological imagination*. New York: Grove Press.

Minninger, J. (1980). *Free yourself to write*. San Francisco: Workshops for Innovative Teaching.

Murray, D. M. (1978). Write before writing. *College Composition and Communication, 29*, 375–381.

Murray, D. M. (1995). *The craft of revision*. New York: Harcourt Brace.

Nelson, B. (1988). Deep-seated causes found for tendency to delay. *New York Times*, April 12, pp. C3 & C8.

Nelson, D. (1980). *Frederick W. Taylor and the rise of scientific management*. Madison: University of Wisconsin Press.

Nixon, H. K. (1928). *Psychology for the writer*. New York: Harper, 1928.

Nurnberger, J. T., & Zimmerman, J. (1970). Applied analysis of human behavior. *Behavior Therapy, 1,* 59–60.

Oatley, K., & Jenkins, J. M. (1992). Human emotions: Function and dysfunction. *Annual Review of Psychology, 43,* 55–85.

Ochse, R. (1990). *Before the gates of excellence*. New York: Cambridge University Press.

Parini, J. (1989). The more they write, the more they write. *New York Times Book Review*, July 30, pp. 10 & 24–25.

Pascarella, E. T., & Terenzini, P. (1991). *How college affects students*. San Francisco: Jossey-Bass.

Pear, J. J. (1977). Self-control techniques of famous novelists. *Journal of Applied Behavior Analysis, 10,* 515–525.

Perkins, D. N. (1981). *The mind's best work*. Cambridge: Harvard University Press.

Perl, S. (1978). *Five writers writing: Case studies of the composing processes of unskilled college writers*. Ph.D. diss., New York University.

Peterson, K. E. (1987). *Relationships among measures of writer's block, writing anxiety, and procrastination*. Ph.D. diss., Ohio State University.

Plax, T. G., and Kearney, P. K. (1992). Teacher power in the classroom. In V. P. Richmond, and J. C. McCroskey (Eds.), *Power in the classroom* (pp. 67–84). Hillsdale, NJ: Erlbaum.

Procrastinators' predictions for the 70s on target. (1980). *New York Times,* Jan. 1, p. 26.

Pronzoni, B., & Malzberg, B. (1979). Prose bowl. *Fantasy & Science Fiction, 57,* 135–156.

Quaytman, W. (1969). Psychotherapist's writing block. *Voices, 4* (14), 13–17.

Rabinbach, A. (1990). *The human motor*. New York: Basic Books.

Rachlin, H. (1995). Self-control: Beyond commitment. *Behavioral and Brain Sciences, 18,* 100–159.

Reddy, M. J. (1993). The language metaphor: A case of frame conflict in our language about language. In A. Ortony (Ed.), *Thought and metaphor* (pp. 164–201). New York: Cambridge University Press.

Rheingold, H. L. (1994). *The psychologist's guide to an academic career*. Washington, DC: American Psychological Association.

Ribot, T. (1906). *Essay on the creative imagination*. Chicago: Open Court.

Rose, M. (1980). Rigid rules, inflexible plans, and the stifling of language: A cognitive analysis of writer's block. *College Composition and Communication, 31,* 389–401.

Rosenbaum, M. (1980). A schedule for assessing self-control behaviors. *Behavior Therapy, 11,* 109–121.

Rosenberg, H., & Lah, M. I. (1982). A comprehensive behavioral-cognitive treatment of writer's block. *Behavioural Psychotherapy, 10,* 356–363.

Ross, E. I. (1985). *How to write while you sleep.* Cincinnati: Writer's Digest Books.

Rothblum, E. D. (1990). The fear of failure: The psychodynamic, need achievement, fear of success, and procrastination models. In H. Leitenberg (Ed.), *Handbook of social and evaluation anxiety* (pp. 387–394). New York: Plenum.

Rothblum, E. D., Solomon, L. J., & Murakami, J. (1986). Affective, cognitive, and behavioral differences between high and low procrastinators. *Journal of Counseling Psychology, 33,* 387–394.

Rothenberg, A. (1990). *Creativity and madness.* Baltimore: Johns Hopkins University Press.

Royce, J. (1898). The psychology of invention. *Psychological Review, 5,* 113–114.

Salovey, P., & Haar, M. D. (1990). The efficacy of cognitive-behavior therapy and writing process training for alleviating writing anxiety. *Cognitive Therapy and Research, 14,* 515–528.

Schneidman, E. S. (1984). Personality and "success" among a selected group of lawyers. *Journal of Personality Assessment, 48,* 609–616.

Schouwenberg, H. C. (1992). Procrastinators and fear of failure: An exploration of reasons for procrastination. *European Journal of Personality, 6,* 225–256.

Schrier, M. F., & Carver, S. C. (1992). Effects of optimism on psychological and physical well-being: Theoretical overview and empirical update. *Cognitive Therapy and Research, 16,* 201–228.

Schuman, E. P. (1981). Writing block treated with modern psychoanalytic interventions. *Psychoanalytic Review, 68,* 113–134.

Seligman, M. E. P. (1991). *Learned optimism.* New York: A. A. Knopf.

Silver, R. C., Wortman, C. B., & Crofton, C. (in press). The role of coping in support provision: The self-presentational dilemma of victims of life crises. In I. G. Sarason, B. R. Sarason, & G. R. Pierce (Eds.), *Social support: An interactional view.* New York: Wiley.

Silverman, S., & Lay, C. (in press). The relations of agitation and dejection to trait procrastination and dilatory behavior over an academic exam period.

Simonton, D. K. (1988). *Scientific genius.* New York: Cambridge University Press.

Simonton, D. K. (1994). *Greatness.* New York: Guilford.

Singer, J. L. (1988). Sampling ongoing unconsciousness and emotional implications for health. In M. J. Horowitz (Ed.), *Psychodynamics and cognition* (pp. 297–348). Chicago: University of Chicago Press.

Skinner, B. F. (1971). *Beyond freedom and dignity.* New York: A. A. Knopf.

Skinner, B. F. (1976). *Particulars of my life.* New York: A. A. Knopf.

Skinner, B. F. (1979a). My experiences with the baby-tender. *Psychology Today, 12* (10), 29–40.

Skinner, B. F. (1979b). *The shaping of a behaviorist.* New York: A. A. Knopf.

Skinner, B. F. (1981). How to discover what you have to say—a talk to students. *Behavior analyst, 4,* 1–7.

Skinner, B. F. (1983). *A matter of consequences.* New York: A. A. Knopf.

Smith, A. (1776). *The wealth of nations.* Oxford: Clarendon Press.

Snyder, C. R., & Higgins, R. L. (1988). Excuses: Their effective role in the negotiation of reality. *Psychological Bulletin, 104,* 23–35.

Solomon, L. J., & Rothblum, E. D. (1984). Academic procrastination: Frequency and cognitive-behavioral correlates. *Journal of Counseling Psychology, 31,* 503–509.

Solomon, L. J., & Rothblum, E. D. (1988). Procrastination Assessment Scale—Students. In M. Hersen & A. S. Bellak (Eds.), *Dictionary of behavioral assessment techniques* (pp. 358–360). New York: Pergamon Press.

Solomon, R., & Solomon, J. (1993). *Up the university: Re-creating higher education in America.* Reading, MA: Addison-Wesley.

Solomons, L. M., & Stein, G. (1896). Normal motor automatism. *Psychological Review, 3,* 492–512.

Stack, R. (1980). Writing as conversation. *Visible Language, 14,* 376–382.

Sternberg, R. J. (1985). *Beyond IQ: A triarchic theory of human intelligence.* New York: Cambridge University Press.

Sternberg, R. J. (1988). *The triarchic mind: A new theory of human intelligence.* New York: Penguin.

Sternberg, R. J. (1990). Prototypes of competence and incompetence. In R. J. Sternberg & J. Kolligan (Eds.), *Competence considered* (pp. 117–145). New Haven: Yale University Press.

Sternberg, R. J., & Lubart, T. I. (1991). An investment theory of creativity and its development. *Human Development, 34,* 1–31.

Sternberg, R. J., Okagaki, L., & Jackson, A. S. (1990). Practical intelligence for success in school. *Educational Leadership, 42,* 35–39.

Stine, J. J. (1994). Psychosocial and psychodynamic issues affecting non-compliance with psychostimulant treatment. *Journal of Child and Adolescent Psychopharmacology, 4*, 75–86.

Stone, G. C. (1979). Patient compliance and the role of the expert. *Journal of Social Issues, 35*, 34–59.

Streigel-Moore, R. H., Silberstein, L. R., & Rodin, J. (1993). The social self in bulimia nervosa: Public self-consciousness, social anxiety, and perceived fraudulence. *Journal of Abnormal Psychology, 102*, 297–303.

Taal, E., Rasker, J. J., Seydel, E. R., & Wiegman, O. (1993). Health status, adherence with health recommendations, self-efficacy, and social support in patients with rheumatoid arthritis. Special Issue: Psychosocial aspects of rheumatic diseases. *Patient Education and Counseling, 20*, 63–76.

Theroux, P. (1980). *The old Patagonian express.* New York: Pocket Books.

Tobias, S. (1990). *They're not dumb, they're different.* Tucson, AZ: Research Corporation.

Tooth, L., McKenna, K., Colquhoun, D. (1993). Prediction of compliance with a post-myocardial infraction home-based walking programme. *Australian Occupational Therapy Journal, 40*, 17–22.

Tremmel, R. (1989). Investigating productivity and other factors in the writer's practice. *Freshman English News, 17*, 19–25.

Tremmel, R. (1993). Zen and the art of reflective practice in teacher education. *Harvard Educational Review, 63*, 434–468.

Trollope, A. (1929). *An autobiography.* New York: Houghton Mifflin.

Turkington, C. (1983). Therapists must dodge procrastinator's traps. *APA Monitor*, Dec., p. 21.

Upper, D. (1974). An unsuccessful self-treatment of "writer's block." *Journal of Applied Behavior Analysis, 7*, 497.

Viinamaki, H., Niskanen, L., Korhonen, T., Tahka, V. (1993). The patient-doctor relationship and metabolic control in patients with Type 1 (insulin-dependent) diabetus mellitus. *International Journal of Psychiatry in Medicine, 23*, 265–274.

Wagner, R. K., & Sternberg, R. J. (1986). Tacit knowledge and intelligence in the everyday world. In R. J. Sternberg & R. K. Wagner (Eds.), *Practical intelligence: Nature and origin of competence in the everyday world.* New York: Cambridge University Press.

Weimer, M., & Lenze, L. F. (1991). Instructional interventions: A review of the literature on efforts to improve instruction. In J. C. Smart (Ed.), *Higher Education: Handbook of theory and research* (pp. 294–333). New York: Agathon.

Wesp, R. (1986). Reducing procrastination through required course involvement. *Teaching of Psychology, 13*, 128–130.

Wessman, A. E. (1993). Personality and the subjective experience of time. *Journal of Personality Assessment, 37*, 103–114.

Wiggers, T. T. (1984). Dealing with the manana syndrome. Paper presented at the American Psychological Association, Toronto.

Williams, J. D. (1985). Covert language behavior during writing. *Research in the Teaching of English, 17*, 301–312.

Wilson, E. O. (1994). *Naturalist*. Washington, DC: Island Press.

Wilson, M. G., & Edmunson, J. (1993). Health values. *Journal of Health Behavior, Education, and Promotion, 17*, 10–20.

Wratcher, M. A. (1988). Facilitating a time management workshop for adult learners. Paper presented at the American College Personnel Association, Phoenix.

Zimmerman, B. J. (1986). Development of a structured interview for assessing student use of self-regulated learning strategies. *American Educational Research Journal, 23*, 614–628.

Zoellner, R. (1969). Talk-write: A behavioral pedagogy for composition. *College English, 30*, 267–320.

Index

Active waiting, 7
Adler, Alfred, 157–160
Anti-interventionism, 9
Anti-compulsivity, 9
Anxiety, 61
Art versus science, 50
Automaticity, 18–22, 56, 86, 134
Autonomy, 53
Avoidance, 38

Baumeister, Roy, *x, xii, xxxvi*, 25,
  44, 47, 48, 70, 71, 83, 93, 114,
  117, 128, 133–135, 148
Behavioral patterns, 71
Behaviorism, *xxiii, xxiv*, 23–26, 41,
  48, 63, 71, 113, 147
Bergler, Edmund, 15–16, 40
Bingeing, 65–69, 117–119, 124–125
Blocking: basic components of,
  122–126; costs of, 47–74; defined, *xii, xix–xx*, 61; and
  fatigue, 7; model of, 139–144;
  parallels to other maladaptive
  behaviors, 93–115; as a taboo

topic, *xiii–xv*. *See also* Procrasti-
  nation
Boyle, Peg, 72
Brande, D., 21
Breaking tasks into small bits of
  work, 39
Burgar, P., 82–83
Burka, Jane, 40
Busyness, *xix,* 2, 60–61, 86, 96

Charting progress, 69
Coaching procrastinators, 104–110
Cognitive therapies, 28, 42, 79,
  84–86
Communication, *xxi*
Confidence, 97
Conrad, J., 126–127
Control, 13
Creative madness, 3, 119–127
Creativity, *xxvii,* 120
Csikszentmihalyi, M., 48, 88, 96

Deadlines, 10, 51, 71, 82
Defensiveness, 52
Denial, 4

McCown, William, 32, 44
MBTI (Myers-Briggs Type Indicator), 29
Medical noncompliance, 146–152
Mental health, 119–137, 179–180
Mentoring, 80
Methodological problems with research, 34–35
Milgram, Norman, 31–32
Mindlessness, 8, 131, 140, 149, 183
Moderation, 8, 74, 142
Moral weakness, 37, 49
Murray, Donald, 7, 98
Myths about PB, 47

Nixon, H.K., 24
Nonadherence. *See* Medical noncompliance

Objectivism, 23, 47. *See also* Behaviorism
Observation of procrastination. *See* Direct observation

Patience, 79, 139
PB. *See* Procrastination; Blocking
Perkins, David, 25, 58, 94, 114
Personality disorders and PB, 128, 136
Personality research, 30–38, 41–42, 44–45, 131–132
Personality traits, 37, 44, 62
Pessimism, 140
Phobias, 33
Pressures, 12
Priorities, 26, 62
Problem-solving, 22, 53, 113–115
Procrastination: basic components of, 128–136; costs of, *xiii, xx, xxii, xxvii*, 4, 7–8, 12, 47–74; defined, *xi, xix–xx*, 4, 7, 61; and eating disorders, 117–119; as medical noncompliance, 146;

model of, 42–44, 139–144; newspaper accounts of, *xxi*; parallels to other maladaptive behaviors, 93–115; related to teaching, 112; short-term benefits of, *xxvii*, 3, 7; as a taboo subject, *xiv–xv, xxv–xxvii*, 6, 50, 56, 83, 111, 119, 143, 145–173
Productivism, 160
Productivity, 67–68
Product versus Product orientations, 11, 28, 43, 55, 60–61, 96–97, 106, 113, 115, 117, 129, 140
Psychoanalysis, 22, 40
Punctuality, 9, 36

Quick starters, 58–59, 71–74, 100

Rabinbach, A., 10, 95
Rachlin, Howard, 25, 70, 126, 148
Release time, 76–77
Romantics, 3. *See also* Humanism
Rothblum, E., 30, 72
Rules for behaving rigidly, 28

Satisficing, 8
Schedules, 11
Self-consciousness, *xx,* 43
Self-control, 9, 41, 48, 89, 134–137
Self-defeating behaviors, 133–135
Self-downing, 39, 88
Self-efficacy, 73. *See* Efficacy
Self-focus, 18
Self-management, 71
Self-regulation, 25, 118, 134, 139, 142
Self-serving evaluations, 41
Seligman, Martin, *x*, 113, 135, 148
Short-term vs. Long-term benefits, 5–8, 47

About the Author

ROBERT BOICE is professor of psychology at the State University of New York, Stony Brook. He is the author of numerous books on faculty development, ethology, and scholarly writing, including *How Writers Journey to Comfort and Fluency* (Praeger, 1994).